The Declaration of Independence and the Constitution

PROBLEMS IN
AMERICAN CIVILIZATION

The Declaration of Independence and the Constitution

Third Edition

Edited and with an introduction by

Earl Latham
Amherst College

D. C. HEATH AND COMPANY
Lexington, Massachusetts Toronto

CARNEGIE LIBRARY
LIVINGSTONE COLLEGE
SALISBURY, N. C. 28144

Copyright © 1976 by D. C. Heath and Company.
Also copyright 1949 and 1956 by D. C. Heath and Company.

All rights reserved. No part of this publication may be reproduced or transmitted in any form or by any means, electronic or mechanical, including photocopy, recording, or any information storage or retrieval system, without permission in writing from the publisher.

Printed in the United States of America.

International Standard Book Number: 0-669-94888-8

Library of Congress Catalog Card Number: 76-5637

342.73
L 352

CONTENTS

100344

INTRODUCTION

With the American Revolution the thirteen colonies became, as the Declaration of Independence says, "Free and Independent States." Each was jealous of its own sovereignty and each adopted its own constitution and set up its own administrative machinery. Necessity alone had forced the states to band together in order to win the war with England. It is not surprising, therefore, that their first political cooperation as independent states took the form of a confederation, which provided that each state was to retain its "sovereignty, freedom and independence and every power, jurisdiction and right" not expressly delegated to the Confederation government.

The years under the Articles of Confederation from the Peace of Paris in 1783 to the Constitutional Convention of 1787 brought critical developments both for the new state governments and for the Confederation. Postwar readjustments—business depression, the funding of state and national debts, the writing of new state constitutions, the functioning of the new confederation, the defining of its relation both to individual states and to foreign governments—all these posed difficult problems of economics and politics. And their solution was complicated by the tension between two needs: the need to maintain and fulfill the egalitarian and democratic promises implied in the Declaration of Independence, and the need to establish and maintain responsible state governments and a strong and stable national government, able and willing to fund its debts and open the channels of domestic and international trade.

Those who valued the first of these needs higher than the second kept the state legislatures close to the electorate and responsive to its wishes. Universally among the states, the legislature tended to become the most powerful governmental body, controlling governor and judiciary alike. If the states adopted acts of sequestration to despoil loyalists of their property; if there was debasement of the currency by the too-free flotation of unbacked paper money; if interstate rivalry took the form of customs barriers to commerce—these acts were the acts of free peoples in the full possession of political power.

But to many of the leaders in government and business, things were moving too fast. Political anarchy and fiscal irresponsibility seemed to threaten the loss of those ideals for which the sacrifices of the war had been made. The Revolution had been fought not only for republican independence but for nationhood, and to men who cherished both, the ideal of national unity seemed threatened by state particularism.

Accordingly, steps were taken to create a new political order with a stronger central authority replacing the loose association that had been the Confederation system. After an abortive meeting of representatives from five states at Annapolis in 1786, the Confederation Congress called into being the convention that met in Philadelphia to revise the Articles of Confederation, but remained, in the hot summer of 1787, to formulate an entirely new Constitution of the United States in order, as it was said in the Preamble of that historic document, to bring about a "more perfect union."

What was the nature of the work the Founding Fathers did at the Constitutional Convention? Was there continuity with the ideals of the Declaration of Independence or was there discontinuity, that is, a sharp departure from the egalitarian and democratic values that had made a new nation only a little more than a decade before? Was the creation of the Constitution the work of noble men of continental vision, patriotic and disinterested, or was it primarily (or, perhaps, also) a reconstruction of political authority for the better protection of the interests of the well-to-do, including the authors of the new fundamental law, with such concessions to the less-well-off as might be necessary to persuade them to accept a new government?

The last revision of this book, in 1956, was published at a time when this issue could be more clearly drawn than it can today, with traditionalist historians arguing that patriotic feeling and not economic motivation was the dynamic principle in the establishment of the new government, and two generations of historians, beginning with Charles A. Beard, asserting the opposite. Since the middle of the 1950s, however, there has been new research and writing into the origins of the ideology of the American Revolution, and a major attack upon the economic interpretation associated with Charles Beard. This book takes into account the new research and the revisionist writing, and leaves it to the reader to determine where the merits of the controversy now lie.

The first four essays—by Ralph Barton Perry, Bernard Bailyn, Jack P. Greene, and John C. Miller—deal with the nature of the American Revolution and its philosophical origins. Perry sees continuity between 1776 and 1787 and argues that the Constitution was a correcting and perfective instrument of government that not only did not abandon the ideals of the Revolution but created new political institutions in a different mood and emphasis through which, historically, revolutionary ideals came to be fulfilled. He remarked that by the time of the Revolution itself, the psychological disposition of the colonials was such that they were prepared for the ultimate act of separation from the mother country.

The source of the psychological preparedness to break away is what Bernard Bailyn and Jack P. Greene disagree about, with Professor Bailyn stressing the importance in the colonies of the so-called "oppositionist" literature produced prodigiously in the political quarrels of early eighteenth-century England. Much of this polemical literature had a very specific target—the man history regards as the first prime minister of England, Sir Robert Walpole—and grew out of party struggles between Tories and Whigs (and within Whig ranks) and dynastic struggles bred by the attempt of the Stuarts to return to the throne of England. Walpole became First Lord of the Treasury and Chancellor of the Exchequer in 1721, after the English people had endured years of political and economic turmoil. He restored stability, but at a price. By corruption and bribery, he obtained a Whig House of Commons, and by similar means he fought against various rivals to maintain his authority for some twenty years, during which he also effected a transfer of power to the Commons from the Court and the House of Lords.

One of Walpole's great adversaries was Bolingbroke, a Tory leader, who associated himself with Jonathan Swift, Alexander Pope, John Gay and other satirists and men of letters. In a series of letters in *The Craftsman* he wrote strong attacks against Walpole and what he called the "Robinocracy," that is, government by a corrupt minister and his accomplices. He was not alone in his attacks but his voice could be heard above those of a varied and vociferous opposition.

The dissent struck not only at the machinations of a master minister of power but at the social texture of a whole society in pursuit of gain. Bailyn says that although these attacks had relatively little effect upon the course of events in England, they were enormously "influential and popular" in the American colonies, providing the colonials not only with a debater's manual and glossary of terms but with a "harmonizing force" for all the discordant and nonconformist elements in the thought of the revolutionary generation in America. All the tributaries of example from the classics, Enlightenment, common law, and religious dissent could be brought together by ideas generated in the English Civil War and the Walpolean controversy and made into a "comprehensive theory of politics" by the colonials to oppose the new regulations laid upon them by the British in 1763.

Professor Jack P. Greene took issue with Bailyn's thesis, saying that it failed to consider older intellectual and political traditions before the Walpolean controversy, and did not undertake to establish how and how far the older traditions were displaced by the newer ones. The older political tradition was the opposition to the Crown in seventeenth-century England, the conflicts between the Stuart kings and Parliament that produced a regicide, and eventually drove the Stuarts from the throne and out of England. The century that began with statements about the divine right of kings ended with the primacy of Parliament—truly a revolution—and all taking place, as Greene said, during "a formative period of colonial life." In Greene's view, the colonials in America reproduced in the eighteenth century a transatlantic version of the seventeenth-century constitutional crisis in England and over the very same issue, namely, the extent of the royal prerogative with the assemblies in the role of Parliament and the governors in the role of the monarch.

However the reader may judge the merits of the difference of view between Bailyn and Greene, it would be well to keep in mind the nature of the ultimate historic act achieved by the colonials, whatever the sources of their inspiration. They came to profess political principles of universal appeal, ethical in character and commanding to the conscience—life, liberty, the pursuit of happiness, and government by the consent of the governed. In the categories of Marxist writers, the American Revolution qualifies as a war of national liberation rather than a social revolution based on class struggle, but more traditional writers, like John C. Miller, whose view is stated in these readings, see the Revolution as a truly radical event.

The fifth and sixth essays—by Merrill Jensen and Andrew C. McLaughlin—express basically different views about the nature of the Confederation government, with a sympathetic view presented by Jensen and a more critical one stated by McLaughlin. The designation "the critical period" for the Confederation years was used in the title of a book on the era by the historian John Fiske, published in 1885, and has been generally accepted as descriptive by writers who believe that the Constitution was a necessary corrective to basic defects in the Articles of Confederation. This view is not accepted by others. Charles Beard in *An Economic Interpretation* gave the question only passing consideration. He noted that the gloomy view of economic conditions under the Confederation government was not shared by all "writers of eminence and authority," and he cited Benjamin Franklin for his statement in January 1787 that although there were complaints, property on the whole was "widespread and obvious." Beard said also that precise facts had not been presented to support the dictum of Fiske that under the Articles of Confederation "the bonds of the social order were dissolving." At the same time he minimized the cruciality of social conditions under the Confederation, however, Beard was throwing away a good argument for his view that the Constitution was—in important part, at least—the product of upper-class economic interests. He rather disparagingly dismissed, or held in little account, the Shays Rebellion that certainly had alarmed men of property in the late 1780s, saying that the "inflamed declarations of the Shaysites are not to be taken as representing accurately the state of the people." It was a tacit assumption of Beard that the Confederation was a successful mode of government, that the Articles were merely an extension of the revolutionary ethic, and that the Constitution was a departure from it.

The seventh essay, by Robert L. Schuyler, is an admirable, short account of the framing and adoption of the Constitution, done with precise scholarship. Much of the historical discussion about the work of the Framers, however, has concerned itself less with what it was the Framers *did* (about which there is general agreement) than with *how* what they did should be *characterized.* A late-nineteenth-century scholar, John W. Burgess, held that the work of the Framers, had it been performed by a Julius or a Napoleon, would have been called a "coup d'etat," which is generally thought to be a sudden (and often violent) political action in which existing government is subverted, overthrown, or displaced. Although it is true that the Framers were sent to the Convention under instructions merely to amend the Articles of Confederation and that they violated these instructions without serious debate in order to create a whole new instrument of government, Burgess's characterization seems excessive to the point of falsity. On the other hand, the argument that the whole procedure was "democratic" (despite its technical illegality) because the proposed Constitution was submitted to the states for ratification by the people, instead of adoption by the Confederation Congress, would seem to go too far in the other direction.

Except for a few rousing fights in ratifying conventions and some hot exchanges in the press, there is not much evidence that the "people" were very much involved in the ratification of the new Constitution. We just do not know how many people voted for delegates to the various ratifying conventions, the nature of the instructions given them, the numbers of delegates who were given any instructions at all, or whether they deviated from their instructions. What is clear is that there was widespread apathy (or at least non-voting, which may not mean the same thing) for delegates to the ratifying conventions, although writers differ on the reasons for the low degree of voter participation. Charles Beard argues that disenfranchisement by property qualifications may have been a principal reason and his most pressing critic, Robert E. Brown, denying this, says that the governing factor was whether there was an issue and how important it was, most people seeing no issue in the new Constitution or at least none important enough to make a fuss about. There was indignation and class feeling in the Massachusetts ratifying convention, and yet the turnout that had elected the delegates was not large. Neither Beard nor Brown can explain the paradox.

There is also a difference in view about the inference to be drawn from the first four ratifications, which were almost immediate: Delaware, December 7, 1787; Pennsylvania, December 12, 1787; New Jersey, December 18, 1787; and Georgia, January 2, 1788. The oddity is that Delaware, New Jersey, and Georgia voted unanimously in favor of the new Constitution with a total of 95 votes for and none against. Robert Brown argued that since three of these four states were "agrarian," Beard's thesis about the salience of the ownership of personalty (by definition the principal form of property in an "agrarian" state is land, not commercial paper), should have led to the conclusion that they would have rejected the proposed Constitution. The late Clinton Rossiter characterized the delegations from all three states to the Convention as "nationalists" of some sort or other (including Patterson of New Jersey, the author of the "small state plan"), and noted that Delaware had ratified after only "five days of friendly and desultory discussion"; that "hapless New Jersey" had given the Constitution the courtesy of a full week; and that what could have been a lively debate in "defenceless Georgia" was stifled because the Creek Indians were a threat to the state. It was his thought that the quick unanimous ratifications in three of the first four states were the product of smart Federalist tactics, with the proponents of the new Constitution "moving into action before the war was fairly begun," pressing for quick approval in states thought to favor the Constitution in order to build up momentum.

The next three selections of this book deal with various aspects of the ratification controversy. Vernon Parrington does not view the Framers with the filio-pietistic awe that characterized much nineteenth-century writing about the period, which tended to accept the Federalist interpretation argued by Hamilton, Madison, and Jay in *The Federalist Papers.* Although Parrington wrote his *Main Currents in American Thought* after Beard's *An Economic Interpretation of the Constitution of the United States,* Parrington is put before Beard because his work is broader, more conceptual, and more literary than that of his predecessor. Parrington's view of the making of the Constitution is basically like that of Beard's, and the perspective of both is balanced in the present collection by the essays of Robert E. Brown and Forrest McDonald. Parrington's view of Number Ten of *The Federalist Papers* is balanced by the inclusion of Madison's famous essay in its entirety, to which Parrington gave so much emphasis and such a selective interpretation. Readers may wish to consider with more than passing notice the interpretation of Number Ten given by Douglass Adair, which takes it out of the category of mere polemics in a New York political fight and makes of it a statement about the just society and the rights of minorities—all minorities—within it. Readers should judge for themselves whether Madison was a mere sectarian propagandist or a philosopher concerned with justice and stability, two values of political ethics of importance now as well as then. In what Parrington called "The Great Debate," contributions were made by modest men as well as the ones that historians tend to emphasize. The piece on *Philadelphiensis* is an account of one such modest man.

The last five essays in this collection deal with the controversy over the correct interpretation of the events that led to the framing and adoption of the Constitution. The first statement is that of Charles Beard, who wrote what he called "an economic interpretation" of the Constitution, and established thereby a canon of historical interpretation that was to predominate among historians for decades. The Beard excerpt is followed by a much later rebuttal written by a distinguished conservative scholar of American constitutional history, Charles Warren. The virtue of the Warren explanation is the emphasis given to constitutional and legal questions, although this emphasis may give less than proper weight to social and economic elements in political change. The tone of Warren's exposition, however, is in great contrast to that of some earlier critics of Beard, such as William Howard Taft—who thought that Beard had produced a muckraking book—or Nicholas Murray Butler, the president of Columbia University, who suggested that the Beard thesis was related to the "crude, immoral, and unhistorical teaching of Karl Marx."

In the 1956 edition of the present work, the last line of the bibliography (added as the book was going to press) said, "For an all-out attack on the economic interpretation see: Robert E. Brown, *Charles Beard and the Constitution: A Critical Analysis of 'An Economic Interpretation of the Constitution'* (Princeton, 1956)." The book by Brown was the first by one of several writers for whom the Beard interpretation had come to be thought inadequate, for various reasons. In the rush to smash the Beard canon, however, some critics committed extravagances of their own, bumping into each other clumsily on both facts and interpretations. For Brown, there were virtually no class distinctions at the time of the Convention, but for Richard B. Morris there were important class distinctions, although no class war. The leaders of the Revolution and the Convention were the same kind of people for Benjamin Fletcher Wright; but not really, said Stanley Elkins and Eric McKittrick, who described different generational outlooks upon the value of firm central authority. Some thought that the Confederation period was indeed critical; others did not. Some thought that there was no conspiracy on the part of a Federalist elite to put the Constitution over; others admired the slickness with which a smooth Federalist elite managed to have its way.

Brown's attack on Beard's *Economic Interpretation* was a chapter-by-chapter refutation, and the reader will want to consult the work itself for the extended analysis. The excerpt reprinted in this book is Brown's criticism of what is perhaps Beard's most famous chapter (Chapter 5), the one concerning the personalty holdings of the Framers. The piece by Brown is followed by a summary of the criticism of Beard made by Forrest McDonald whose own work, *We the People,* argued that the Beard interpretation was wrong because his economic categories were too simplistic and unworkable and that Brown's central idea was right in that the Convention represented the country at large and did not serve special economic class interests. McDonald's position is criticized by Jackson T. Main in the next selection, and McDonald's rebuttal to Main follows.

The attacks on Beard during the last two decades have been made by writers who may fairly be said to be as much creatures of their own time as they have said Beard was of his—tending to lay stress on *consensus* in the Dwight Eisenhower–Lyndon Johnson mode whereas Beard laid stress on *conflict* in the Populist–Progressive mode. But as fashions in interpretation change with national moods, so it may happen that writers may come again to think less well of consensus that conceals corruption and continuity that perpetuates it, and rather more of conflict as the key term of politics, which is what Beard did.

Ralph Barton Perry

THE DECLARATION OF INDEPENDENCE

Not all revolutions are alike. Some merely effect a transfer of power from one set of officials to another without touching the social life of the community in any serious way, leaving basic social and economic groups in approximately the same relation to each other as before, without significant changes in their material well-being or their relative political positions. Other revolutions, however, not only effect the transfer of power from one set of officials to another but radically reconstruct social and economic institutions, abolishing the privileges of those who ruled and elevating the interests of those over whom rule was enforced.

The American Revolution was not a struggle of lower colonial classes against upper colonial classes, as were the classical social revolutions of France and Russia. It was a struggle of entire colonies against what was believed to be the usurpation of the power of self-government by outsiders. The "usurpers" were not foreigners, of course, as the British were in India or the French in Algeria, since the American colonials, most of whom came from the British Isles, felt close ties with England. The "usurpers" were the ministers of the Crown who had become tyrannical and oppressive.

Although parties as we know them did not exist at the time of the Revolution, there were two broad political formations in both the colonies and England—the Tories and the Whigs—with the Tories strongly against rebellion. The colonial Whigs, however, were divided on the issue of rebellion right up to the Declaration of Independence, with Conservative Whigs like John Dickinson of Delaware tending to oppose, and Liberal Whigs like Thomas Jefferson and John Adams tending to support separation from Britain. When the time for decision came, almost all of the colonial Whigs closed ranks in support of the struggle against England, although some who had been Patriot leaders before the Declaration became Loyalists when it was proclaimed.

Although the loose political alignment of Tories and Whigs did not represent a strict array of social groups pitted against each other, it would be a mistake to suppose that the colonials were a classless society without social orders and status levels. The speeches and other public expressions of the time contain many references to the "better sort," the "middle sort," and the "meaner sort," although it must also be said that the "middling classes" were expanding most rapidly.

Not all historians agree on the fundamental nature of the American Revolution, even after two hundred years, and some have argued, as did Carl Becker almost seventy years ago, that the struggle was not only about home rule but about who should rule at home, while some deny that there was any significant movement at home for a more democratic society. There

From *Puritanism and Democracy* by Ralph Barton Perry, copyright 1944 by Ralph Barton Perry. Reprinted by permission of the Vanguard Press, publisher.

is general agreement, however, that the agitation that culminated in the Revolution produced an earnest intellectual debate about the fundamentals of politics in which the best minds of the country participated, and that the American Revolution was a triumph of the principle of republicanism over monarchy.

The essay by Ralph Barton Perry that follows speaks of the changing argument about concepts and principles, legal and philosophical—first, the rights of the colonists, then the rights of Englishmen, and finally the rights of man as expressed in the Declaration of Independence. As the author says, "The Declaration of Independence contains the essential ideas of American democracy, and has remained its creed and standard throughout the years of its subsequent development." The federal Constitution, in his view, did not reject these principles but represented a "different mood and emphasis."

The American Revolution was a successful rebellion against the constituted authority. It was not a crusade undertaken in behalf of a creed formulated in advance, but a summary effect of interests and of mental dispositions, compounded among themselves and facilitated by the circumstances of time and place. Nevertheless, since the revolution assumed the form of a deliberate enterprise, calling for unanimity, prolonged effort, and sacrifice, it was necessary to invoke "reasons." There was need of an approving conscience, an assenting judgment, and a confirmation by the disinterested opinion of mankind. There was need for these because they are elements of strength and bonds of effective union. The rebellious colonists, then, took certain "grounds": first, a legal ground; and then, in the last resort, a philosophical ground.

The first attempt of the colonists to justify their resistance to authority looked to the existing body of law.[1] This attempt proceeded from more specific to more general grounds. It was first argued that the imperial authority was justified in imposing external taxes and trade regulations, but not direct internal taxes, such as the stamp tax. This distinction broke down, partly because it was difficult to draw the line, and partly because if it were drawn, it became increasingly clear that the colonists did not propose to submit to *any* kind of taxation. The famous slogan "No taxation without representation" took the broader ground that Parliament's prerogative of taxation was based on its representative character: the colonists sent no member to Parliament, and their interests, being remote, had no

[1] Carl Becker, *The Declaration of Independence: A Study in the History of Political Ideas,* Harcourt Brace (now Alfred A. Knopf), 1922, Chap. III. By permission of the author.

effective spokesman in that body. But even this ground was too narrow, since it was limited to the power of taxation. Hence the next step was to insist that as constituents of the British Empire the colonists owed allegiance not to Parliament, but only to the King. This claim has been supported by recent authorities, on the precedent of Ireland,[2] and was in line with the subsequent development of the British Empire. But it afforded no justification of the defiance of the King, and when it became evident that the colonists did not propose to obey British authority at all, this, like the other and narrower legal arguments, lost its force.

There was, finally, the appeal from the British imperial constitution to "natural law," or "the fundamental rights of Englishmen." This would have been a legal justification had it been submitted to duly constituted judicial authorities. But the colonists did not propose to submit to British judges any more than to Parliament or the King. They proposed to make up their minds for themselves as to the "justice" of their cause. The issue was to be submitted to the arbitrament of reason, and that authority spoke within their own breasts. At this point their justification became extralegal—a justification of illegality in terms of the philosophical principles on which law itself is based. A political philosophy, says Leslie Stephen, is usually "the offspring of a recent, or the symptom of an approaching revolution."[3] It arises when the habit of obedience is broken: when men have, in effect, suspended their allegiance until their interests and intellectual faculties shall have been satisfied.

On July 2, 1776, the Continental Congress, on the motion of Richard Henry Lee, adopted the following resolution: "That these United Colonies are, and of right ought to be, free and independent States, that they are absolved from all allegiance to the British Crown, and that all political connection between them and the State of Great Britain is, and ought to be, totally dissolved."[4] The resolve and the act were unmistakably and uncompromisingly illegal. The Declaration of Independence, which was adopted two days later, was a philosophical creed designed to justify the action of men who had taken the law

[2] Cf. C. H. McIlwain, *The American Revolution: A Constitutional Interpretation* (Macmillan, 1923).
[3] *History of English Thought in the Eighteenth Century* (2 vols.; London, 1902), Vol. II, p. 131.
[4] Carl Becker, op. cit., p. 3.

into their own hands. It was at one and the same time a justification of rebellion and a statement of those common principles on which was to be founded a new state. It is as though men should say: "This is what government and law are for. Judged by this standard, the existing authority has forfeited its claim to obedience. This is at the same time the ground on which to erect a new authority which shall in the future be obeyed as commending itself to our reason and conscience." History affords few parallel instances of a state thus abruptly created, and consciously dedicated to a body of ideas whose acceptance constitutes its underlying bond of agreement.

This American democratic creed, designed to justify the past and chart the future, began as follows:

> *When in the Course of human events, it becomes necessary for one people to dissolve the political bands, which have connected them with another, and to assume among the powers of the earth, the separate and equal station to which the Laws of Nature and of Nature's God entitle them, a decent respect to the opinions of mankind requires that they should declare the causes which impel them to the separation.—We hold these truths to be self-evident, that all men are created equal, that they are endowed by their Creator with certain unalienable Rights, that among these are Life, Liberty and the pursuit of Happiness.—That to secure these rights, Governments are instituted among Men, deriving their just powers from the consent of the governed,—That whenever any Form of Government becomes destructive of these ends, it is the Right of the People to alter or to abolish it, and to institute new Government, laying its foundation on such principles and organizing its powers in such form, as to them shall seem most likely to effect their Safety and Happiness.*[5]

Not the least extraordinary feature of this remarkable document is the compactness and simplicity of statement with which a complete system of philosophy is embraced within a few brief paragraphs. It contains a political philosophy, setting forth the reasons that justify the authority of the state and define the fundamental rights which underlie the positive law; an ethics, which sets up the aggregate happiness of individuals as the supreme end; and a theistic and creationist doctrine of the origins of nature and man.

The Declaration of Independence was composed by Thomas Jefferson. It owes much to his intellect as well as to his pen, for he was no phrasemaker, ghost-writer, or unconscious plagiarist. But in this

[5] The Declaration of Independence as it reads in the parchment copy, as quoted by Carl Becker, op. cit., pp. 185–86.

document he was giving the imprint of his genius to the current wisdom of the age. To quote Jefferson himself:

> *With respect to our rights, and the acts of the British government contravening those rights, there was but one opinion on this side of the water. All American whigs thought alike on these subjects. When forced, therefore, to resort to arms for redress, an appeal to the tribunal of the world was deemed proper for our justification. This was the object of the Declaration of Independence. Not to find out new principles, or new arguments, never before thought of, not merely to say things which had never been said before; but to place before mankind the common sense of the subject, in terms so plain and firm as to command their assent, and to justify ourselves in the independent stand we are compelled to take. Neither aiming at originality of principle or sentiment, not yet copied from any particular and previous writing, it was intended to be an expression of the American mind, and to give to that expression the proper tone and spirit called for by the occasion. All its authority rests then on the harmonizing sentiments of the day, whether expressed in conversation, in letters, printed essays, or in the elementary books of public right, as Aristotle, Cicero, Locke, Sidney, &c.*[6]

The question of Jefferson's sources is one on which authorities disagree. The earlier view that he was inspired by Rousseau has long since been abandoned. Rousseau's *Social Contract* was not published until 1762, and the essential ingredients of the thought of the Declaration were current in America before that time. There is no clear evidence, furthermore, that Jefferson had read Rousseau. A recent authority attaches importance to the fact that Jefferson had read and summarized the tracts of Lord Kames, the Scottish jurist, and traces Jefferson's political thinking to Anglo-Saxon history and jurisprudence: the Jeffersonian democracy "was born under the sign of Hengist and Horsa, not of the Goddess of Reason."[7] But to attribute the Declaration of Independence to any single source, whether French or English, is to miss its historical significance altogether. If special importance be attributed to the influence of Locke, this is not because of the fact that Jefferson is known to have been familiar with Locke's writings, or because of close parallels between the text of the Declaration and that of Locke's *Second Treatise of Civil Government;* but because Locke was the greatest and most representative

[6] Letter of May 8, 1825, to Henry Lee, from *The Writings of Thomas Jefferson,* ed. P. L. Ford (10 vols.; New York, 1892–99), Vol. X, p. 343, courtesy of G. P. Putnam's Sons.
[7] Gilbert Chinard, *Thomas Jefferson, the Apostle of Americanism* (Little, Brown, 1929), p. 87.

exponent of the thought of the Enlightenment—which, arising in England in the seventeenth century, gave a distinctive character to the mind of Europe and America in the century that followed.

The political ideas of the Declaration, while explained in the language and the temper of the Enlightenment, were in full accord with the principles embodied in the earliest colonial charters. For one hundred and fifty years the American mind had been prepared for their reception. The charter of Maryland (1632) provided that Lord Baltimore and his heirs should make laws "consonant to Reason" and "Agreeable to the Laws, Statutes, Customs and Rights of . . . England."[8] Similar provisions were contained in the Fundamental Orders of Connecticut (1639), in the Massachusetts Body of Liberties (1641), and in William Penn's Frame of Government of Pennsylvania (1682). In the First Continental Congress John Adams was insistent that the colonies should "recur to the law of nature, as well as to the British constitution, and our American charters and grants," because he foresaw a necessity of avoiding any implied acceptance of existing authority.[9] But whether they were termed "natural," as became usual after 1760; or were referred to as "fundamental" or "ancient," or "customary," as "the laws of God," or as "the rights of Englishmen,"[10] in any case there were recognized basic principles which might be invoked against the powers of any human government, and which found their sanction in reason, conscience, and piety.

The Declaration of Independence was an ex post facto justification of the American Revolution, as Locke's *Treatises of Civil Government* were an ex post facto justification of the English Revolution of 1688. Both wordings were avowedly apologetic. The Declaration of Independence was animated by "a decent respect to the opinions of mankind." Locke's *Treatises* were written

> *to establish the throne of our great restorer, our present king William; to make good his title, in the consent of the people . . . and to justify to the world the people of England, whose love of their just and natural rights,*

[8] *Select Charters . . . of American History, 1606–1775,* pp. 56–57.
[9] Notes on the debates in the First Continental Congress as summarized later in his Autobiography, John Adams, *Works,* ed. C. F. Adams (10 vols.; Little, Brown, 1850–56), Vol. II, p. 374.
[10] Cf. Benjamin F. Wright, Jr., *American Interpretations of Natural Law* (Harvard University Press, 1931), Chaps. II–IV.

> *with their resolution to preserve them, saved the nation when it was on the very brink of slavery and ruin.*[11]

Jefferson, like Locke, gathered and reaffirmed the reasons. This does not imply that these reasons were first in the mind of the revolutionary party, in advance of any other condition or interest; and that they were then executed by purposeful action. They were the reasons by which the revolution was justified to its proponents, to its opponents, and to neutral observers. They constituted the defense of the revolution against the scruples of its own agents; they were designed to enlist the support of adherents in the enemy's camp; and to win the approval of the world and of posterity. Through this rationalization it was hoped that the revolution might be put on higher ground than sordid or partisan interest. But because it was a rationalization, the Declaration of Independence was not insulated from the stream of historical events. It expressed, and in turn affected, the minds of men. It was, in short, a *cause*—not the initial cause, not the only cause, not the sufficient cause, but, for all one can know to the contrary, a *necessary* cause. It occurred in response to a felt need, as the condition of a full and enduring concert of action.

That the Declaration of Independence should have been a social cause, reinforcing the effects of interest, habit, and passion, does not imply that its doctrines were not true. Whether they were or were not true in the sense in which political, moral, or religious doctrines can be true, is for philosophers to determine. In any case, they were intended as true, and taken as true. They expressed and were designed to invoke the "enlightenment" of their age; and by the same token they lend themselves either to reaffirmation, or to correction, in terms of the more advanced enlightenment of later times.

The author of the best book on the Declaration of Independence, a book distinguished by its wit as well as by its penetration, delivers himself of the following judgment on the subject: "To ask whether the natural rights philosophy of the Declaration of Independence is true or false is essentially a meaningless question." As though in defense of his pronouncement, Professor Becker proceeds to show that the philosophy of the Declaration, like similar philosophies pro-

[11] *Works* (10 vols.; London), Vol. V, p. 209.

fessed under similar conditions, is appealed to "in justification of actions which the community condemns as immoral or criminal." Revolutionists formulate the sort of philosophy which brings their action, despite its conflict with established law and custom, "into harmony with a rightly ordered universe, and enables them to think of themselves as having chosen the nobler part." They invoke a "higher law," which may be a law of God, or of conscience, or of nature. Such a law, says the author, when it provides "emotional inspiration," is "true" to them whom it so fortifies; but, we are allowed to infer, not *really* true (or false) at all.[12]

This argument employs the method unhappily characteristic of the newer school of critical historians. It rests upon an unformulated philosophy of truth, which is itself assumed to be true. If the terms "laws of nature," "God," "self-evident," "rights," "equality," "just," and "happiness," meant anything to the Americans of 1776, then the propositions containing these terms were of necessity either true or false; and if we can recover the meanings, we can detect the truth or falsehood. That they *did* mean something can be proved only by setting forth their meanings—which I shall hope to do, ably assisted by the critical historians themselves.

The belittlement of the doctrines of the Declaration of Independence takes other forms. Thus Alvin Johnson has recently written:

> *American democracy has proved itself an irrepressible force for the reason that it is not a matter of philosophical definition or legal status but a complex of impulses more or less trained and of experience more or less substantial deep in the heart of the individual democrat. Three centuries of life almost wholly civil in character, within an environment rich enough to offer opportunity for independence to most men, represent the chief conditioning circumstances for the development of this peculiar and tenacious plant, the American democratic spirit.*[13]

This judgment is true in what it affirms, and false in what it denies. It is false to deny that American democracy is "a matter of philosophical definition or legal status"—peculiarly false. No polity in human history has owed so much to philosophy and jurisprudence. To hold to this indisputable historical fact is quite consistent with an

[12] Op. cit., pp. 277–79.
[13] "The Substance of American Democracy," in Max Ascoli and Fritz Lehmann, *Political and Economic Democracy* (Norton, 1937), pp. 323–24.

ample recognition of the debt which American democracy owes to its environment and experience.

It was inevitable that historians of today should rewrite the history of the American Revolution in terms of "propaganda" and the "ruling class":

> *The work of the propagandists has spoken for itself; by their fruits we have known them. Without their work independence would not have been declared in 1776 nor recognized in 1783. . . . The provincial ruling class, threatened in its position, used legal agencies of government and already established social institutions to undermine and ultimately to overthrow the British control. Through propaganda they spread the alarm to all classes. The propagandists identified the interests of the provincial ruling class with national interests and created a war psychosis. It was the propagandists who made inchoate feelings articulate opinion and provided the compulsive ideals which led to concrete action. . . . Nationalism was not the cause of the revolution, nor was it democratic in its origin, but the work of the revolutionary propagandists aided in developing the feeling of nationalism and in stimulating the ideals of a new democracy.*[14]

This account adds nothing and subtracts nothing. Leaders, statesmen, philosophers, men of influence, and founding fathers remain the same when they are called "the provincial ruling class"; and persuasion, argument, or emotional appeal is not changed in character when it is called "propaganda." It remains as necessary as ever to acknowledge, define, interpret, and explain "the feeling of nationalism" and "the ideals of a new democracy."

The Declaration of Independence contains the essential ideas of American democracy, and has remained its creed and standard thoughout the years of its subsequent development. "For the first time in the history of the world," says Professor Corwin, "the principles of revolution are made the basis of settled political institutions."[15] These principles have been challenged by individual thinkers, and even, as in the epoch of the Civil War, by sections or classes, but they have invariably been invoked in times of crisis or of patriotic fervor as constituting the moral bond of American national-

[14] Philip Davidson, *Propaganda and the American Revolution, 1763–1783* (University of North Carolina Press, 1941), p. 410.
[15] Edward S. Corwin, "The 'Higher Law' Background of American Constitutional Law," *Harvard Law Review* 42 (1929): 403. By permission of the publisher and the author.

ity. The later history of the ideas of the Declaration concerns us only so far as may be necessary to establish their permanence and pervasiveness. They were promptly embodied, if they had not been anticipated, in the constitutions of the several states. Their public reading on successive anniversaries has solemnized the national memory and aspiration. They have proved broad enough to embrace partisan differences and cycles of political change.

When the Federal Constitution was under discussion in the year 1787–88 the problem of the colonists had shifted from revolution to reconstruction. It was a time of recoil and suspended activity. Even the conquest of the continent had lost much of its momentum. Men felt the pains and costs of change rather than its impetus. In 1803 the Reverend Jedediah Morse was minded to say, "Let us guard against the insidious encroachments of *innovation,* that evil and beguiling spirit which is now stalking to and fro through the earth, seeking whom he may destroy."[16] The "political bands which [had] connected them with another" had been dissolved, and it was now imperative for Americans "to form a more perfect union" among themselves.

The sentiment and emphasis which are effective for purposes of revolution are the precise opposites of those required "to institute new Government." Revolution is associated with the defiance of authority and the resort to violence; it is the task of political reconstruction to persuade men once again to obey. Revolution begets the feeling that a man can have what he wants; reconstruction compels him again to submit his particular interest to law and to the general good. The problem of reconstruction is to escape from that state of nature to which, in the act of revolution, society has reverted. In 1783 factionalism and personal jealousies were rife. The defects of human nature and the evils of anarchy were everywhere apparent. It was natural that in such a mood, and in response to the exigencies of such a crisis, there should be a swing toward political conservatism.

The Federal Constitution, then, expressed a fear of the excesses of revolutionary democracy, and of the mind of the masses. These fears inspired John Adams, Alexander Hamilton, and other leaders of the Federalist party; they represented the mood of reconstruction, as had Samuel Adams that of revolution. The motive of these leaders was to

[16] Quoted by Henry Adams in his *History of the United States of America during the First Administration of Thomas Jefferson* (2 vols.; Scribner, 1909), Vol. I, p. 78. . . .

set such limits to popular government as should save it from self-destruction. Neither they nor Burke and the Whig party in England had any intention of denying popular government, but they desired that government should express the sober second thought of the people rather than their haste or passion. To this end they retarded the popular will and multiplied its intermediaries.[17] They sought to accomplish their purpose not by strengthening the executive, but by a division of powers, and by the six-year term of senators. *The Federalist* defended this last provision as follows:

> *To a people as little blinded by prejudice or corrupted by flattery as those whom I address, I shall not scruple to add that such an institution may be sometimes necessary as a defense to the people against their own temporary errors and delusions. As the cool and deliberate sense of the community ought, in all governments, and actually will, in all free governments, ultimately prevail over the views of its rulers; so there are particular moments in public affairs when the people, stimulated by some irregular passion, or some illicit advantage, or misled by the artful misrepresentations of interested men, may call for measures which they themselves will afterwards be most ready to lament and condemn. In these critical moments, how salutary will be the interference of some temperate and respectable body of citizens in order to check the misguided career, and to suspend the blow meditated by the people against themselves, until reason, justice, and truth can regain their authority over the public mind.*[18]

While the Federal Constitution represented a different mood and emphasis, it did not reject the doctrine of the Declaration of Independence. It rested upon the principle that men erect governments by agreement, and for their good as they consciously envisage it. In

[17] Cf. C. Edward Merriam, *A History of American Political Theories* (Macmillan, 1920), pp. 126, 131. For Burke, cf. John MacCunn, *The Political Philosophy of Burke* (London, 1913).

[18] "The Senate," *The Federalist*, Paper LXIII, Colonial Press, p. 348. (Whether this Paper was written by Madison or Hamilton is a subject of controversy.) Cf. also E. M. Burns, *James Madison, Philosopher of the Constitution* (Rutgers University Press, 1938), Chap. III and p. 154. That men judge government from the standpoint of their interests, and that among these their economic interests will take a leading place, cannot be doubted. It follows that in protecting property against the consolidated power of the impecunious masses the Constitution of 1788 would appeal to the propertied classes. Political conservatism coincides with the desire for stability, fulfillment of contractual obligations, and the protection of minority rights on the part of men who enjoy a comparatively advantageous position in the existing distribution of wealth. Cf. Charles A. Beard's famous *An Economic Interpretation of the Constitution of the United States* (Macmillan, 1913), Chap. VI.

the last analysis, the sovereignty lay in the will of the people—if possible their thoughtful will, but nonetheless their will. The state rested upon sound moral premises, and was devoted to a moral end. Its purpose was to keep the peace among men in order that as individuals they might enjoy their fundamental rights and attain a maximum of personal development and happiness. Whenever the controversy over the Constitution turned on the fundamentals of political philosophy it was to the doctrine of natural law and natural rights that all parties appealed. As has been abundantly proved and documented by a recent political writer, "it seems safe to say that no member of the convention . . . ever questioned the validity of this concept." They took it for granted as the common ground of their differences.[19]

It should be added that the Federalists represented not only a conservative emphasis on strong government and a delay of the popular will, but also the economic interest of the financial and mercantile classes of the eastern seaboard. These motives tend to agree, since creditors are more dependent than debtors upon public order and stability. At the moment when a debt is to be paid it is the debtor who suffers, and the creditor who profits, by a strict compliance with the law. The debtor is more disposed to welcome, if he does not actually foment, a state of disorder which permits of repudiation. He can "afford" to be more reckless.

During its later history American democracy has had, under various names, its constitutional and its revolutionary parties. The constitutional party has emphasized the system of government in its integrity and has insisted on legality of procedure. It has attracted those whose advantage lay in economic stability, and in the status quo. The revolutionary party, on the other hand, has emphasized the popular will as directly expressed in the vote of the majority, and has attracted those whose advantage lay in change. The second of these parties represents the forward impulses of American democracy; the first, its sober thought. The second has been retarded by the first, but never stopped or reversed. The history of American democracy is a gradual realization, too slow for some and too rapid for others, of the implications of the Declaration of Independence.[20]

[19] B. F. Wright, Jr., *American Interpretations of Natural Law,* pp. 125, 248–51, 342–43, and Chap. VI, passim. . . .

[20] Cf. J. B. McMaster, *The Acquisition of Political, Social and Industrial Rights of Man in America* (Cleveland, Ohio, 1903).

Bernard Bailyn

IDEOLOGICAL ORIGINS OF THE AMERICAN REVOLUTION

It is the common wisdom that the intellectual father of the American Revolution was John Locke, the philosopher of the Glorious Revolution of 1688. And indeed both John Locke and Thomas Jefferson did lay intellectual foundations for republicanism and revolution in colonial America. But Locke was only one intellectual source—although admittedly a major one—in the development of the revolutionary spirit *in the colonies, and the recent research and writing of Professor Bernard Bailyn of Harvard University have contributed much to an understanding of the breadth and depth of the flow of inspiration to the colonials from the struggles in the home country between the Stuarts and Parliament in the seventeenth century, and the political struggles in the early eighteenth, in which Sir Robert Walpole was the controversial center. Professor Bailyn's principal thesis is that the roots of the American Revolution grew from oppositionist agitation against the Stuart regime and the Walpole ministry, with special emphasis on the latter.*

The point of view of Ralph Barton Perry—that the American Revolution was a successful rebellion against constituted authority, not a crusade for a creed formulated in advance but a "summary effect of interests and mental dispositions"—still leaves somewhat unanswered the question why the colonists wanted to rebel in the first place. Professor Bailyn's work does much to establish the nature of these "mental dispositions" in his investigation of the ideological sources of the revolutionary rhetoric, making more understandable the quickness of the colonials to react against a relatively "innocuous" Stamp Act, the Townshend duties, which were repealed, and the Boston Massacre, which was little more than an "urban riot." It is Professor Bailyn's position that these incidents were "incendiary" because of the predispositions that shaped the perception of them.

In Bailyn's view, an integrated pattern of political attitudes had developed in the colonies before 1763 that disposed the colonists to see, with suspicion of sinister design, the various policies and acts of King and Parliament after the Seven Years' War. Contributions to this ideology flowed from several sources, some of which, philosophically, were at variance with others. Thus, there was the heritage of classical antiquity, which supplied texts for some and footnotes for others in the debates about colonial politics. Philosophies of universal Reason were available in the works of "major figures of the European Enlightenment." The English common law, on the other hand, stressed tradition and custom to balance the unstabilizing

Reprinted by permission of the author and publishers from *The Ideological Origins of the American Revolution* by Bernard Bailyn, Cambridge, Massachusetts: The Belknap Press of Harvard University Press, © 1967 by the President and Fellows of Harvard College.

influence of "right reason" in social life. Another ideological source of revolutionary ideology was the social and political gospel of New England Puritanism. What brought these "disparate strands of thought" together in the revolutionary consciousness of the colonials was the work of radical political thinkers of the seventeenth century and of writers in the early eighteenth opposed to Sir Robert Walpole and his "Robinocracy."

The following is an excerpt from Bailyn's principal statement of these points.

The intellectual history of the years of crisis from 1763 to 1776 is the story of the clarification and consolidation under the pressure of events of a view of the world and of America's place in it only partially seen before. Elements of this picture had long been present in the colonies—some dated from as far back as the settlements themselves—but they had existed in balance, as it were, with other, conflicting views. Expressed mainly on occasions of controversy, they had appeared most often as partisan arguments, without unique appeal, status, or claim to legitimacy. Then, in the intense political heat of the decade after 1763, these long-popular, though hitherto inconclusive ideas about the world and America's place in it, were fused into a comprehensive view, unique in its moral and intellectual appeal. It is the development of this view to the point of overwhelming persuasiveness to the majority of American leaders and the meaning this view gave to the events of the time, and not simply an accumulation of grievances, that explains the origins of the American Revolution. For this peculiar configuration of ideas constituted in effect an intellectual switchboard wired so that certain combinations of events would activate a distinct set of signals—danger signals, indicating hidden impulses and the likely trajectory of events impelled by them. Well before 1776 the signals registered on this switchboard led to a single, unmistakable conclusion—a conclusion that had long been feared and to which there could be only one rational response.

What were the sources of this world view? From whom, from what, were the ideas and attitudes derived?

Study of the sources of the colonists' thought as expressed in the informal as well as the formal documents, in the private as well as the public utterances, and above all in the discursive, explanatory pamphlets, reveals, at first glance, a massive, seemingly random eclecticism. To judge simply from an enumeration of the colonists' citations, they had at their finger tips, and made use of, a large portion of the inheritance of Western culture, from Aristotle to Molière, from Cicero to "Philoleutherus Lipsiensis" [Richard Bentley], from Vergil to Shakespeare, Ramus, Pufendorf, Swift, and Rousseau. They liked to display authorities for their arguments, citing and quoting from them freely; at times their writings become almost submerged in annotation: in certain of the writings of John Dickinson the text disappears altogether in a sea of footnotes and footnotes to footnotes. But ultimately this profusion of authorities is reducible to a few, distinct groups of sources and intellectual traditions dominated and harmonized into a single whole by the influence of one peculiar strain of thought, one distinctive tradition.

Most conspicuous in the writings of the Revolutionary period was the heritage of classical antiquity. Knowledge of classical authors was universal among colonists with any degree of education, and references to them and their works abound in the literature. From the grammar schools, from the colleges, from private tutors and independent reading came a general familiarity with and the habit of reference to the ancient authors and the heroic personalities and events of the ancient world. "Homer, Sophocles, Plato, Euripides, Herodotus, Thucydides, Xenophon, Aristotle, Strabo, Lucian, Dio, Polybius, Plutarch, and Epictetus, among the Greeks; and Cicero, Horace, Vergil, Tacitus, Lucan, Seneca, Livy, Nepos, Sallust, Ovid, Lucretius, Cato, Pliny, Juvenal, Curtius, Marcus Aurelius, Petronius, Suetonius, Caesar, the lawyers Ulpian and Gaius, and Justinian, among the Romans"—all are cited in the Revolutionary literature; many are directly quoted. "It was an obscure pamphleteer indeed who could not muster at least one classical analogy or one ancient precept."

But this elaborate display of classical authors is deceptive. Often the learning behind it was superficial; often the citations appear to have been dragged in as "window dressing with which to ornament a page or a speech and to increase the weight of an argument," for classical quotation, as Dr. Johnson said, was "the *parole* of literary men all over the world." So Jonathan Mayhew casually lumped Plato with Demosthenes and Cicero as the ancients who in his youth had initiated him "in the doctrines of civil liberty"; Oxenbridge Thacher too thought Plato had been a liberty-loving revolutionary, while Jefferson, who actually read the *Dialogues*, discovered in them only the "sophisms, futilities, and incomprehensibilities" of a "foggy mind" —an idea concurred in with relief by John Adams, who in 1774 had cited Plato as an advocate of equality and self-government but who was so shocked when he finally studied the philosopher that he concluded that the *Republic* must have been meant as a satire.

Yet Jefferson was a careful reader of the classics, and others too—James Otis, for example, who wrote treatises on Latin and Greek prosody—were thorough scholars of the ancient texts. What is basically important in the Americans' reading of the ancients is the high selectivity of their real interests and the limitation of the range of their effective knowledge. For though the colonists drew their citations from all portions of the literature of the ancient world, their detailed knowledge and engaged interest covered only one era and one small group of writers. What gripped their minds, what they knew in detail, and what formed their view of the whole of the ancient world was the political history of Rome from the conquests in the east and the civil wars in the early first century B.C. to the establishment of the empire on the ruins of the republic at the end of the second century A.D. For their knowledge of this period they had at hand, and needed only, Plutarch, Livy, and above all Cicero, Sallust, and Tacitus—writers who had lived either when the republic was being fundamentally challenged or when its greatest days were already past and its moral and political virtues decayed. They had hated and feared the trends of their own time, and in their writing had contrasted the present with a better past, which they endowed with qualities absent from their own, corrupt era. The earlier age had been full of virtue: simplicity, patriotism, integrity, a love of justice and of liberty; the present was venal, cynical, and oppressive.

For the colonists, arguing the American cause in the controversies of the 1760s and 1770s, the analogies to their own times were compelling. They saw their own provincial virtues—rustic and old-fashioned, sturdy and effective—challenged by the corruption at the center of power, by the threat of tyranny, and by a constitution gone wrong. They found their ideal selves, and to some extent their voices, in Brutus, in Cassius, and in Cicero, whose Catilinarian orations the enraptured John Adams, aged 23, declaimed aloud, alone at night in his room. They were simple, stoical Catos, desperate, self-sacrificing Brutuses, silver-tongued Ciceros, and terse, sardonic Tacituses eulogizing Teutonic freedom and denouncing the decadence of Rome. England, the young John Dickinson wrote from London in 1754, is like Sallust's Rome: " 'Easy to be bought, if there was but a purchaser.' " Britain, it would soon become clear, was to America "what Caesar was to Rome."

The classics of the ancient world are everywhere in the literature of the Revolution, but they are everywhere illustrative, not determinative, of thought. They contributed a vivid vocabulary but not the logic or grammar of thought, a universally respected personification but not the source of political and social beliefs. They heightened the colonists' sensitivity to ideas and attitudes otherwise derived.

More directly influential in shaping the thought of the Revolutionary generation were the ideas and attitudes associated with the writings of Enlightenment rationalism—writings that expressed not simply the rationalism of liberal reform but that of enlightened conservatism as well.

Despite the efforts that have been made to discount the influence of the "glittering generalities" of the European Enlightenment on eighteenth-century Americans, their influence remains, and is profusely illustrated in the political literature. It is not simply that the great *virtuosi* of the American Enlightenment—Franklin, Adams, Jefferson—cited the classic Enlightenment texts and fought for the legal recognition of natural rights and for the elimination of institutions and practices associated with the *ancien régime.* They did so; but they were not alone. The ideas and writings of the leading secular thinkers of the European Enlightenment—reformers and social critics like Voltaire, Rousseau, and Beccaria as well as conservative analysts like Montesquieu—were quoted everywhere in the colonies, by everyone who claimed a broad awareness. In pamphlet after pamphlet the American writers cited Locke on natural rights and on the social and governmental contract, Montesquieu and later Delolme on the character of British liberty and on the institutional requirements for its attainment, Voltaire on the evils of clerical oppression, Beccaria on the reform of criminal law, Grotius, Pufendorf, Burlamaqui, and Vattel on the laws of nature and of nations, and on the principles of civil government.

The pervasiveness of such citations is at times astonishing. In his two most prominent pamphlets James Otis cited as authorities, and quoted at length, Locke, Rousseau, Grotius, and Pufendorf, and denounced spokesmen, such as Filmer, for more traditional ideas of political authority. Josiah Quincy, Jr. referred with approval to a whole library of enlightened authors, among them Beccaria, Rousseau, Montesquieu, and the historian Robertson; and the young Alexander Hamilton, seeking to score points against his venerable antagonist, Samuel Seabury, recommended with arch condescension that his adversary get himself at the first opportunity to some of the writings of Pufendorf, Locke, Montesquieu, and Burlamaqui to discover the true principles of politics. Examples could be multiplied almost without end. Citations, respectful borrowings from, or at least references to, the eighteenth-century European illuminati are everywhere in the pamphlets of Revolutionary America.

The citations are plentiful, but the knowledge they reflect, like that of ancient classics, is at times superficial. Locke is cited often with precision on points of political theory, but at other times he is referred to in the most offhand way, as if he could be relied on to support anything the writers happened to be arguing. Bolingbroke and Hume are at times lumped together with radical reformers, and secondary figures like Burlamaqui are treated on a level with Locke. Nor were the critical, reforming writings of the Enlightenment, even some of the most radical, used exclusively by the left wing of the Revolutionary movement. Everyone, whatever his position on Independence or his judgment of Parliament's actions, cited them as authoritative; almost no one, Whig or Tory, disputed them or introduced them with apology. Writers the colonists took to be opponents of Enlightenment rationalism—primarily Hobbes, Filmer, Sibthorpe, Mandeville, and Mainwaring—were denounced as frequently by loyalists as by patriots; but almost never, before 1776, were Locke, Montesquieu, Vattel, Beccaria, Burlamaqui, Voltaire, or even Rousseau. Mercy Otis Warren listed the contents of a hypothetical Tory library in her play *The Group*; but with the exception of Filmer none of the authors she mentions there were in fact referred to favorably by the Tories. James Chalmers, the Maryland loyalist, attacked Paine not with Hobbes, Sibthorpe, Wedderburn's speeches, and the statutes of Henry VIII, which, according to Mrs. Warren, he should have done, but with Montesquieu, Hutcheson, even Voltaire and Rousseau. The New York loyalist Peter Van Schaack reached his decision to oppose Independence on the basis of a close and sympathetic reading of Locke, Vattel, Montesquieu, Grotius, Beccaria, and Pufendorf, and in 1777 justified his defiance of the state of New York with reference to "the sentiments of Mr. Locke and those other advocates for the rights of mankind whose principles have been avowed and in some instances carried into practice by the congress." The Pennsylvania loyalist

Joseph Galloway also cited Locke and Pufendorf as readily as his antagonists did; and when Charles Inglis looked for the source of Paine's anti-monarchism in order to attack it, he found it not in Enlightenment theory, whose exponents he praised, but in an obscure treatise by one John Hall, "pensioner under Oliver Cromwell."

Referred to on all sides, by writers of all political viewpoints in the colonies, the major figures of the European Enlightenment and many of the lesser, contributed substantially to the thought of the Americans; but except for Locke's, their influence, though more decisive than that of the authors of classical antiquity, was neither clearly dominant nor wholly determinative.

Also prominent and in certain ways powerfully influential was yet another group of writers and ideas. Just as the colonists cited with enthusiasm the theorists of universal reason, so too did they associate themselves, with offhand familiarity, with the tradition of the English common law. The great figures of England's legal history, especially the seventeenth-century common lawyers, were referred to repeatedly—by the colonial lawyers above all, but by others as well. Sir Edward Coke is everywhere in the literature: "Coke upon Littleton," "my Lord Coke's Reports," "Lord Coke's 2nd Institute"—the citations are almost as frequent as, and occasionally even less precise than, those to Locke, Montesquieu, and Voltaire. The earlier commentators Bracton and Fortescue are also referred to, casually, as authorities, as are Coke's contemporary Francis Bacon, and his successors as Lord Chief Justice, Sir Matthew Hale, Sir John Vaughan, and Sir John Holt. In the later years of the Revolutionary period, Blackstone's *Commentaries* and the opinions of Chief Justice Camden became standard authorities. Throughout the literature, trial reports—Raymond's, Salkeld's, Williams', Goldsboro's—are referred to, and use is made of standard treatises on English law: Sullivan's *Lectures on the Laws of England*; Gilbert's *Law of Evidence;* Foster's *Crown Law;* Barrington's *Observations on the More Ancient Statutes.*

The common law was manifestly influential in shaping the awareness of the Revolutionary generation. But, again, it did not in itself determine the kinds of conclusions men would draw in the crisis of the time. Otis and Hutchinson both worshiped Coke, but for reasons that have nothing to do with the great chief justice, they read significantly different meanings into his opinion in *Bonham's Case.* The law was no science of what to do next. To the colonists it was a repository of experience in human dealings embodying the principles of justice, equity, and rights; above all, it was a form of history—ancient, indeed immemorial, history; constitutional and national history; and, as history, it helped explain the movement of events and the meaning of the present. Particularly revealing, therefore, though vague in their intent, are the references in the pamphlets to the seventeenth-century scholars of the law, especially of the history of the law, whose importance in the development of English historical thought we have only recently become aware: Henry Spelman, Thomas Madox, Robert Brady, and William Petyt. English law—as authority, as legitimizing precedent, as embodied principle, and as the framework of historical understanding—stood side by side with Enlightenment rationalism in the minds of the Revolutionary generation.

Still another tradition, another group of writers and texts, that emerges from the political literature as a major source of ideas and attitudes of the Revolutionary generation stemmed ultimately from the political and social theories of New England Puritanism, and particularly from the ideas associated with covenant theology. For the elaborate system of thought erected by the first leaders of settlement in New England had been consolidated and amplified by a succession of writers in the course of the seventeenth century, channeled into the mainstream of eighteenth-century political and social thinking by a generation of enlightened preachers, and softened in its denominational rigor by many hands until it could be received, with minor variations, by almost the entire spectrum of American Protestantism.

In one sense this was the most limited and parochial tradition that contributed in an important way to the writings of the Revolution, for it drew mainly from local sources and, whatever the extent of its newly acquired latitudinarianism, was yet restricted in its appeal to those who continued to understand the world, as the original Puritans had, in theological terms. But in another sense it contained the broadest ideas of all, since it offered a context for everyday events nothing less than cosmic in its dimensions. It carried on into the eighteenth century and into the minds of the Revolutionaries the idea, originally worked out in the sermons and tracts of the settlement period, that the colonization of British America had been an event designed by the hand of God to satisfy his ultimate aims. Reinvigorated in its historical meaning by newer works like Daniel

Neal's *History of the Puritans* (1732–1738), his *History of New England* (1720), and Thomas Prince's uncompleted *Chronological History of New England in the Form of Annals* (1736), this influential strain of thought, found everywhere in the eighteenth-century colonies, stimulated confidence in the idea that America had a special place, as yet not fully revealed, in the architecture of God's intent. "Imparting a sense of crisis by revivifying Old Testament condemnations of a degenerate people," it prepared the colonists for a convulsive realization by locating their parochial concerns at a critical juncture on the map of mankind's destiny. Their own history, it was clear, would provide the climax for those remarkable *"Connections"* from which they liked to quote, Samuel Shuckford's *Sacred and Profane History of the World Connected* (which contains a map fixing the exact geographical location of the Garden of Eden) and Humphrey Prideaux's *The Old and New Testament Connected.*

But important as all of these clusters of ideas were, they did not in themselves form a coherent intellectual pattern, and they do not exhaust the elements that went into the making of the Revolutionary frame of mind. There were among them, in fact, striking incongruities and contradictions. The common lawyers the colonists cited, for example, sought to establish right by appeal to precedent and to an unbroken tradition evolving from time immemorial, and they assumed, if they did not argue, that the accumulation of the ages, the burden of inherited custom, contained within it a greater wisdom than any man or group of men could devise by the power of reason. Nothing could have been more alien to the Enlightenment rationalists whom the colonists also quoted—and with equal enthusiasm. These theorists felt that it was precisely the heavy crust of custom that was weighing down the spirit of man; they sought to throw it off and to create by the unfettered power of reason a framework of institutions superior to the accidental inheritance of the past. And the covenant theologians differed from both in continuing to assume the ultimate inability of man to improve his condition by his own powers and in deriving the principles of politics from divine intent and from the network of obligations that bound redeemed man to his maker.

What brought these disparate strands of thought together, what dominated the colonists' miscellaneous learning and shaped it into a coherent whole, was the influence of still another group of writers, a group whose thought overlapped with that of those already mentioned but which was yet distinct in its essential characteristics and unique in its determinative power. The ultimate origins of this distinctive ideological strain lay in the radical social and political thought of the English Civil War and of the Commonwealth period; but its permanent form had been acquired at the turn of the seventeenth century and in the early eighteenth century, in the writings of a group of prolific opposition theorists, "country" politicians and publicists.

Among the seventeenth-century progenitors of this line of eighteenth-century radical writers and opposition politicians united in criticism of "court" and ministerial power, Milton was an important figure—not Milton the poet so much as Milton the radical tractarian, author of *Eikonoklastes* and *The Tenure of Kings and Magistrates* (both published in 1649). The American Revolutionary writers referred with similar respect if with less understanding to the more systematic writing of Harrington and to that of the like-minded Henry Neville; above all, they referred to the doctrines of Algernon Sidney, that "martyr to civil liberty" whose *Discourses Concerning Government* (1968) became, in Caroline Robbins' phrase, a "textbook of revolution" in America.

The colonists identified themselves with these seventeenth-century heroes of liberty: but they felt closer to the early eighteenth-century writers who modified and enlarged this earlier body of ideas, fused it into a whole with other, contemporary strains of thought, and, above all, applied it to the problems of eighteenth-century English politics. These early eighteenth-century writers—coffeehouse radicals and opposition politicians, spokesmen for the anti-Court independents within Parliament and the disaffected without, draftsmen of a "country" vision of English politics that would persist throughout the eighteenth century and into the nineteenth—faded subsequently into obscurity and are little known today. But more than any other single group of writers they shaped the mind of the American Revolutionary generation.

To the colonists the most important of these publicists and intellectual middlemen were those spokesmen for extreme libertarianism, John Trenchard (1662–1723) and Thomas Gordon (d. 1750). The former, a west-country squire of ample means and radical ideas, was a 57-year-old veteran of the pamphlet wars that surrounded the Glorious Revolution when in 1719 he met Gordon, "a clever young Scot . . . fresh from Aberdeen University, [who had come] to London to make his fortune, equipped with little but a sharp tongue and a ready wit." They joined forces to produce, first, the weekly *Indepen-*

dent Whig to attack High Church pretensions and, more generally, the establishment of religion, fifty-three papers of which were published in book form in 1721; and *Cato's Letters,* a searing indictment of eighteenth-century English politics and society written in response to the South Sea Bubble crisis, which appeared first serially in *The London Journal* and then, beginning in 1720, in book form. Incorporating in their colorful, slashing, superbly readable pages the major themes of the "left" opposition under Walpole, these libertarian tracts, emerging first in the form of denunciations of standing armies in the reign of William III, left an indelible imprint on the "country" mind everywhere in the English-speaking world. In America, where they were republished entire or in part again and again, "quoted in every colonial newspaper from Boston to Savannah," and referred to repeatedly in the pamphlet literature, the writings of Trenchard and Gordon ranked with the treatises of Locke as the most authoritative statement of the nature of political liberty and above Locke as an exposition of the social sources of the threats it faced.

Standing with Trenchard and Gordon as early eighteenth-century "preceptors of civil liberty" was the liberal Anglican bishop, Benjamin Hoadly. This "best hated clergyman of the century amongst his own order," as Leslie Stephen described him—honored and promoted by an administration that despised him but could not do without him—achieved fame, or notoriety, in England for his role in the elaborate clerical polemics of the "Bangorian Controversy" (1717–1720), in which he had been assisted by Gordon. In the course of this bitter and voluminous debate he had become an object of scorn and vituperation as well as of admiration in England; but in the colonies he was widely held to be one of the notable figures in the history of political thought. Anglicans in America, it was true, like their codenominationalists at home, could scarcely endorse his extraordinary denial of sacerdotal powers for the Church hierarchy or his almost unbelievable repudiation of the whole idea of the church visible, nor could they, in theory at least, accept his extreme toleration of dissent. But their attention focused not on his views of the Church but on the crucial battles he had fought early in the century against the nonjurors and their doctrines of divine right and passive obedience, and on the extreme statements of Whig political theory in his treatise *The Original and Institution of Civil Government Discussed* (1710) and in certain of his many tracts, especially *The Measures of Submission to the Civil Magistrates Considered* (1705). Ultimately, Hoadly came to embody physically the continuity of the conglomerate tradition of English radical and opposition thought, for though he had been active at the end of the seventeenth century, he lived on until 1761, associating in his very old age with the English radicals of Jefferson's generation and establishing contact with such spokesmen of advanced American thought as Jonathan Mayhew.

With Hoadly, among his contemporaries, though below him in importance to the Americans, was the outstanding opponent in Parliament of Walpole's administration, the leader of a coterie of early eighteenth-century freethinking Whigs, Robert Viscount Molesworth. Friend of Trenchard and Gordon, encomiast of *Cato's Letters* (they were frequently attributed to him), he was known particularly in the colonies for his *Account of Denmark* (1694), which detailed the process by which free states succumb to absolutism. An opposition leader of another sort who contributed in a more complicated way to the colonists' inheritance of early eighteenth-century thought was the spectacular Jacobite politician, writer, and philosopher, Henry St. John, Viscount Bolingbroke. His *Craftsman,* appearing weekly or semiweekly for a full ten years, from 1726 to 1736, roasted Walpole's administration in crackling fires of ridicule and denunciation. Its savage, bitter, relentless attacks were indistinguishable from *Cato's* polemics on major points of political criticism. *The Craftsman,* in fact, quoted the writings of Trenchard and Gordon freely, and otherwise, in almost identical language, decried the corruption of the age and warned of the dangers of incipient autocracy. The Scottish philosopher, Francis Hutcheson, and the nonconformist schoolmaster, Philip Doddridge, were also figures of this generation the colonists knew and cited in the same general context, as was Isaac Watts, the hymnologist and writer on questions of church and education.

The tradition continued into the Revolutionaries' own generation, promoted by Richard Baron, republican and dissenter, associate and literary heir of Thomas Gordon, who republished in the 1750s political works of Milton and Sidney and issued also an anthology of the writings of the later radicals, including Jonathan Mayhew; and promoted even more effectively by that extraordinary one-man propaganda machine in the cause of liberty, the indefatigable Thomas Hollis, whose correspondence in the 1760s first with Mayhew and then with Andrew Eliot illustrates vividly the directness of the influence of this radical and opposition tradition on the ideological origins of the Revolution. In the Revolutionary years proper a group of still younger writers renewed the earlier ideas, extended them still further, and, together with the leading spokesmen for the colonies, applied them to the Anglo-American controversy. Foremost among these later English advocates of reform in politics and religion were Richard Price, Joseph Priestley, and John Cartwright; but the key book of this generation was the three-volume *Political Disquisitions* published in 1774 by the schoolmaster, political theorist, and moralist, James Burgh. The republican historian Catharine Macaulay, whose *History of England* has aptly been called "an imaginative work in praise of republican principles under the title of a History of England," was also an important intellectual figure of this generation to the colonists, but among the many Whig historians the Americans knew and referred to—including Bulstrode Whitelock, Gilbert Burnet, William Guthrie, and James Ralph—their preference was for the exiled Huguenot, Paul de Rapin-Thoyras. His "inestimable treasure," the vast, radically Whiggish *Histoire d'Angleterre,* published in English between 1725 and 1731, together with his earlier sketch of the whole, *A Dissertation on the . . . Whigs and Tories* (1717; reprinted in Boston in 1773), provided indisputable proof of the theories of all of the radical and anti-establishment writers by demonstrating their validity through a thousand years of English history. But all history, not only English history, was vital to the thought of the Revolutionary generation, and it is a matter of particular consequence that among the best, or at least the most up-to-date, translations of Sallust and Tacitus available to the colonists were those by the ubiquitous Thomas Gordon, "under whose hands [Tacitus] virtually became an apologist for English Whiggery"; he prefaced his translations with introductory "Discourses" of prodigious length in which he explained beyond all chance of misunderstanding the political and moral meaning of those ancient historians.

To say simply that this tradition of opposition thought was quickly transmitted to America and widely appreciated there is to understate the fact. Opposition thought, in the form it acquired at the turn of the seventeenth century and in the early eighteenth century, was devoured by the colonists. From the earliest years of the century it nourished their political thought and sensibilities. There seems never to have been a time after the Hanoverian succession when these writings were not central to American political expression or absent from polemical politics. James Franklin's *New England Courant* began excerpting *Cato's Letters* eleven months after the first of them appeared in London; before the end of 1722 his brother Benjamin had incorporated them into his Silence Dogood papers. Isaac Norris I in 1721 ordered his London bookseller to send him the separate issues of *The Independent Whig* as they appeared, and that whole collection was reprinted in Philadelphia in 1724 and 1740. John Peter Zenger's famous *New York Weekly Journal* (1733 ff.) was in its early years a veritable anthology of the writings of Trenchard and Gordon. By 1728, in fact, *Cato's Letters* had already been fused with Locke, Coke, Pufendorf, and Grotius to produce a prototypical American treatise in defense of English liberties overseas, a tract indistinguishable from any number of publications that would appear in the Revolutionary crisis fifty years later. So popular and influential had *Cato's Letters* become in the colonies within a decade and a half of their first appearance, so packed with ideological meaning, that, reinforced by Addison's universally popular play *Cato* and the colonists' selectively Whiggish reading of the Roman historians, it gave rise to what might be called a "Catonic" image, central to the political theory of the time, in which the career of the half-mythological Roman and the words of the two London journalists merged indistinguishably. Everyone who read the *Boston Gazette* of April 26, 1756, understood the double reference, bibliographical and historical, that was intended by an anonymous writer who concluded an address to the people of Massachusetts—as he put it without further explanation—"in the words of Cato to the freeholders of Great Britain."

Testimonies to the unique influence of this opposition literature—evidences of this great "hinterland of belief" from which would issue the specific arguments of the American Revolution—are everywhere in the writings of eighteenth-century Americans. Sometimes they are explicit, as when Jonathan Mayhew wrote that, having been "initiated, in youth, in the doctrines of civil liberty, as they were taught by such men . . . as Sidney and Milton, Locke, and Hoadly, among the moderns, I liked them; they seemed rational"; or when John Adams insisted, against what he took to be the massed opinion of informed Englishmen, that the root principles of good government could be found only in "Sidney, Harrington, Locke, Milton, Nedham, Neville, Burnet, and Hoadly"; or again, when he listed the great political thinkers of 1688 as "Sidney, Locke, Hoadly, Trenchard, Gordon, Plato Redivivus [Neville]"; or when Josiah Quincy, Jr., bequeathed to his son in 1774 "Algernon Sidney's works,—John Locke's works,—Lord Bacon's works,—Gordon's *Tacitus,*—and *Cato's Letters.* May the spirit of liberty rest upon him!" More often, the evidence is implicit, in the degree to which the pamphleteers quoted from, plagiarized, and modeled their writings on *Cato's Letters* and *The Independent Whig.* Above all, their influence may be seen in the way the peculiar bent of mind of the writers in this tradition was reflected in the ideas and attitudes of the Americans.

The fact is easily mistaken because on the main points of theory the eighteenth-century contributors to this tradition were not original. Borrowing heavily from more original thinkers, they were often, in their own time and after, dismissed as mere popularizers. Their key concepts—natural rights, the contractual basis of society and government, the uniqueness of England's liberty-preserving "mixed" constitution—were commonplaces of the liberal thought of the time. But if the elements of their thought were ordinary, the emphasis placed upon them and the use made of them were not. Pride in the liberty-preserving constitution of Britain was universal in the political literature of the age, and everyone agreed on the moral qualities necessary to preserve a free government. But where the mainstream purveyors of political thought spoke mainly with pride of the constitutional and political achievements of Georgian England, the opposition writers, no less proud of the heritage, viewed their circumstances with alarm, "stressed the danger to England's ancient heritage and the loss of pristine virtue," studied the processes of decay, and dwelt endlessly on the evidences of corruption they saw about them and the dark future these malignant signs portended. They were the Cassandras of the age, and while their maledictions "were used for party purposes . . . what [they] said about antique virtue, native liberty, public spirit, and the dangers of luxury and corruption was of general application" and was drawn from the common repository of political lore. They used the commonplaces of the age negatively, critically. They were the enemies of complacence in one of the most complacent eras in England's history. Few of these writers would have agreed with the sentiment expressed by the Lord Chancellor of England in 1766 and concurred in by the overwhelming majority of eighteenth-century Englishmen: "I seek for the liberty and constitution of this kingdom no farther back than the [Glorious] Revolution; there I make my stand." Few of them accepted the Glorious Revolution and the lax political pragmatism that had followed as the final solution to the political problems of the time. They refused to believe that the transfer of sovereignty from the crown to Parliament provided a perfect guarantee that the individual would be protected from the power of the state. Ignoring the complacence and general high level of satisfaction of the time, they called for vigilance against the government of Walpole equal to what their predecessors had shown against the Stuarts. They insisted, at a time when government was felt to be less oppressive than it had been for two hundred years, that it was necessarily—by its very nature—hostile to human liberty and happiness; that, properly, it existed only on the tolerance of the people whose needs it served; and that it could be, and reasonably should be, dismissed—overthrown—if it attempted to exceed its proper jurisdiction.

It was the better to maintain this vigil against government that they advocated reforms—political reforms, not social or economic reforms, for these were eighteenth- not nineteenth- or twentieth-century English radicals—beyond anything admissible in Walpole's age, or indeed in any age that followed in England until well into the nineteenth century. At one time or another, one or another of them argued for adult manhood suffrage; elimination of the rotten borough system and the substitution of regular units of representation systematically related to the distribution of population; the binding of representatives to their constituencies by residential requirements and by instructions; alterations in the definition of seditious libel so as to permit full freedom of the press to criticize government; and the total withdrawal of government control over the practice of religion.

Such ideas, based on extreme solicitude for the individual and an equal hostility to government, were expressed in a spirit of foreboding and fear for the future. For while they acknowledged the existing stability and prosperity of England, they nevertheless grounded their thought in pessimism concerning human nature and in the discouraging record of human weakness. Their resulting concern was continuously deepened by the scenes they saw around them. Politics under Walpole may have been stable, but the stability rested, they believed, on the systematic corruption of Parliament by the executive, which, they warned, if left unchecked, would eat away the foundations of liberty. The dangers seemed great, for they say, as J. G. A. Pocock has written in outlining "the 'Country' vision of English politics as it appears in a multitude of writings in the half century that follows, 1675," that

> *the executive possesses means of distracting Parliament from its proper function; it seduces members by the offer of places and pensions, by retaining them to follow ministers and ministers' rivals, by persuading them to support measures—standing armies, national debts, excise schemes—whereby the activities of administration grow beyond Parliament's control. These means of subversion are known collectively as corruption, and if ever Parliament or those who elect them—for corruption may occur at this point too—should be wholly corrupt, then there will be an end of independence and liberty.*

This was their major theme, their obsessive concern, and they hammered away at it week after week, year after year, in ringing denunciations of Walpole's manipulation of Parliament and of the dissoluteness of the age that permitted it. The outcries were as loud, the fear as deep, on the "left" of the opposition spectrum as on the "right." So "Cato" warned, again and again, that

> *public corruptions and abuses have grown upon us; fees in most, if not all, offices, are immensely increased; places and employments, which ought not to be sold at all, are sold for treble value; the necessities of the public have made greater impositions unavoidable, and yet the public has run very much in debt; and as those debts have been increasing, and the people growing poor, salaries have been augmented, and pensions multiplied.*

Bolingbroke was even more insistent that England was faced with the age-old and associated dangers of ministerial usurpation and political corruption. And the prose of his jeremiads—echoed in the more artistic productions of the great Tory satirists of the age, in the writings of Swift, Pope, Gay, Mandeville, even in the less partisan, critical-patriotic rhapsodies of James Thomson, *Liberty and Britannia*—was even more vivid, more memorable than that of "Cato." He devised a new terminology to describe the urgent danger. *"Robinocracy,"* he wrote, was what was developing under the "prime"-ministry (a term of derogation) of Robert Walpole. Robinocracy, he explained, was a form of government in which the chief minister maintained the façade of constitutional procedures while he in fact monopolized the whole of governmental power:

> *The* Robinarch, *or chief ruler, is nominally a* minister *only and creature of the prince; but in reality he is a sovereign, as despotic, arbitrary a sovereign as this part of the world affords. . . . The* Robinarch . . . *hath unjustly engrossed the whole power of a nation into his own hands . . .* [*and*] *admits no person to any considerable post of trust and power under him who is not either a* relation, *a* creature, *or a* thorough-paced tool *whom he can lead at pleasure into any dirty work without being able to discover his designs or the consequences of them.*

The modes of Robinarcal control of a once-free legislature were clear enough. The corrupt minister and his accomplices systematically encourage "*luxury* and *extravagance,* the certain forerunners of *indigence, dependance,* and *servility.*" Some deputies

> *are tied down with* honors, titles, *and* preferments, *of which the* Robinarch *engrosses the disposal to himself, and others with* bribes, *which are called pensions in these countries. Some are persuaded to prostitute themselves for the lean reward of* hopes *and* promises; *and others, more senseless than all of them, have sacrificed their principles and consciences to a set of* party names, *without any meaning, or the vanity of appearing in favor at* court.

Once in power the Robinarcal ministry feeds on its own corruption. It loads the people with taxes and with debts, and ends by creating a mercenary army ostensibly for the purpose of protecting the people but in fact to perfect its dominance in just those ways, Bolingbroke wrote, that Trenchard had explained years before in his tracts on standing armies.

Solutions of different forms were advocated by "left" and "right": the former urged those institutional, political, and legal reforms which would finally be realized a full century later in the Reform Acts of the nineteenth century; the latter argued the need for that romantic ideal, the Patriot Prince, who should govern as well as reign, yet govern above parties and factions, in harmony with a loyal and independent commons. But if their solutions were different their basic observations and the fears they expressed were identical. Everywhere, they agreed, there was corruption—corruption technically, in the adroit manipulation of Parliament by a power-hungry ministry, and corruption generally, in the self-indulgence, effeminizing luxury, and gluttonous pursuit of gain of a generation sunk in new and unaccustomed wealth. If nothing were done to stop the growth of these evils, England would follow so many other nations into a tyranny from which there would be no recovery.

But if these dark thoughts, in the England of Walpole and Gibbon, attained popularity in certain opposition, radical, and nonconformist circles, they had relatively little political influence in the country at large. In the mainland colonies of North America, however, they were immensely popular and influential. There, an altered condition of life made what in England were considered to be extreme, dislocating ideas sound like simple statements of fact. There, the spread of independent landholding had insensibly created a broad electorate. There, the necessity of devising systems of representation at a stroke and the presence of persistent conflict between the legislatures and the executives had tended to make representation regular and responsible and had limited the manipulative influence of any group in power. There, the multiplicity of religious groupings, the need for continuous encouragement of immigration, and the distance from European centers of ecclesiastical authority had weakened the force of religious establishments below anything known in Europe. There the moral basis of a healthy, liberty-preserving polity seemed already to exist in the unsophisticated lives of the independent, uncorrupted, landowning yeoman farmers who comprised so large a part of the colonial population. Yet there the threat of ministerial aggrandizement seemed particularly pressing and realistic, for there, in all but the charter colonies, the executive branches of government—venal surrogates, it so often seemed, of ill-informed if not ill-disposed masters—held, and used, powers that in England had been stripped from the crown in the settlement that had followed the Glorious Revolution as inappropriate to the government of a free people.

In such a situation the writings of the English radical and opposition leaders seemed particularly reasonable, particularly relevant, and they quickly became influential. Everywhere groups seeking justification for concerted opposition to constituted governments turned to these writers. When in 1735 John Peter Zenger's lawyer sought theoretical grounds for attacking the traditional concept of seditious libel, he turned to Trenchard and Gordon's *Cato's Letters.* When, four years later, an opposition writer in Massachusetts drew up an indictment of the governor so vehement the Boston printers would not publish it, he did so, he wrote, with "some helps from *Cato's Letters,* which were wrote upon the glorious cause of liberty." When in 1750

Jonathan Mayhew sought to work out, in his celebrated *Discourse Concerning Unlimited Submission,* a full rationale for resistance to constituted government, he drew on—indeed, cribbed wholesale—not Locke, whose ideas would scarcely have supported what he was saying, but a sermon of Benjamin Hoadly, from whom he borrowed not only ideas and phrases but, in abusing the nonjuror Charles Leslie, the Bishop's enemies as well. When in 1752–1753 William Livingston and his friends undertook to publish in a series of periodical essays a sweeping critique of public life in New York, and in particular to assault the concept of a privileged state, they modeled their publication, *The Independent Reflector,* on Trenchard and Gordon's *Independent Whig,* and borrowed from it specific formulations for their central ideas. And when [in] Massachusetts in 1754 opponents of a stringent excise act sought models for a campaign of opposition, they turned not only generally to the literature of opposition that had been touched off by Walpole's excise proposal of 1733 but specifically to Bolingbroke's *Craftsman* of that year, from which they freely copied arguments and slogans, even figures of speech. Everywhere in America the tradition that had originated in seventeenth-century radicalism and that had been passed on, with elaborations and applications, by early eighteenth-century English opposition publicists and politicians brought forth congenial responses and provided grounds for opposition politics.

But it did more. It provided also a harmonizing force for the other, discordant elements in the political and social thought of the Revolutionary generation. Within the framework of these ideas, Enlightenment abstractions and common law precedents, covenant theology and classical analogy—Locke and Abraham, Brutus and Coke—could all be brought together into a comprehensive theory of politics. It was in terms of this pattern of ideas and attitudes—originating in the English Civil War and carried forward with additions and modifications not on the surface of English political life but in its undercurrents stirred by doctrinaire libertarians, disaffected politicians, and religious dissenters—that the colonists responded to the new regulations imposed by England on her American colonies after 1763.

Jack P. Greene

THE COLONIAL ASSEMBLIES AND REVOLUTIONARY IDEOLOGY

After The Ideological Origins of the American Revolution, *Professor Bailyn published another work,* The Origins of American Politics, *which built upon and extended his interpretation of the intellectual sources of the American Revolution. He said that the leading explanation of the origins of American politics at present was the view that the colonial assemblies became little "Parliaments" and thought of themselves as such. This view, he believed, was mere institutional history that omitted dynamic elements. It was Bailyn's opinion that the rise of the assemblies* was *important but that it was not a "sufficient explanation" of the Revolution because it ignored what the revolutionaries said about themselves. They had said that the cause of their distress was the deliberate design—a conspiracy—of ministers of state to overthrow the British constitution in England and America and to diminish British liberties, an enterprise bred and nourished in corruption.*

Issue was taken by Professor Jack P. Greene with Bailyn's interpretation of the ideological origins of the American Revolution. He said that Bailyn had concentrated upon the pamphlets of the Revolution and thought that this limitation of evidence to pamphlets and newspaper essays was a defect of Bailyn's research design. Of most serious importance, however, according to Greene, Bailyn had failed to consider or to give proper weight to the behavior of colonial legislators during the eighteenth century and their persistent preoccupation with the dangers of prerogative power. This preoccupation was rooted in the pre-Walpolean opposition of Parliament to the Crown in seventeenth-century England, and the central issue was always the nature and extent of the royal prerogative. The English revolution consisted precisely in the defeat of the claims of kings that they had a right to act independently of the consent of their subjects as represented in their elected legislature, the Parliament. England settled this conflict in favor of the people in the Glorious Revolution of 1688 and thereafter the fundamental question of power was not in issue. But what had been settled in England was not settled in the colonies, or at least was not perceived to have been settled; but continued to have force in the imaginations and behavior of colonial legislators right up to the Revolution itself. Saying that an explanation for this phenomenon must be tentative, Greene suggested that the phenomenon appeared by the action of "powerful mimetic impulses within colonial society." But imitation and cultural lag could not alone account for the tensions between colonial legislatures and colonial governors. The lines

Reprinted by permission from the authors and publisher from: Jack P. Greene, "Political Mimesis: A Consideration of the Historical and Cultural Roots of Legislative Behavior in the British Colonies in the Eighteenth Century," Bernard Bailyn, "A Comment," and Jack P. Greene, "A Reply," *The American Historical Review* 75 (December 1969): 337–67 (footnotes omitted).

of tension between the Stuarts and their recalcitrant parliaments were in fact *reproduced on the American continent because the same conditions that created them in England in the seventeenth century created them in America in the eighteenth.*

Bernard Bailyn replied to Greene's strictures and said that Greene was under certain misconceptions. He was wrong in assuming that because Bailyn emphasized eighteenth-century beliefs, the seventeenth-century political conflicts that preceded were ignored. It seemed to Bailyn self-evident that the eighteenth-century intellectual and political dialog was a continuation of that of the seventeenth, although the fears of autocracy were expressed in "new, more up-to-date and realistic form." The worry both in England and the colonies in the eighteenth century was not over the prerogatives of the King for the very good reason that no one in the colonies mistook the governors for the King. The worry both in England and the colonies was over the acts of his ministers and other "Crown underlings," including colonial governors. Hence, said Bailyn, "the whole crucial subject of corruption . . . lay at the heart of colonial political thought." It was not until the Revolution was near that the focus of attack shifted from the supposed conspiracy of ministers and centered upon the King. It was then *that the colonials felt that they were reenacting the political drama of seventeenth-century England. Greene's documentation proved that the "Rise of the Assembly" really took place, but Bailyn believed that the "process of politics is not explained by it."*

Greene then replied to Bailyn's statement of defense of his thesis, laying emphasis upon what he believed to be shortcomings in Bailyn's historical methodology.

The next essay is Professor Greene's first criticism of Professor Bailyn, and is followed by their exchange of comments.

Until comparatively recently, most investigations of government and politics in the eighteenth-century American colonies concentrated upon the recurrent contests between governors and elected lower houses of assembly and "the growth of colonial self-government" as reflected in the repeated triumphs of the assemblies in those struggles. There was an almost total consensus, as Charles M. Andrews wrote in 1943 after a lifetime of study, that "the most conspicuous feature" of "the political and institutional aspects . . . of the eighteenth century . . . was the rise of the colonial assembly with its growth to self-conscious activity and de facto independence of royal control." Perhaps because the focus in these studies was primarily upon institutional development and the process by which the assemblies increased their authority, none of the studies made much attempt to handle the problem of motivation, to explain in any detail why the assemblies acted as they did. The early assumption of nineteenth-century patriotic American historians that the assemblies, obviously representing the natural desire of all men to be free, were fighting for liberty and democracy against executive oppression and tyranny simply gave way to the equally vague and untestable supposition of H. L. Osgood, Andrews, and their students. They contended that the assemblies, responding to environmentally induced social and intellectual tendencies that diverged sharply from those of the mother country, were seeking to secure as much self-government as possible, to attain, in the words of one writer, "the largest measure of local home rule compatible with whatever might be necessary to retain the advantages of the British connection."

Around the beginning of this century, a few historians adopted a more promising line of investigation by focusing upon the political divisions that existed in almost every colony at many points during their history and that invariably cut across institutional boundaries. Because these historians often sought to explain those divisions in terms of a crude social dichotomy between upper and lower classes, the earliest of their studies did not much advance our understanding of the psychology of colonial politics. But they did show, as Andrews acknowledged late in his career, that any complete explanation of colonial political life required an "understanding of the social and propertied interests involved, class distinctions and personal rivalries, the motives of majorities, and the ambitions of political leaders." Despite the often fragmentary records of colonial politics, many detailed studies written during the past twenty-five years have provided a wealth of solid information on the nature of political rivalries, the social, economic, and religious motivation that lay behind those rivalries, and the substantive issues in dispute. In the process, they have shifted attention almost entirely away from the emergence of the assemblies, but they have revealed that rivalries were so diverse, motivation so complex, and issues so varied—not only from colony to colony but also from time to time within colonies—that it has been extremely difficult to construct an alternative general framework of interpretation that has so comprehensive an applicability.

Bernard Bailyn has considered this problem at some length in his recent studies of the relationship among society, politics, and ideology in the eighteenth-century colonies. Earlier writers had described many of the central ingredients of colonial political thought and had pointed out the remarkable degree to which they were "a proudly conscious extension of political thought in England," but Bailyn was the first to try to show which strands of English political thought were most important in the colonies and how those strands affected colonial political behavior. In the introduction to the first volume of his *Pamphlets of the American Revolution* he analyzed in greater detail than any previous scholar the intellectual content of American arguments against British policy between 1763 and 1776. He found that, although Americans drew heavily upon the heritage of classical antiquity, the writings of Enlightenment rationalism, the tradition of the English common law, and the political and social theories of New England Puritanism, it was the writings of "a group of early eighteenth-century radical publicists and opposition politicians in England who carried forward into the eighteenth century and applied to the politics of the age of Walpole the peculiar strain of anti-authoritarianism bred in the upheaval of the English Civil War" that dominated revolutionary political thought, "shaped it into a coherent whole," and, to a remarkable degree, determined the ways American leaders interpreted and responded to British regulatory and restrictive measures after 1763. In a new and expanded version of this work Bailyn argued on the basis of an investigation of earlier political writings that this same "configuration of ideas and attitudes . . . could be found [in the colonies] intact—completely formed—as far back as the 1730s" and "in partial form . . . even . . . at the turn of the seventeenth century."

That this opposition vision of politics—this pattern of thought that viewed contemporary Britain "with alarm, 'stressed the dangers of England's ancient heritage and the loss of pristine virtue,' studied the processes of decay, and dwelt endlessly on the evidences of corruption . . . and the dark future these malignant signs portended"—was the single most important intellectual ingredient in "American politics in its original, early eighteenth-century form" has subsequently been contended by Bailyn in a series of recent essays. He seeks to explain why this conception of politics acquired in the colonies a place in public life far more significant than it had ever had in England, why it became so "determinative of the political understanding of eighteenth-century Americans" that it formed the "assumptions and expectations" and furnished "not merely the vocabulary but the grammar of thought, the apparatus by which the world was perceived." In constructing an answer to this question, Bailyn manages to weave "into a single brief statement of explanation" his own findings on political ideology, many of the discoveries of those writers who stressed the rise of the assemblies, and the conclusions of the students of internal political divisions. What gave the opposition view of politics a "sharper relevance" in America, according to Bailyn, was the "bitter, persistent strife" that characterized colonial politics, strife between executives and legislatures and, infinitely more important, among the chaotic and continually shifting factions that, he suggests, were endemic to colonial life. This strife was rooted in two anomalies. First, while the theoretical powers of colonial executives were greater than those of their English counterparts, their actual powers were much smaller because they had at their disposal few of the "devices by which in England the executive" exerted effective political control. Second, the intense competition for status, power, and wealth generated by an unstable economic and social structure made what in England were only "theoretical dangers" appear in the colonies to be "real dangers" that threatened the very essentials of the constitution and created an atmosphere of suspicion and anxiety that made the opposition vision of politics seem especially appropriate.

Although the interpretation presented by Bailyn in *The Origins of American Politics* accommodates more aspects of colonial political life than any previous explanation, it is not, by itself, a sufficient explanation. Above all, it is insufficient because it does not fully take into account or put in clear perspective one of the main features of colonial political life, the very feature almost invariably singled out for comment by contemporaries in the colonies and subsequently treated as the central theme of colonial political development by so many later historians: the persistent preoccupation of colonial legislators with the dangers of prerogative power. Bailyn is, to be sure, at some pains to show the excessiveness, by English standards, of the governors' assigned powers. But he pays little attention to the colonial response to this situation. Instead, he stresses the executive weakness and the economic and social instability that made public life so brittle as presumably to give the opposition's frenzied charges of influence, conspiracy, and ministerial corruption such extraordinary explanatory power in the colonies. But this neglect and this emphasis were, in large measure, predetermined by Bailyn's research design. Limiting his investigation mostly to pamphlets and newspaper essays and ignoring other relevant sources such as legislative journals, he approached his study of early eighteenth-century political thought in search of the intellectual *origins* of the American Revolution and the *origins* of mid-eighteenth-century American politics, and he found precisely what he was looking for: instances of colonial use of the writings of John Trenchard and Thomas Gordon, Viscount Bolingbroke, and other writers of the opposition to Sir Robert Walpole, and the colonial conditions that made the message of those writers congenial. The result of this focus is that his study is both incomplete and, to the extent that it does not give adequate attention to other, perhaps more central aspects of early eighteenth-century politics, anachronistic. Specifically, in relation to the subject of this article, it does not consider changes in the nature and content of colonial political thought over time. It neither explores older intellectual and political traditions that preceded colonial acceptance of the Walpolean opposition conception of politics nor seeks to explain under what conditions and to what extent newer conceptions replaced those older traditions. What Bailyn has failed to do for the early eighteenth century is thus precisely what he has correctly accused earlier writers of not doing for the revolutionary era: he has not been sensitive to what colonial political leaders "themselves . . . professed to be their own motivations." He has not considered the importance of how they saw themselves and how they conceived of the dimensions and function of the political roles into which they were cast.

It is this problem as it specifically relates to the behavior of colonial legislators during the eighteenth century that I shall attempt to explore. My argument is that colonial legislative behavior was initially and deeply rooted in an older political tradition. I shall try to identify and explain the nature of that tradition, the sources and ways through which it may have been transmitted to the colonies, the intellectual and institutional imperatives it required of its adherents, the internal political and social circumstances that contributed to its acceptance and perpetuation in the colonies long after it had spent most of its force in England, and the extent to which it continued to inform and shape colonial legislative behavior right down to the American Revolution.

The older political tradition to which I refer is, of course, the seventeenth-century tradition of opposition to the Crown as it developed out of the repeated clashes between the first two Stuarts and their Parliaments during the first half of the century and, even more important because it occurred during a formative period in colonial political life, out of the Whig opposition to Charles II and James II in the 1670s and 1680s. Initially emerging from attempts by James I to challenge some of the "ancient Privileges" of the House of Commons, this tradition, as Thornhagh Gurdon remarked in the early eighteenth century, was a product of the "Apprehensions and Fears" among "Parliament and People . . . that instead of the ancient Constitution of *England,* a Monarchy limited by original Contract, between the ancient Princes and their People, established, and known by Custom and Usage," James "aimed at a . . . despotick Government." The ensuing "Strife and Debate," as eighteenth-century opposition writers were fond of pointing out, could be interpreted, fundamentally, as another effort in behalf of liberty in its age-old struggle against arbitrary power from whatever source it emanated. But because the Crown in this instance was the offending party and the House of Commons was still conceived of as the chief bulwark of the people's liberties, the contest became a fight by the House of Commons to restrain the prerogative of the King, an attempt by the Commons to define what one later writer described as "the just Limits between Prerogative and Privilege." The specific issues in dispute changed from Parliament to Parliament under the early Stuarts, but the debate over them was almost invariably cast in this form. Even after the contest had escalated in the early 1640s to the point where the ultimate issue became whether King or Parliament would exercise sovereign power, parliamentary leaders tended to see and to justify their actions as necessary protests or preventive measures against arbitrary use of royal prerogatives.

In part because Parliament itself had been so obviously guilty of abusive use of governmental power during the Civil War and Interregnum and in part because Parliament's existence no longer appeared to be in jeopardy, the conditions under which Charles II returned to the throne created strong pressures toward cooperation between King and Parliament. For a decade and a half after the Restoration, the opposition talked not about the dangers of excessive prerogative but about the potential evils of royal influence in the second Long Parliament. But as the "prerogative reached unparalleled heights" in the late 1660s and as the very existence of Parliament increasingly seemed to the emerging Whig opposition "to be far too precarious and desperately in need of stronger protection," the "uneasy cooperation of the first few years after the Restoration gave way, in the 1670s to a series of charges by the Commons that the King was acting unconstitutionally." It was widely assumed, as a later speaker declared, that the King had had "a surfeit of Parliaments in his father's time, and was therefore extremely desirous to lay them aside." Moved by the same old fears that had plagued its predecessors during the first half of the century, the House of Commons once again "leapt at any chance to question the royal prerogative" and to demand "constitutional safeguards . . . to protect the role of Parliament." As Betty Kemp has pointed out, the last six years of the reign of Charles II "and the whole reign of James II, showed that the more fundamental dangers of dissolution and absence of parliament had not passed" with the significant result that the Commons was "recalled . . . from a seemingly premature concern with influence to their earlier concern with prerogative." Opposition writers reminded their readers that the history of relations between Crown and Commons had been a "Series of . . . Invasions upon the *Privileges of Parliaments*" by the Crown and dilated upon the theme that, in the later words of Thomas Hanmer, it was not cooperation with but "distrust of the executive" that was the chief "principle on which the whole of our Constitution is grounded." Although the conviction that "serious restrictions" had to be imposed "on the King's prerogative in relationship to Parliament" was inextricably intertwined with fears of popery and concern over the Crown's arbitrary interference with all sorts of established institutions, and although it was held in check by vivid memories of what happened when Parliament went too far in its assault upon the Crown in the 1640s, it was central to Whig and parliamentary opposition under the last two Stuarts and was one of the primary justifications for the Revolution of 1688. Once these restrictions had been achieved by the settlement of 1689, they provided the basis for working out in the eighteenth century those methods "for cooperation between King and Commons" described by Betty Kemp, J. H. Plumb, and others. Though the fear of prerogative always lurked not far beneath and occasionally even appeared above the surface of political life, it ceased to be an animating force in English politics. Opposition writers concerned themselves instead with the dangers of ministerial influence and corruption.

In the colonies, by contrast, the seventeenth-century opposition tradition, with its overriding fear of prerogative power and its jealous concern with protecting the privileges and authority of the House of Commons, continued to occupy a prominent place in politics at least until the middle of the eighteenth century and did not entirely lose its force until after the Declaration of Independence.

Any explanation for this phenomenon must at this point be highly tentative. A partial explanation is to be found, however, in the powerful mimetic impulses within colonial society. At work to some extent in all areas of colonial life from the beginning of English colonization, these impulses are another example of the familiar tendency of provincial societies to look to the cultural capital for preferred values and approved models of behavior. If, as Peter Laslett has remarked, English colonization contained within it a strong urge to create in America "new societies in its own image, or in the image of its ideal self," the impetus among the colonists to cast their societies in that same ideal image was (except in places like Massachusetts Bay, where men actually hoped to improve upon and not merely to duplicate English patterns) infinitely more powerful. Conditions of life in new and relatively inchoate and unstable societies at the extreme peripheries of English civilization inevitably created deep social and psychological insecurities, a major crisis of identity, that could be resolved, if at all, only through a constant reference back to the one certain measure of achievement: the standards of the cultural center. The result was a strong predisposition among the colonists to cultivate idealized English values and to seek to imitate idealized versions of English forms and institutions.

These mimetic impulses, which became increasingly intense through the eighteenth century and, ironically, were probably never greater than they were on the eve of the American Revolution, were given more power and made more explicit by two simultaneous developments in the late seventeenth and early eighteenth centuries. The first was the emergence of recognizable and reasonably permanent colonial elites with great political influence, whose economic activities carried them directly into the ambit of English society and thereby subjected them, to an even greater degree than earlier colonials, to the irresistible pull of English culture. The second was the extensive expansion of English governmental influence into the colonies after the Restoration and the largely successful attempt by imperial authorities to substitute something resembling an English model of government for a welter of existing political forms that had grown up in the colonies.

That this model was only superficially English, that the analogy between King, Lords, and Commons in England on the one hand and the governors, councils, and assemblies in the colonies on the other was so obviously imperfect only stimulated the desire of colonial political leaders to make it less so. Nowhere was this desire more manifest than in the behavior of the lower houses of assembly and of the men who composed them. Because the governors and councils so clearly rested upon a less independent foundation, they might never be more than "imperfect" equivalents of their English counterparts. But the lower houses had so "exact" a "resemblance" to "that part of the British constitution," which they stood for in the colonies that it was entirely plausible to entertain the heady possibility that each of them might indeed come to be the very "epitome of the house of commons." Because they were "called by the same authority," derived their "power from the same source, [were] instituted for the same ends, and [were] governed by the same forms," there was absolutely no reason why each of them "should not have the same powers . . . and the same rank in the system of" its "little community, as the house of Commons" had "in that of Britain."

In their attempt to convert this possibility into reality, to model their lower houses as closely as possible after the English House of Commons, colonial legislators had a wide range of sources to draw upon. They had, to begin with, some of the proceedings of the House of Commons as published, for the period from 1618 to the execution of Charles I, along with many other relevant documents in John Rushworth's eight-volume *Historical Collections* (London, 1659–1701) and, for the 1670s and 1680s, in the separately printed journals of each session of the House. They had, as well, much of the vast literature of the Whig opposition to the later Stuarts, including both the major philosophical disquisitions of Henry Neville, Algernon Sydney, and John Locke (each of which carefully defined the functions of the House and elaborated the proper relationship between prerogative and Parliament), and many of the vast number of occasional pieces, some of which were reprinted following the Glorious Revolution in the two-volume collection of *State Tracts* (London, 1689–93) and others of which were later issued together in the sixteen-volume edition of *Somers Tracts* (London, 1748–52). Finally, they had such terse and comprehensive statements of Whig theory as Henry Care's *English Liberties: or, The Free-Born Subject's Inheritance* (London, 1682), which was reprinted several times in the colonies; the Whig contributions to the extensive debate over the antiquity of Parliament; early Whig histories, especially that of Paul de Rapin-Thoyras, the Huguenot who sailed with William of Orange and who interpreted the events of the seventeenth century from the perspective of the most radical wing of Whig thinkers; and, probably most important of all, the several parliamentary commentaries and procedural books published in the seventeenth century, including those of William Hakewell, Sir Edward Coke, Henry Scobell, Henry Elsynge, and, most significantly, George Petyt. Petyt's work was reprinted by Andrew Bradford in 1716 in both New York and Philadelphia and was the last such treatise of major proportions until John Hatsell published his four-volume work in 1781.

As Petyt remarked in his preface, these procedural books served as a comprehensive introduction to "*the admirable method* of Parliamentary Proceedings; *the Exactness and Decency of their* Orders; *the Wisdom and Prudence of their* Customs; *the Extent of their* Powers; *and the Largeness of their* Privileges." They adumbrated in detail and cited appropriate precedents concerning mechanics of conducting elections, the necessary qualifications for members and electors, the methods of examining election returns and deciding disputed elections, the power of the House over its own members, the method of electing a speaker and the correct way for him to conduct his office, the ways of selection and the roles of other House officers, the proper procedures for passing bills and conducting debates, the several categories of committees and the structure and function of each, the customary form of a session, the privileges of members, and the usual distribution of function and patterns of relationship among the three branches of Parliament.

The importance of such manuals in the exportation of parliamentary government to distant plantations can scarcely be overemphasized. If, as Anthony Stokes later remarked, "the Journals of the Houses of Parliament" were "the precedents by which the Legislatures in the Colonies conduct[ed] themselves," these manuals provided a convenient distillation of the several pertinent matters in those journals. The extent to which colonial legislators probably used them in the process of taking, as the Pennsylvania Speaker David Lloyd phrased it, "their rules from the *House of Commons,*" of copying its forms and procedures may be inferred from the work of several earlier scholars, most notably Mary Patterson Clarke, and requires no further comment here.

What has been much less clearly perceived, however, and what, in fact, has been largely missed by earlier writers, is the remarkable extent to which these parliamentary commentaries and the later Stuart opposition literature shaped not merely the form and procedure of the lower houses but also the understanding and behavior of their members. For, in addition to spelling out the method and manner of parliamentary proceedings, they prescribed explicitly in detail a whole set of generalized and specific institutional imperatives for representative bodies, a particular pattern of behavior for their members, and a concrete program of political action.

The central assumptions behind this prescription were, first, that there was a natural antagonism between the "King's Prerogative" and the "Rights, Liberties and Properties of the People," and, second, that the primary function of the House of Commons, as Henry Care declared, was "to preserve inviolable our Liberty and Property, according to the known Laws of the Land, without any giving way unto or Introduction of that absolute and arbitrary Rule practiced in Foreign Countries." To that end the House was expected always to be careful never to relinquish possession of the "Keys to unlock Peoples Purses" and always to be on the alert for any indications of arbitrary government in order that they might be checked before they could "wound the Body Politick in a vital Part." The role of the House of Commons was thus essentially negative and defensive. To "redress Grievances, to take notice of Monopolies and Oppressions, to curb the Exorbitances of great Favourites, and pernicious Ministers of State, to punish such mighty Delinquents, who are protected by the King, that they look upon themselves too big for the ordinary reach of Justice in Courts of Common Law, to inspect the conduct of such who are intrusted with the Administration of Justice, and interpret the Laws to the prejudice of the People, and those who dispose the publick Treasure of the Nation"—there were the many grave and weighty responsibilities that fell to and could only be handled by that "great Assembly." The House was the subject's single most important governmental hedge against "arbitrary Violence and Oppression" from the prerogative or any other source and final guarantor of the liberty that was the peculiar and precious "Birth-right of Englishmen."

Such extraordinary responsibilities required both a strong House of Commons and a membership devoted to maintaining that strength. Voters had, therefore, always to be especially careful to elect only such men to Parliament who had sufficient "Wisdom and Courage" that they could "not be hectored out of their Duties by the Frowns and Scowls of Men" and who were "resolved to stand by and maintain the *Power and Privileges of Parliaments,*" which were the very "Heart-strings of the Common-Wealth." It was incumbent upon all men elected to *"that honourable Station"* to make sure that they were *"thoroughly skill'd in* Parliamentary Affairs *to know their own* Laws *and* Customs, *their* Powers *and* Privileges, *that they may not at any time suffer Invasions to be made upon them, by what plausible* Pretences *soever.*"

Because many—perhaps most—of those "Invasions" could be expected to derive directly from and even to be protected by the excessive "Privileges and Prerogatives" invested in the Crown, it was absolutely necessary that the House of Commons have sufficient powers and privileges to contest the Crown on equal, perhaps even superior, grounds. The House had to have legal guarantees that it would meet frequently, have full investigative powers, and have complete control over its own officers. Its members must have freedom of speech and debate, freedom from arrest during sessions, and exemption from punishment outside the House for anything said or done in or on behalf of the House. In short, the House had to be a law unto itself responsible only to its constituents and to its own special law, the "Lex & Consuetudo Parliamenti."

Bent upon turning their lower houses into "epitomes of the House of Commons," "so fond," as one Jamaica governor reported, "of the notion to be as near as can be, upon the foott of H[is] M[ajesty's] English subjects that the desire of it allmost distracts them [*sic*]," and prone, like all provincials, to take the ideals of their cultural capital far more seriously than they are ever taken in the capital itself, colonial representatives adopted *in toto* this entire system of thought and action along with its patterns of perception and its cluster of imperatives, roles, and conventions. This system supplied them with a special frame of reference, an angle of vision that helped them to put their own problems and actions in historical, seemingly even cosmic, perceptive, gave them a standard of behavior, determined how they conceived of the lower houses and of their own political roles, and, most important, shaped into predictable and familiar forms their perceptions of and responses to political events.

So deeply was this system of thought and action imbedded in their political culture that the remembrance of the terrible excesses of Stuart despotism, of those infamous times "when prerogative was unlimited, and liberty undefined" and "arbitrary power, under the shelter of unlimited Prerogative was making large strides over the land," was throughout the eighteenth century always near the surface of political consciousness. Colonial representatives scarcely needed to be reminded of "what extraordinary Progress was made" in the attempt "to raise Royalty above the Laws and Liberties of the People, by the chimerical Ideas of Prerogative" during the "three last hereditary Reigns of the *Stuarts,* what Toil, what Fatigue, what Slaughter the Nation underwent before the Delirium of *Charles* the 1st, could be vanquished. What Lengths were run, what large Compliances made under *Charles* the Second, . . . how near fatal the Blow was to Freedom and Liberty under his Brother *James,*" and how all of these evil efforts were defeated only because they were "constantly and strictly opposed by Parliament" under the leadership of those noble House of Commons men—Sir John Eliot, Sir Edward Coke, Edward Littleton, John Pym, John Hampden, William Jones—"who stood forth at that critical period, in defense of the Constitution."

With such vivid memories always before them, colonial legislators had a strong predisposition to look at each governor as a potential Charles I or James II, to assume a hostile posture toward the executive, and to define with the broadest possible latitude the role of the lower house as "the main barrier of all those rights and privileges which British subjects enjoy." Ever ready to stand "in the gap against oppression," they were, in the best tradition of seventeenth-century English opponents of the Crown, constantly worried lest "Prerogative" gain "a considerable Advantage over *Liberty*" or a governor extend "his Power, beyond what any King in *England* ever pretended to, even in the most despotick and arbitrary Reigns." Especially sensitive to any encroachments "upon their jurisdiction" that might "(if submitted to) strip them of all authority, and [thereby] disable them from either supporting their own dignity or giving the people . . . that protection against arbitrary power, which nothing but a free and independent Assembly" could "give," they invariably, in imitation of the English House of Commons, opposed all attempts to make innovations "contrary to . . . the constant Practice of all English Assemblies" or "to Govern otherwise than according to the Usage and Custom of the Country since the first Settlement thereof." In the words of Elisha Cooke, Jr., they "Warily observed and tim[or]ously Prevented" any precedents that might, by making "little Changes in

Fundamentals," lead to the collapse of the whole constitution. In their determination to discover and root out all examples of arbitrary executive power, they were particularly concerned "to enquire into the abuses and corruptions of office, the obstructions of public justice, and the complaints of subjects, oppressed by the hand of power, and to bring the offenders in such cases to justice."

The governors of the colonies themselves encouraged colonial representatives in this conception of the function of the lower houses and the mode of behavior it implied. For the legislators were not the only group imprisoned by the rhetoric, anxieties, and peculiar political myopia of Stuart England. Like the Stuart monarchs and their supporters, governors, occupying similar roles in the political order, could scarcely avoid interpreting any questioning of executive actions and any opposition to gubernatorial programs or imperial directives as, covertly and fundamentally at least, a challenge to the essential prerogatives of the Crown or proprietors. From every colony came charges from the governors and their adherents that the lower houses were "exceeding their due and reasonable Bounds; strengthening themselves with pretences of publick Good and their own Privileges as the Representatives of the People." Everywhere, the executive complained that the lower houses were declaring "themselves a House of Commons," assuming "all the Privileges of it, and" acting "with a much more unlimited Authority." It was widely echoed, and believed, that the lower houses, like the first Long Parliament in the "Period that every good Man wishes could be struck out of our Annals," were actually endeavoring "to wrest the small Remains of Power out of the Hands of the Crown," "to assume the Executive Power of the Government into their own Hands," and perhaps even "to weaken, if not entirely to cast off, the Obedience they owe to the Crown, and the Dependance which all Colonies ought to have on their Mother Country." From the governors' chairs, the leaders of the legislative opposition appeared to be not patriots struggling in the glorious cause of liberty but exactly as the leaders of the House of Commons had seemed to the Stuarts: "designing and malicious Men imposing upon and deluding the People" until they were "so far infatuated, as to seem insensible of their . . . true interest." Every recalcitrant lower house appeared to be bent on pursuing "the example of the parliament of 1641" and every leader to be "a great Magna-Carta Man & Petition-of-Right maker" determined to persuade his fellow legislators "to dance after the Long Parliament's pipe." Both sides, then, were playing out roles and operating within a conception of politics that derived directly from the revolutionary situation in Stuart England, a conception that conditioned them to view politics as a continuing struggle between prerogative and liberty, between executive and legislative power.

For the governors and legislators alike, this conception of their behavior and their disagreements gave them an enlarged purpose that transcended the narrow bounds of their several localities and, by investing their actions with national—not to say, universal—meaning, linked them directly to their cultural inheritance and helped to satisfy their deepest mimetic impulses. What was equally important, at least in the case of the legislators, that enlarged purpose also supplied them and their institutions with the prestige, standing, and political power within their respective communities, which seem to be so necessary to the psychological needs of emergent elites.

But the fact that this specific conception of politics had such a powerful hold on men's minds in England at exactly the same time that colonial legislators were self-consciously beginning to cultivate English political values and to imitate the procedures and behavior of the House of Commons does not completely account for the adoption of that conception in the colonies. What also accounts for its adoption as well as for its continued vitality in the colonies long after it had become in England little more than a series of political clichés and hackneyed constitutionalisms that were largely irrelevant to the realities of political life was the survival in the colonies during the eighteenth century of the very conditions and circumstances that had initially spawned it in seventeenth-century England. For, as Bailyn had recently reminded us, explicit restrictions of the kind Parliament successfully imposed upon the prerogative in England following the Glorious Revolution were never achieved in the colonies. As a result, the institutional cooperation made possible by the revolutionary settlement in England was rarely attainable in the colonies, and the specter of unlimited prerogative thus continued to haunt colonial legislators.

For legislators "in love with . . . [the English] Constitution," striving diligently to achieve a "form of government" that resembled "that of England, as nearly as the condition of a dependent Colony" could "be brought to resemble, that of its mother country," and culturally programmed to be ever on guard against the dangers of unlimited prerogative, this situation was a source of perpetual anxiety. Not only did it directly frustrate their mimetic impulses by blatantly reminding them of the great gap between their aspirations and reality; it also put them into continual fear lest some evil governor employ his excessive power to introduce the most pernicious form of tyranny. It seemed absolutely inexplicable, as an anonymous Jamaican declared in 1714, "that in all the Revolutions of State, and Changes of the Ministry" in England since the Restoration "the several Colonies which compose the *British* Empire in *America*" and were inhabited by supposedly freeborn Englishmen "should . . . lye still so much neglected, under such a precarious Government and greivous [*sic*] Administration, as they have, for the most part, labour'd under, both before and since the late signal Revolution." Indeed, from the perspective of that Revolution in which the rights and privileges of subjects in England had been so fully "confirmed; and the knavish Chicanes, and crafty Inventions, that were introduced to deprive the Subject of his Rights . . . abolished," it seemed especially grievous—and frighteningly dangerous—"that a Governour of any Colony . . . so far distant from the Seat of Redress . . . should be vested with a Power to govern, in a more absolute and unlimited manner there, than even the Queen herself can, according to Law, or ever did attempt to exercise in *Great Britain,*" that a lower house should have "less Sway and Weight" in a colony "than the *House of Commons* had in *Great Britain.*"

The dangers of this situation were not merely imaginary. They were vividly confirmed by the many "Instances" in which both royal and proprietary governors, lacking in many cases even a remote sense of identity of interests with the colonists, had used their preponderant powers "to gripe and squeeze the People . . . for [no] . . . other Reason, than their own private Gain," "usurped more Authority than [even theoretically] belonged to them," and attempted to exercise "Arbitrary Power, unknown in our Mother-Country since the glorious Revolution of 1688." It was well known "that all [of the many] Contentions and Animosities . . . between the Governour and Inhabitants of" the colonies took "their first Rise, from some grievous and intolerable Acts of Oppression, in the Administration." As Richard Jackson remarked, it was the governors who always acted the *"offensive Part,"* who "set up unwarrantable Claims" and employed "Snares, Menaces, Aspersions, Tumults, and every other unfair Practice" in an attempt either to bully or to wheedle "the Inhabitants out of the Privileges they were born to." Like the House of Commons, the lower houses thus always acted "on the *defensive only*"; their members courageously struggled with true British patriotism against the wicked machinations of "hungry, ignorant, or extravagant" governors and their "crafty, active, knavish, . . . servile, fawning" adherents, the very "trash of mankind" who alone would enter into such unsavory alliances against the people's rights and liberties as represented by the lower houses.

Whatever images they held of themselves, however, colonial representatives could not, in the situation, act "on the *defensive only.*" Precisely because the King's governors claimed to "be more Absolute in the Plantations than" the King himself was "in England," because some governors actually sought to use their exorbitant powers to increase the prerogative at the expense of liberty, and because, as a Barbadian complained in 1719, it was not always possible to secure redress against such grievances in London in face of the superior influence of the governors with men in power—for all of their reasons so "generally [well] Known in *America*" the lower houses found themselves—and were frequently and correctly accused of—trying to secure checks on the prerogative and power over executive affairs well beyond any exercised by the House of Commons. It was "a received opinion" that "Right without Power to maintain it, is the Derision and Sport of Tyrants." To defend such deviations from the imperial norm, colonial legislators were forced to fall back upon that ultimate defense of the seventeenth-century House of Commons, *"Perpetual Usage"* and "established custom," and to claim that, like the Commons, each legislature had a "Lex & Consuetudo Parliamenti" of its own. Despite the depth and genuineness of their imitative impulses, the mimesis of the House of Commons by the colonial lower houses and of the imperial government by the several provincial governments could never be exact because of the Crown's exaggerated claims for prerogative in the plantations and the immoderate responses those claims evoked from the legislatures. The result, a source of amusement, derision, and amazement among imperial administrative supporters in the colonies, was the ironic spectacle of men determined to form their "assemblies . . . on the Plan of an *English* Parliament" forced into defending their peculiar practices on the obvious grounds that it was "altogether . . . absurd to prescribe [exactly] the same form of government to people differently circumstanced."

The lower houses in most colonies were able through such innovative practices to bridle the governors, both because, unlike the king, the governors were never protected from attack by the aura of the concept that the king could do no wrong and because, as Bailyn has so fully and effectively argued, most governors did not have at their command those "devices by which in England the executive" was able to exert its control over politics and secure its goals. But this ability to restrain the governors never completely allayed the colonial legislators' fears of prerogative power and arbitrary government. As long as the Crown or proprietors refused to abandon the claims of such extravagant powers for their governors or to recognize the actual limitations imposed upon the prerogative by the lower houses, there was always the terrifying possibility that imperial authorities might unleash the unlimited might of the parent state to enforce its claims, perhaps even by bringing the force of Parliament itself against the lower houses. Although some colonial leaders wishfully hoped that *"that August Assembly,* the Protectors of English Liberties," might actually side with its sister institutions in the colonies, there was an uneasy awareness as well of "how deeply" parliamentary intervention might "enter into our *Constitution* and affect our most *valuable privileges.*" Such extreme vulnerability meant, of course, that colonial legislators could never feel entirely secure "against the assaults of arbitrary power . . . [upon] their lives, their liberties, or their properties.

The resulting anxiety, only partly conscious and appropriately expressed through the classic arguments of the seventeenth-century opposition to the Stuarts, ensured that, at least until such a time as the colonies were granted "a free Constitution of Government" equivalent to that enjoyed by Englishmen at home, those arguments would continue to be especially relevant to colonial politics and to give form and coherence to much of its outward appearance. However, because those arguments and the conception of politics from which they derived were seemingly so explanatory of the peculiar circumstances of colonial politics and apparently so well suited to meet the psychological needs produced by these circumstances, they became so integral a part of colonial political culture and so determinative of the sensibilities of colonial politicians that they ran far "deeper than the Surface of things." They ran so deep, in fact, that they created a strong predisposition to interpret virtually all political

CARNEGIE LIBRARY
LIVINGSTONE COLLEGE
SALISBURY, N. C. 28144

conflict as struggles between prerogative and liberty. Even factional fights over tangible economic issues that obviously cut across institutional lines and had nothing ostensible to do with constitutional questions were perceived as, and thereby to some extent actually converted into, such struggles.

It is important, of course, to keep in mind that in colonial, as in all, politics there was frequently, if not invariably, a considerable difference between the ostensible and the real; any comprehensive interpretation will have to distinguish between and describe both "the dress parade of debate" and "the program of opportunist political tactics" and concrete social and economic interests that lay behind that debate. But it is equally important to comprehend the powerful hold of this older opposition political conception upon the minds of colonial politicians and the remarkable extent to which it conditioned them to conceive of and to explain—even to themselves—behavior and actions arising out of the most self-interested and sordid ambitions as essential contributions to the Englishman's heroic struggle against the evils of unlimited prerogative.

But the hold of this older political conception upon colonial politicians was not so powerful as to prevent them from receiving and employing later English conceptions. Through the middle decades of the eighteenth century, the economies of the home islands and the colonies became ever more tightly connected, the last two intercolonial wars provided a new and compelling focus of common attention, and the colonial elites developed an increasing cultural and political self-consciousness and became more aware of the great social gulf between the colonies and Britain. As a result, the attractive force of English culture and the explicit desires of the elites to cultivate English styles and values and to Anglicize their societies greatly intensified. Under certain conditions, this intensification of colonial mimetic impulses led to the supplementation and, in a few cases, the virtual submersion of the older seventeenth-century political tradition by either, or parts of both, of two newer systems of political thought imported directly from Walpolean England. This process of supplementation and submersion was rendered especially easy because of the close similarity among the older and newer traditions of basic assumptions about human nature, the corrosive effects of unbridled power, the functions of governments and constitutions, and the preferred qualities for rulers.

The first of these traditions, which Bailyn has labeled "mainstream thought," was developed by administrative supporters in the half century after the Glorious Revolution and especially during Walpole's ministry. Within the House of Commons itself, this tradition was fostered by and epitomized by the behavior of Arthur Onslow, who was speaker continuously from 1727 to 1761. He enjoyed a great reputation in both Britain and the colonies and served as a model for speakers of the colonial lower houses. The nuances of this tradition cannot be described here, but its central imperative was the desirability of institutional cooperation among all branches of government. Governors and administrative supporters in all the colonies cultivated this ideal in every sort of political situation. But the ideal could only become the dominant political tradition—among legislators as well as among the administration—in colonies where there was no threat from the prerogative either through direct challenges made by governors who were intent upon exercising the full range of their assigned powers or through the corruption or manipulation of the legislature through the use of patronage.

Among the mainland colonies, at least, such a situation existed only in Virginia. There, Lieutenant Governor William Gooch had practically no patronage at his disposal to raise fears of undue executive influence and had sufficiently strong connections at home to keep the Board of Trade from insisting that he take steps to obtain legislative recognition of his assigned prerogative powers. By cooperating closely with Sir John Randolph and John Robinson, two speakers of the House of Burgesses who were obviously inspired by and frequently compared to the great Onslow, Gooch managed both to extirpate faction in the colony and to gain such widespread acceptance of the theory of institutional cooperation as to avoid almost all conflict with the legislature and seriously to undermine the older conception that politics was a struggle between prerogative and liberty.

The second tradition was, of course, that of the Walpolean opposition, which has been so fully and penetratingly analyzed by Bailyn, J. G. A. Pocock, Caroline Robbins, Isaac Kramnick, and others that it requires little elaboration here. What I would like to call attention to, however, is the emphasis in this tradition upon the necessity of maintaining a clear separation of powers and upon the dangers of executive influence in the House of Commons. To some degree, of course, the theory of balanced government was integral to every English political tradition from the middle of the seventeenth to the early part of the nineteenth century, and colonials had conventionally employed it in political arguments. Even such a militant antiprerogative politician as Elisha Cook, Jr., subscribed to it. In 1720 he wrote that "the Kings Prerogative when rightly used, is for the good & benefit of the People, and the Liberties and Properties of the People are for the Support of the Crown, and the Kings Prerogative when not abused."

Significantly, however, most colonial legislators, like Cooke, seem to have employed the idea of balance primarily as a defense of liberty and property against prerogative. Confronted as they were with executive claims for such extensive prerogative powers, they manifested little interest in imposing any restraints upon their own legislative powers. Indeed, as Corinne Comstock Weston has implied in her revealing study, *English Constitutional Theory and the House of Lords, 1556–1832,* that theory seems to have been attractive primarily to groups whose powers or prerogatives were under attack and who were operating from a position of practical political weakness. Just as Charles I, seeking to stem the assault of the first Long Parliament, was chiefly responsible for popularizing and thrusting into the center of political consciousness the doctrine of balanced government in England during the seventeenth century, so in the colonies during the eighteenth century the governors and various administrative adherents in places where the executive was unusually weak—men such as Cadwallader Colden and Archibald Kennedy in New York and James Logan and the Reverend William Smith in Pennsylvania—were its earliest and most vociferous exponents and were most deeply committed to it.

Among the colonial political community at large, however, it appears to have received primary emphasis only where the threat of administrative corruption of the legislature was sufficiently great to make the desirability of a strict separation of powers especially obvious. Such a situation seems to have existed in Maryland, where the proprietor always had extensive patronage at his command; in New Hampshire, where after 1750 Governor Benning Wentworth established a powerful patronage machine; in New York, where in the 1740s and 1750s James De Lancey, first as chief justice and then as lieutenant governor, managed to achieve such an invulnerable position in the government that he was able to establish a system very much resembling a "Robinarchical" corruption; and, preeminently, in Massachusetts, where William Shirley, governor from 1741 to 1756, put together a peculiar combination of superb talents for political management, strong connections in Britain, and local patronage sufficient to enable him to secure an effective "influence" over the Massachusetts legislature.

In such a situation the real danger of "subversion and Change of the Constitution" derived not from "the Wantonness and Violence of Prerogative," but from "the Power of the People trusted with their Representatives," and the charges of conspiracy, corruption, and influence associated with the Walpolean opposition and the whole system of thought connected with them took on a heightened relevance. Shirley's Massachusetts provided real substance to the charge that there was a *"deep Plot"* among "all the Men *in the P--v--ce of the Massachusetts* that have grown very remarkably Rich and Great, High, and Proud, since the Year 1742," who "by Cunning, and by Power; through Lust of Power, Lust of Fame, Lust of Money," and "love of *Prerogative*"; "through Envy, Pride, Covetousness, and *violent* Ambition" were intent upon "killing . . . our CONSTITUTION," destroying the very "Freedom, the Liberty and Happiness of the People of *New-England.*" In such a situation, in which a grasping administration was intent upon corrupting the whole legislature, the legislature could no longer be trusted to safeguard the constitution. That responsibility then fell directly upon the people, who were urged to bind their representatives by positive and inflexible instructions to prevent them from selling their constituents' liberty for pelf or position.

The extraordinary flowering in Shirley's Massachusetts of political literature cast in the intellectual mold of the Walpolean opposition suggests the possibility that prior to 1763 the ideas of that opposition were fully relevant to and predominant in only those colonial political situations that bore some reasonable resemblance to that of Walpole's England. These were situations in which the administration actually had at its command many of the devices of the informal constitution which Walpole had used to give his administration its effective influence over Parliament and to achieve that "high degree of public harmony" and "peaceful integration of political forces" that, much to the chagrin and worry of the opposition, accounted for the stability and marked the success of his ministry. If this suggestion turns out to be true, if the acceptance and widespread utilization of the political conceptions of the Walpolean opposition prior to 1763 were concentrated in, or even limited to, those places where the governors had enough practical political power to enable them to dominate the lower houses and where an informal constitution similar to the one that existed in England was most fully developed, then Bailyn's arguments that the Walpolean opposition tradition became dominant everywhere in the colonies during the decades before the Revolution and that the "swollen claims and shrunken powers" of the executive were among the most important sources of that development may have to be substantially qualified.

I would suggest, in fact, that before the 1760s in most colonies both the mainstream and opposition Walpolean traditions supplemented rather than supplanted the older tradition of the seventeenth-century opposition to the Stuarts. The older tradition had been so institutionalized in colonial politics and so internalized among colonial politicians that it could never really be displaced until the conditions that had given rise to and nourished it had disappeared, until "the principles of the British constitution" had been fully extended to the colonies and, as James Otis remarked as late as 1762, "all plantation Governors" had resolved to "practice upon those principles, instead (as most of them do) of spending their whole time in extending the prerogative beyond all bounds." In Virginia, even while Randolph was praising Lieutenant Governor Gooch for his mild administration and dilating upon the necessity and virtues of cooperation between legislature and executive, he worried about "those Governors" elsewhere "who make Tyranny their Glory." How close the fears of unlimited prerogative remained to the surface of Virginia politics was dramatically revealed during the early 1750s in the pistole fee controversy when Gooch's successor, Robert Dinwiddie, tried to levy a fee without the consent of the House of Burgesses. Similarly, in Shirley's Massachusetts the Walpolean opposition fear of the administration's influence, of "an ambitious or designing Governour" who might "be able to *corrupt* or *awe* your Representatives," was often—and probably usually—combined with the older concerns about the "large Strides Prerogative" was "daily making towards absolute and despotick Power," much in the same way that earlier in the century the apprehensions of prerogative had frequently been accompanied by complaints that avaricious courtiers were assisting prerogative in its unending efforts to "compleat" its "Conquest . . . over Liberty."

What finally led to the submersion of the older opposition tradition and what rendered the Walpolean mainstream tradition totally irrelevant was the series of restrictive measures taken by Crown and Parliament against the colonies after 1763. Even farther removed from the center of politics than the English opposition, the colonists, as Bailyn has so brilliantly and convincingly argued, could only interpret British behavior in opposition terms. Even then, however, it was not the corruption of local legislatures by local executives about which they were primarily worried, nor was it the relevance of the message of the Walpolean opposition to local politics that made it so attractive to them. Rather it was the corruption of Parliament by the ministry and the extraordinary extent to which that corruption seemed to explain what was being done to the colonies by the imperial government. Even after 1763, however, the submersion of the older tradition by the newer was not total. Because so many of the objectionable measures of the British government between 1763 and 1776 stemmed directly from the Crown and were immediate challenges to the customary powers of the colonial lower houses, the old fears of unlimited prerogative persisted. The Declaration of Independence can and must be read as an indictment of not merely a corrupt Parliament under the influence of a wicked king but also of the unjust and arbitrary misuse of the royal prerogative to undermine the liberties of the people and their lower houses.

The degree to which this seventeenth-century conception of politics as a continual struggle between prerogative and liberty was fundamental to the political system of the old English Empire is perhaps best indicated by the fact that the conception continued to exercise a powerful sway over men's minds and to have an important influence in political life in all these colonies that did not revolt as long as the old pattern of political and constitutional relationships persisted. Over sixty years after the American Revolution it was still true, as Lord Durham reported in 1839, that "it may fairly be said . . . that the natural state of government in all these colonies is that of collision between the executive and representative body." That such collisions were the "natural state of government" in the older colonies in the eighteenth century as well was the reason why the tradition of the seventeenth-century opposition to the Stuarts continued down to the early 1760s to be such a primary element in colonial political culture and profound shaping influence upon the behavior of colonial legislators.

A COMMENT by Bernard Bailyn

There is no point in attempting to comment in any detail on the various arguments and accusations in Mr. Greene's article, but there are two underlying misconceptions that I think are of general interest and for that reason deserve particular comment.

1. No one can doubt—it certainly never occurred to me to doubt—that the eighteenth-century beliefs I emphasized in my *Origins of American Politics* were based on seventeenth-century notions of the threat of prerogative power to liberty and reflect the ancient struggle between king and Commons. It seems to me self-evident, and I cannot see why anyone needs to argue the point, that eighteenth-century opposition views absorbed, supplemented, and updated older, seventeenth-century views. This "older" opposition ideology, far from being submerged and superseded (something I never claimed), remained very much alive, in modified and modernized form. The late seventeenth-century and early eighteenth-century opposition writers whom I have discussed carried forward this ancient fear of autocracy in new, more up-to-date, and realistic form. And these new forms were as relevant in the colonies as they were in England for the very good reason that no one in the colonies mistook governors for the King and everyone knew the prerogatives of the Crown itself had been reduced by the Glorious Revolution; no one consequently worried in seventeenth-century terms about the direct and immediate force of Crown prerogatives as such—in the colonies any more than in England. What they were worried about in both places was not the direct autocracy of George I or George II but the manipulation, corruption, and misuse of executive powers by Crown underlings, unworthy Crown adherents: ministers in England, venal governors in the colonies. Hence the whole crucial subject of corruption, in the precise up-to-date terms that were worked out, as J. G. A. Pocock has demonstrated, during and after the Exclusion Crisis and that formed the core of opposition attacks on the eighteenth-century ministries, lay at the heart of colonial political thought. For this reason, if for no other, the opposition literature fitted the needs of the colonial legislative leaders—fitted them in some cases more precisely than it did opposition leaders in England (see, for example, the peculiar political relevance of the much-reprinted essay from *Cato's Letters* I quoted on pp. 137-38 nn. [in *Origins*])—and was used continuously, in a conflation of terminology

and reference, with the heightened meaning that I tried to explain in my book.

And it was used generally. Mr. Greene attempts to reduce the applicability of these ideas to colonies in which gubernatorial patronage powers approximated in their political effect the power of the Crown's "influence" in Parliament, and he sets up the correlation: the greater the gubernatorial patronage the greater the use of this literature. This is mistaken in conception and insupportable in fact. For, first, though there were degrees of difference in gubernatorial patronage in the colonies, in only one or two colonies, and at particular points only, did patronage approximate in its political force the relative power of the Crown's patronage in England—a fact that Mr. Greene himself incidentally admits. Second, the applicability of opposition arguments in the colonies did not rest on the governors' use of patronage power alone; it rested as well on the mere existence of irresponsible and corruptible, if not actually corrupt, gubernatorial proconsuls, whether they had much patronage or not, and hence was generalized through the culture. Third, there is in fact no such correlation as Mr. Greene claims: the use of opposition writings was if anything *less* prominent in New Hampshire, where, late in the colonial period, the governor's patronage power was extremely high, than it was in South Carolina, where patronage barely existed at all. James De Lancey may seem to Mr. Greene to have controlled the legislature in New York in quasi-Walpolean fashion, but twenty years earlier William Cosby did not, though it was then that the opposition made the most celebrated use of the anti-Walpolean literature. Each of the examples Mr. Greene passingly cites can be similarly refuted.

And far from the relevance of seventeenth-century ideas giving way finally to the eighteenth-century opposition ideas only in the revolutionary crisis, something like the exact opposite would seem to be true. The colonists felt they were re-enacting the seventeenth-century struggle most precisely not in the benign reigns of George I and George II, when the political evils they experienced were known to be the work of corrupt underlings, but when they were—reluctantly and late in the revolutionary agitation—forced to believe that George III, like Charles I and James II before him, was himself directly involved in an autocratic venture against constituted liberties, especially those associated with legislative rights.

Yet Mr. Greene has much documentation. What does it prove? It proves, yet once again, that that familiar old phenomenon, the Rise of the Assembly, really took place. The Rise of the Assembly undeniably took place, and it undeniably involved the multiple re-enactment on a provincial scale of a phase of seventeenth-century English constitutional history—undeniably on both points because Mary P. Clarke, following Charles M. Andrews, established it all, in the terms Mr. Greene is using, twenty-five years ago in her *Parliamentary Privilege in the American Colonies,* and because more recently Mr. Greene too has written a substantial book on the subject. But the process of politics is not explained by it.

2. Mr. Greene's charge that, knowing what I wanted to prove, I looked only where I was likely to find what I was after—in the pamphlets and newspapers—is not only false as a matter of fact but misconceived as an approach to the questions involved. For the argument rests on the presumption that politicians dealing with the hard realities of politics thought one thing, drew on one body of ideas and developed them, while the pamphleteers and newspaper writers thought another way, drew on another body of ideas and developed them. But were there different groups saying different things in different places in these minuscule political communities? No one knows better than Mr. Greene that James Bland and Landon Carter were the political leaders in the House of Burgesses who led the opposition to Robert Dinwiddie over the pistole fee and to the clergy over the Two-Penny Acts: who but the same two men were the opposition pamphleteers? Who actually struggled against the DeLancey interest in the bitter political infighting in New York in the early 1750s and after? William Livingston, William Smith, and John Morin Scott—were they mere littérateurs? mere belletrist-plagiarists of Trenchard and Gordon? Were the writers who used *Cato's Letters* to argue in newspapers against William Shirley in Massachusetts simply pundits, uninvolved in legislative politics? Were not Lewis Morris and the other newspaper polemicists who struggled in print against Cosby, politicians—indeed, the principal politicians of the time?

The point, of course, is that there was no American Grub Street that produced one thing in pamphlets and newspapers while the politicians thought another. The same people were involved in both, and they used what they could from the whole of their cultural heritage, including seventeenth-century arguments when they fitted, and more ancient and more modern ideas than those when they fitted. The problem is to decide which of the ideas that they used effectively explained to them the nature of the political world around them. As far as I can judge—from all the categories of sources, needless to say, newspapers, pamphlets, legislative debates, letters—they appear to be as I described them in *The Origins of American Politics,* and nothing in what Mr. Greene writes suggests any reason for thinking otherwise.

But it is a tricky business deciding that a writer went only to the sources that he knew beforehand would support his case. Might one suggest, for example, that Mr. Greene's "counter"-demonstration is drawn largely from English parliamentary handbooks, which by definition can only reflect the seventeenth-century struggle between king and Commons?

We agree, however, on one thing. There is much to be said about the details of prerevolutionary politics—so long, in my view, as they are conceived as a process, and not reduced to some master abstraction of institutional growth like the Rise of the Assembly. Anyone interested in the subject will be eager to read Mr. Greene's forthcoming book on Virginia. But not much will be gained by reworking a threadbare cliché under a fashionable title, and by assuming that the publicist and political worlds were moving in separate paths and that eighteenth-century Americans found relevance for seventeenth-century but not for eighteenth-century English ideas.

A REPLY
by Jack P. Greene

I have read Bailyn's comments on my article with great interest, the more especially because they underline, once again, several problems that must be solved before we can achieve a more satisfactory understanding of early American politics.

First and most obvious is the problem I specifically alluded to in my article: the tendency to view colonial politics from the vantage point of the American Revolution. There is, of course, much to be said for looking at a relatively stable and inconspicuous segment of the past from the perspective of a later upheaval. Invariably, the upheaval identifies and brings sharply into focus potentially disruptive tensions, issues, and trends that had previously been either partially submerged beneath or, at the very least, undifferentiated from many other facets of life. But such a perspective also carries with it some rather great dangers. First, what is seen to be most important about the earlier period is often determined by what seems to be most significant in the subsequent upheaval. Second, matters of more pressing concern to contemporaries in the earlier period will, consequently, often be overlooked or deemphasized. And third, events in the earlier period will frequently appear to be worthy of consideration only insofar as they can be interpreted as origins of the later event. Parenthetically, one may add that, as Marc Bloch has warned, origins are by definition beginnings and very often—and very dangerously—beginnings that are "a complete explanation" or, to use Bailyn's perhaps somewhat more updated terminology, "a sufficient explanation." But the problem under discussion is what effect Bailyn's perspective has had upon his interpretation not of the Revolution but of early eighteenth-century politics, and the three dangers listed above are precisely the ones I suggested Bailyn had not wholly avoided. My point was not that he had formulated a hypothesis about colonial politics and then deliberately set out to look exclusively for evidence to support it, but rather that his own earlier and highly persuasive reading of American political thought during the prerevolutionary controversy had exerted a powerful influence upon his interpretation of earlier colonial political culture by making him more sensitive to the importance of some ideas—the very ideas he had shown to have been so determinative of American political understanding just prior to the Revolution—than he was to others. My understanding of Bailyn's comment suggests that it does rather more to confirm these suspicions than to dispel them.

A second problem is the tendency to look at colonial politics too much in terms of contemporary British politics. Over the past decade our knowledge of colonial political life has been greatly enriched by studies of the intimate relationship between virtually all aspects of British and colonial politics and especially of the dependence of the colonies upon the parent culture for their major political conceptions. But there is a danger in refracting provincial life through the lenses of a contemporary metropolis that is similar to that of viewing an earlier period from the perspective of a later one: critical differences may be obscured at the same time that important similarities are illuminated. With regard to the subject under discussion, the potentiality for such distortion is particularly great because of obvious and fundamental differences between conditions of politics in Britain and the colonies. Because the Crown continued throughout the eighteenth century to claim for—and through—its governors prerogative powers in the colonies that it had given up for itself in the home islands, colonial politicians continued to worry about the dangers of prerogative, not, of course, the prerogative of the king in Britain but that of the governors in the colonies. That the governors could not by any stretch of the imagination be mistaken for the king tended not to lessen but to intensify these fears by making the anomalous and persistent claims of the governors more conspicuous, and hence far more ominous. These fears were, to be sure, accompanied—and exacerbated—by the many evidences of corruption and malfeasance by men in the colonial administration precisely in the same way they had been in seventeenth-century England and America. But far from being the distinguishing feature of either colonial political culture or early eighteenth-century British opposition political thought, as Bailyn suggests in his comment, the concerns generated by such behavior would appear to be common to all opposition groups at every point in Anglo-American history during the seventeenth and eighteenth centuries. It is doubtful that such a generalized phenomenon merits the heavy emphasis given it by Bailyn. The focus of opposition attention in Britain was, in fact, not so much upon corruption itself as upon the devices that made the corruption possible: excessive prerogative powers in the seventeenth century and, as Isaac Kramnick, J. G. A. Pocock, and Caroline Robbins have shown, the new mechanisms of "finance, bureaucracy, [and] the standing army" in the eighteenth century. In Pocock's words, the "Civil List," the direct product of these new mechanisms, became the "historical successor to the feudal prerogative" as the primary object of opposition attacks. For the obvious reasons that none of these mechanisms [was] present to anything like the same degree in any but the few colonial situations I mentioned in my article and that only that small number of colonial administrations could possibly be mistaken for the British court, the Walpolean opposition fear that the executive would use its extensive civil list and Treasury Funds to corrupt the body politic was not fully and effectively "generalized through the culture" of the colonies.

A third and subsidiary problem arises from the tendency to assume that colonial use of opposition *writings* automatically means that opposition *ideas* had the same power, relevance, and meaning in the colonies as they had in Britain. No one doubts that colonial writers borrowed heavily from contemporary opposition polemicists in Britain, but the question is not whether they borrowed from opposition writings but how and to what extent they used opposition ideas. My point about Bailyn's heavy reliance upon pamphlets and newspaper essays was not that political writers were a different group from politicians in power; not even the merest novice would make that assumption. Rather, it was that the many literary allusions and blatant examples of wholesale borrowing from metropolitan writers by provincial essayists might be a more misleading index to the essential concerns of colonial politics than spare legislative journals or unadorned letters, diaries, and other personal and private records. But it is not absolutely necessary to turn to such sources; one may use the many eighteenth-century colonial pamphlets that formed the core of my "counter"-documentation to discover that, however extensively opposition writings were cited and copied, they did not always function in the same ways, have the same force and meaning, or dominate the political understanding to the same extent in the colonies that they did among their adherents in Britain. Even when they were used in obviously relevant situations to condemn the corrupt behavior of a Boone, a Reynolds, a Knowles, or a Cosby, they were only an incomplete reproduction of the thought of the anti-Walpoleans because the corruption could not be traced, as in the case of Walpole, to the misuse of the governor's scanty patronage powers or the few unappropriated surplus funds under their control. And I still suspect that the Walpolean opposition tradition was fully relevant to, predominant in, and operated in a manner comparable to the way it operated in Britain only in those situations in which the governors had at their disposal money, patronage, and influence proportionate to that of Walpole at home.

A fourth and final problem is the impulse to try to fit the whole of eighteenth-century colonial politics into a single, relatively simple model. An explanation that rests upon the undifferentiated attribution to all circumstances of one strand of political thought (however greatly attenuated) that is said to have depended for its force and use upon nothing more than the existence of corrupt governors (who, for the most part, lacked the means for effective corruption) and chronically unstable political conditions that everywhere produced a system that can be characterized under one generic rubric called "chaotic factionalism" itelf threatens to become a "master abstraction" as lifeless and as little explanatory of the whole process of colonial politics as that old and much-flogged horse, the Rise of the Assembly. I agree with Bailyn that more study needs to be given to prerevolutionary politics. But I disagree that only the details need to be filled in. Still to be worked out is a more comprehensive and refined general framework that will take into account differences in the structure, process and content of colonial political life from time to time and from place to place. In the meantime, The *Origins of American Politics,* as I pointed out in my review, will be very useful in precisely the way I used it in my article—not as a focal point for debate but as the most satisfactory general explanation of the colonial political process we have to date and a convenient starting point for the further discussion of those features of that process that it does not adequately comprehend.

John C. Miller

THE AMERICAN REVOLUTION AS A DEMOCRATIC MOVEMENT

Because we celebrate the Declaration of Independence and the dissolution of the political bonds with England with speeches and parades, it should not be thought that the event we commemorate is of the same order and magnitude as, say, burning the mortgage on the church after the loan has been paid off. What we celebrate is revolution, *the violent overthrow of tyrannical government which had become an intolerable oppression to the people; and if we have put the authors of it in history's Hall of Fame, we should realize the fully radical nature of the deed they accomplished. They replaced a monarchy with a republic, set a political example for the world, and changed the course of history.*

The central political doctrine of the revolutionaries was popular sovereignty—governments are legitimate only so long as they have the consent of the governed—and their political ethic was a system of natural rights said to be inherent in the people and beyond the power of magistrates to alter or amend. Fully as important as popular rule to the men of the Revolution were the ethical principles of liberty and equality.

The seven years of the Revolutionary War were not only years of military action, they were also years of intensive political creation. It is one thing to say that ultimate political power rests with a mythical "people" against real and very specific oppressors, and it is another thing for very real and specific people to materialize from the rhetoric and actually to wield the power the philosophers and tractarians said they had. But this is what occurred after May 1776, when the Continental Congress called upon the colonies to suppress all forms of royal authority and to organize new governments. What followed was a remarkable period of constitution-making in the former colonies. Although only one of them, the Massachusetts Constitution of 1780, was actually submitted to the "people" for ratification in a convention specially called for the purpose, the new constitutions clearly embodied the central doctrine of the Revolution that the "people" should rule, that legislatures should be strong, and that executives should not.

But principles of liberty and equality were also part of the doctrine of the Declaration, and in service to these principles, all of the states but one had abolished the slave trade within ten years after the Revolution; proceeded to disestablish state churches and extend religious freedom; and to abolish certain forms of hereditary privilege such as primogeniture and entail which had formed the foundation of European aristocracies. The vigor of this liberation spirit is well expressed by John C. Miller in his Origins of the

From John C. Miller, *Origins of the American Revolution* (Boston: Little, Brown and Company, 1943), pp. 491–505. Copyright 1943 by John C. Miller. Reprinted by permission of Little, Brown and Company and the Atlantic Monthly Press.

American Revolution, *a portion of which follows. He makes it clear that before the break with Britain the radicals and the conservatives in the Revolution had somewhat different ends to serve, with the radicals more enthusiastically bent upon projects of social reform than their conservative compatriots who had in mind a "revolution of limited liability."*

The Declaration of Independence represented not merely the triumph of Whigs over Tories but the victory of the radical wing of the Whig Party over the conservative wing. Conservative patriots had opposed independence hardly less vehemently than had the Tories and with hardly less effectiveness. What chiefly distinguished the Tories from the conservative Whigs was that the Tories staunchly refused to accept independence after it had been declared, whereas the Whigs, after a sharp struggle with their consciences, threw in their lot with the rebels. Although the revolutionary movement had taken what seemed to them a wrong turning, they remained loyal to the cause of American liberty. To take a conspicuous example, although John Dickinson had sacrificed his popularity by leading the fight against independence, he declared that he would dedicate his life to "the defense and happiness of those unkind Countrymen whom I cannot forbear to esteem as fellow Citizens amidst their Fury against me."[1] And thereupon he enlisted as a private in the American army. It is also true that many conservatives refused to surrender their hopes of reconciliation even after the Declaration of Independence; in the Middle colonies, independence was often spoken of as a strategic move designed to put the colonies in a better bargaining position. It was widely believed that Americans could walk back into the empire as easily as they had walked out. Some months after the Declaration, Richard Henry Lee asked in exasperation: "Shall we never cease to be teased with the Bugbear Reconciliation, or must we hang for ever on the hagger'd breast of G. Britain?"[2]

Whatever their hopes of restoring British sovereignty, the conservative Whigs were determined to prevent the revolutionary movement from becoming a social upheaval. In general, this was true of American revolutionaries; radical as regards American rights against Great Britain, they had no wish to usher in democracy in the United States. They were not making war upon the principle of aristocracy and they had no more intention than had the Tories of destroying the tradition

[1] *The Thomson Papers,* 29, 31.
[2] Richard Henry Lee to Samuel Adams, July 29, 1776, Adams MSS., New York Public Library.

of upper-class leadership in the colonies. Although they hoped to turn the Tories out of office, they did not propose to open these lush pastures to the common herd. They did believe, however, that the common people, if properly bridled and reined, might be made allies in the work of freeing the colonies from British rule and that they—the gentry—might reap the benefits without interference. They expected, in other words, to achieve a "safe and sane" revolution of gentlemen, by gentlemen, and for gentlemen. They conceived that the American Revolution was to be a revolution of limited liability from the point of view of the upper classes and that it was to be modeled upon the "glorious revolution" of 1688 which had redounded largely to the advantage of the aristocracy.

Many Virginia planters certainly did not intend that the revolutionary movement should break its leash and run with that mongrel, democracy. The rights of property, they insisted, must be kept uppermost and the rights of gentlemen ought never to be subordinated to the rights of man. "Is it right," they said, "that men of *birth* and *fortune,* in every government that is free, should be invested with power, and enjoy higher honours than the people? If it were otherwise, their privileges would be less, and they would not enjoy an equal degree of liberty with the people."[3] "We are not contending," said another Southern aristocrat, "that our rabble, or all unqualified persons, shall have the right of voting, or not be taxed; but that the freeholders and electors, whose right accrues to them from the common law, or from charter, shall not be deprived of that right."[4]

Like the conservative Whigs, the Tories dreaded the effect of revolutionary ideals upon the common people; but unlike the Whigs they did not believe that if revolution broke out in America it could be kept under control by its upper-class sympathizers. They held a catastrophic theory of revolutions: the plebeians would inevitably turn against the aristocracy and overwhelm all gentlemen, whether Whig or Tory. The Tories placed no trust in the "giddy-headed multitude": they held the common people to be "damned villains," "like the Mobility in all Countries, perfect Machines, wound up by any Hand who might first take the Winch."[5] They suspected that the "loud unlettered orators of the republican tribe" whom the conserva-

[3] *Virginia Gazette* (Rind's), June 9, 1768.
[4] Ibid., March 31, 1768.
[5] Peter Oliver, *Origin and Progress of the American Rebellion,* 1781, Egerton MSS., Gay Transcripts, Mass. Hist. Soc., 90.

tive Whigs expected to use for their own purposes would soon set the people to robbing the rich and pulling down the well-born. "I have seen the same trick practised in the Play-house," remarked a Tory; "where a set of wretches with a view of plunder, have given the alarm of fire; and while the terrified spectators were scampering over one another's heads, those villains have made a large collection of earrings, watches &c. before the cheat could be discovered."[6] They deplored that any "crack-brained zealot for democracy" should be listened to in America where the people already enjoyed "the best, the most beautiful political fabric which the sun ever beheld."[7] Edward Biddle of Philadelphia declared that he "sickened" at the thought of "thirteen unconnected petty democracies; if we are to be independent," he exclaimed, "let us, in the name of God, at once have an empire, and place Washington at the head of it."[8] "God forbid," they prayed, "that we should ever be so miserable as to sink into a Republick"—yet they believed that the Whigs were headed directly for this slough of despond.[9] For this reason, the Tories came to believe that they were holding the front line against democracy which, if victorious in America, might sweep across the Atlantic and overwhelm Great Britain itself. But they made little effort to save the people from the Whigs; for the most part, they were content to enjoy that last gratification of doomed aristocrats—damning the people roundly over their port and Madeira.

The menace of colonial democracy caused the Tories' love for the mother country to grow visibly fonder. Great Britain was the sheet anchor of colonial conservatism; the British government had repeatedly intervened in the colonies to save the aristocracy from the common people; and the Tories believed that, despite the unkind cuts of British imperialists, the authority of the mother country was still their best security against the rising tide of democracy. They concluded that it would be safer both for liberty and for property to be under the authority of the British Parliament and "subject to all the duties and taxes which they might think fit to impose, than to be under the government of the *American sons of liberty,* without paying any duties or taxes at all." If obliged to choose between "two of the greatest of human evils, the arbitrary conduct of a Prince: to the

[6] *Rivington's New York Gazetteer,* August 11, 1774.
[7] Inglis, *The True Interest of America Impartially Stated,* 52–54.
[8] Graydon, 301.
[9] *New York Gazette and Weekly Mercury,* April 23, 1770.

tyranny of an insolent and aspiring demagogue," the Tories regarded the despotism of a prince as the lesser evil.[10]

Tory fears that the Revolution would lead to a democratic upheaval were not altogether without foundation; certainly some Americans regarded the principles of the Declaration of Independence as presaging a new social and political order. They were not content with the mere name of republic; in their eyes, the Revolution was a struggle not only against British tyranny but against those aristocrats at home who longed for the power exercised by "Turkish Bashaws, French Grandees, and the Romish Clergy."[11] They were resolved to sweep away all "Foreign or Domestic Oligarchy" in America and to establish a society in which every citizen would enjoy equal rights and receive his "just share of the wealth."[12] There was growing insistence that the doctrine of no taxation without representation be applied in America itself as well as against Great Britain; and some even decried all government as "a combination among a few to oppress the many." Evidences of class hostility multiplied as the revolutionary movement progressed. As early as 1773, it was observed that "both employers and the employed no longer live together with any thing like attachment and cordiality on either side: and the labouring classes instead of regarding the rich as their guardians, patrons, and benefactors, now look on them as so many over-grown colossuses whom it is no demerit in them to wrong."[13] Even titles were called in question. Charles Lee denounced the practice of using such "tinsel epithets" as "his Excellency and His Honour, The Honourable President of the Honourable Congress, or the Honourable Convention." "This fulsome nauseating cant," said Lee, "may be well enough adapted to barbarous monarchies; or to gratify the adulterated pride of the *Magnifici* in pompous Aristocracies, but in a great free manly equal Commonwealth it is quite abominable."[14] Some Americans began to demand that all institutions be subjected to the test of reason. There was, as one radical put it, "a great deal of contemptible, but superstitiously worshipped rubbish, both in Church and State, which has been swept down to us from hea-

[10] *New York Gazette and Weekly Mercury,* June 25, 1770.
[11] *New York Gazette or Weekly Post Boy,* January 29, 1770.
[12] *Pennsylvania Evening Post,* April 30, 1776.
[13] Boucher, *A View of the Causes and Consequences of the American Revolution,* 309.
[14] *The Lee Papers,* II, 178.

thenism and popery, by the great net of time. It is now high time to examine the net, cull out the good fishes, and cast the bad away!"[15]

The demand that the revolution be directed against abuses at home as well as tyranny abroad was strengthened by the efforts of many American merchants to pile up fortunes during the war at the expense of the people. Profiteering was rife; the price of many necessities soared beyond the reach of the common people; and the merchants grew rich by speculation and cornering commodities. "If affairs continue any time in their present condition," exclaimed a Philadelphian in 1776, "they (the great Whig merchants) will have the whole wealth of the province in their hands, and then the people will be nearly in the condition that the East India Company reduced the poor natives of Bengal to."[16] When refugees from Boston and Charlestown began to stream into Connecticut, they found themselves at the mercy of landlords who promptly doubled their rents. To the patriots, these profiteers were "the rankest Tories of America." Did Americans "flee from the rage of Fire and Violence of bloody Men," it was asked, "to be plundered" by exploiters who called themselves Whigs but who in all but name were Tories? It was believed that the Tories opposed independence because it would mean that "their visions of golden mountains, and millions of acres of tenanted soil, will all vanish, and themselves remain in the despised rank of their honest and contented neighbours."[17] Americans did not propose to allow Whig profiteers and speculators to despoil their fellow citizens behind the screen of patriotism.

Resentment against these profiteers was particularly strong among the mechanics and laborers of the towns who were pinched more severely than any other class by their exactions. The town workers were the first to recognize that while Americans were engaged in defending their liberties from tyrants overseas they were in danger of losing their liberties to monopolists at home. In their eyes, the greatest threat to American freedom was that wealth would be concentrated in the hands of a few and that American farmers and workers, victorious against the British and Tories, might find themselves under the heel of new masters. The profiteers, they declared,

[15] *American Archives,* Fourth Series, V, 1157.
[16] *Pennsylvania Evening Post,* April 30, 1776.
[17] *Pennsylvania Gazette,* March 6, 1776. *New York Gazette and Weekly Mercury,* March 4, 1776.

were as great enemies of revolutionary ideals as were the Tories and they merited no better treatment; unless they were struck down, it seemed certain that the common people of America would shed their blood merely in order to exchange the rule of one oligarchy for that of another no less oppressive and self-seeking.[18]

The town artisans were also the chief sufferers by the property requirements placed upon the suffrage in the new state constitutions. Few of them possessed sufficient property to qualify as voters and so they remained an unrepresented group, keenly aware that the Revolution had passed them by. In vain they demanded the recognition of their "inalienable Right" to ratify all laws enacted by the assembly and to pass upon the proposed state constitutions, and protested against the system whereby in politics a workingman was no better than "a Jew or a Turk."[19] When they declared that "*every man in the country* who manifests a disposition *to venture his all for the defence of its Liberty,* should have *a voice in its Councils,*" their voices were drowned out by their opponents' denunciations of "this cursed spirit of levelling."[20] The conservatives who held the reins were determined not to trust themselves on a runaway democracy; on the contrary, they recognized that it was "time the Tradesmen were checked. They take too much upon them. They ought not to intermeddle in State Affairs. They ought to be kept low. They will become too powerful."[21] These measures were taken in time; although the town workers grew increasingly restive and radical in their demands for reform, they were unable to break the grip of the aristocracy.

While kicking against the pricks of Old England, conservative patriots had never overlooked the menace of New England, and the Declaration of Independence by no means extinguished their fear of New England levelism. Particularly dreaded were the New England soldiers, the most democratic element in that hotbed of democracy. It was suspected that these men spread subversive ideas wherever they went, thereby causing Americans to become social revolutionaries instead of God-fearing patriots whose energies were wholly taken up in combating British tyranny. Southern gentlemen who frowned upon democracy and all its works considered the New England army to be a horrible example of the effects of the popular delusion that one

[18] *New York Journal or General Advertiser,* January 4, March 7, 1776. *New York Gazette and Weekly Mercury,* April 8, June 10 and 17, 1776.
[19] C. H. Lincoln, *The Revolutionary Movement in Pennsylvania,* 80, note.
[20] *Pennsylvania Packet,* April 29, 1776.
[21] *Pennsylvania Gazette,* September 22, 1772.

man was as good as another. There were, they pointed out, too many officers in proportion to men in the regiments and the pay of officers and men was too nearly equal. New Englanders, on their part, warmly defended their equalitarianism and branded Southerners' demands that the pay of officers be raised and that of privates lowered as "incompatible with freedom."[22] The absence of gentlemen in the New England army was also distressing to conservatives: some even looked upon the minute-men with apprehension because they were "composed of people of the smallest property, and perhaps of the least virtue"—and might therefore be tempted to turn their arms against the landowning gentry. Although these skittish Whigs found a few men of good family and "decent breeding" among the higher ranks in the New England army, they reported that "anything above the condition of a clown, in the regiments we came in contact with, was truly a rarity." As for General Nathaniel Ward, a New Englander who had risen to high command in the continental army, he was held to be merely "a drivelling deacon."[23] . . .

Until the end of the War of Independence, conservatives generally succeeded in stemming the democratic tide and in keeping the revolutionary movement within the narrow channel of resistance to Great Britain. Their confidence that they had embarked upon a revolution of limited liability was little shaken before 1782. It was not until after the Peace of Paris when Americans put away their arms and vigorously sought to apply the ideals for which they had fought to conditions at home that the conservative patriots saw that the Tories had been true prophets. The forces unleashed by the Revolution could not long remain under the control of Whigs who aspired to step into the shoes of the former Tory aristocrats and to rule the masses in the name of the rich, the wise, and the good. The "principles of 76" were a powerful solvent upon the old aristocratic society that the Whig leaders hoped to perpetuate in the United States. Many years later, Harrison Gray Otis wrote to a friend of revolutionary days: "You and I did not imagine, when the first war with Britain was over, that revolution was just begun."

It has not yet ended.

[22] Joseph Hawley to Samuel Adams, November 12, 1775, Adams MSS., New York Public Library.
[23] Graydon, 154. *The Writings of George Washington,* III, 49. *American Archives,* Fourth Series, VI, 219.

Merrill Jensen

THE ARTICLES OF CONFEDERATION

The Revolution in effect created not one new country on the colonial side of the Atlantic but thirteen new countries, all legally independent of Britain and of each other. If they cooperated in the prosecution of the war, it was because they chose to, not because they could be forced to. The Continental Congress was an assembly of ambassadors from the states, not a government with power to enforce rule against the thirteen former colonies. To put it another way, Revolutionary enthusiasm provided some unity, but the Congress was primarily a council for a coalition of assertive allies. It was not the center of a government that could make its writ run throughout the new nation. Imperial Britain had performed certain necessary central functions for which the Continental Congress was an inadequate substitute, such as the raising and maintenance of armies, the levying of taxes to support the central authority, the conduct of military and diplomatic affairs with countries outside North America, the regulation of trade among the new states and with foreign nations. For all of these services the Congress had to depend upon the cooperative good will of the revolutionary alliance, and could not command it.

It was felt by responsible patriots—almost immediately upon the break with Britain—that a form of central government less provisional than that of the Continental Congress would have to be created, and to that end a new government under the Articles of Confederation was eventually established. Although the Articles were prepared as early as 1777, they were not ratified for another three and a half years, the chief obstacle being the question of the western lands. When the states with overlapping claims to western lands ceded them all to the Confederation government, the Articles were ratified.

The new system of governance was greatly decentralized; the states were not ready to recreate on the North American continent a domestic version of the imperial authority wielded by Britain, but declared that under the new system each of the states was independent and sovereign, and reserved to them the final decision as to whether they would comply with levies of men and money proposed by the central authority. So each state retained an absolute veto on any amendments to the original Articles. The libertarian spirit of the Revolution, then, worked to influence the form of the Confederation and to keep it weak.

The new regime experienced serious difficulties. In the eyes of later historians the Confederation years came to be known as the "Critical Period" because in their view the infirmities of the regime were so great—political and economic—that it would have collapsed unless serious steps were taken to create a stronger central authority.

From Merrill Jensen, *The Articles of Confederation* (Madison: University of Wisconsin Press, 1940), pp. 239–45. Reprinted by permission of the publishers.

The regime under the Articles is sympathetically described, however, in the following essay by Merrill C. Jensen, whose The Articles of Confederation *has helped to counteract generally prevailing conservative accounts of this period in American history.*

The Articles of Confederation were the constitution of the United States from 1781 to 1789, when the Confederation Congress held its last session and turned over the government of the thirteen states to the new national government. The fact that the Articles of Confederation were supplanted by another constitution is no proof either of their success or of their failure. Any valid opinion as to the merits of the Articles must be based on a detailed and unbiased study of the confederation period. Though no such comprehensive study has yet been made, it is possible to draw certain tentative conclusions by approaching the history of the period from the point of view of the American Revolution within the American states rather than from the point of view that the Constitution of 1787 was a necessity, the only alternative to chaos.

An analysis of the disputes over the Articles of Confederation makes it plain that they were not the result of either ignorance or inexperience. On the contrary, they were a natural outcome of the revolutionary movement within the American colonies. The radical leaders of the opposition to Great Britain after 1765 had consistently denied the authority of any government superior to the legislatures of the several colonies. From 1774 on, the radicals continued to deny the authority of a superior legislature whether located across the seas or within the American states. The reiteration of the idea of the supremacy of the local legislatures, coupled with the social and psychological forces which led men to look upon "state sovereignty" as necessary to the attainment of the goals of the internal revolution, militated against the creation of such a centralized government as the conservative elements in American society desired. It can be said that the constitution which the radicals created, the Articles of Confederation, was a constitutional expression of the philosophy of the Declaration of Independence.

Today "states' rights" and "decentralization" are the war cries of the conservative element, which is not wielding the influence in national affairs it once did and still longs to do. But in the eighteenth century decentralization and states' rights meant local self-government, and local self-government meant a form of agrarian democracy. The mass of the population was composed of small farmers, who in the long run could control the politics of their individual states. Since this was the belief of the fathers of the constitution of 1787, who were thus in substantial agreement with the radical leaders of 1776, the testimony might very well be regarded as conclusive.

The writing of the Articles of Confederation brought to the fore political issues that were to be of vast significance in the history of the United States. Many a debate in later years was merely a reiteration or an elaboration of arguments used in 1776 and 1777. Those ideas upon which it is necessary to place the inadequate but necessary label of "conservative" were as well expressed in 1776 as in 1787, and often by the same men: John Dickinson and James Wilson, for instance. The vital change which took place between 1776 and 1787 was not in ideas nor in attitudes but in the balance of political power. The radical organization which had brought about the Revolution disintegrated with success, for the radicals had won their real goal, local self-government. Radical leaders returned to their states to enjoy the results of their efforts unhampered by a central government of extensive power. The conservatives, on the other hand, made only occasional gains in the states, as in Massachusetts, where their rule was met by open rebellion in 1786. In other states the attack upon their position was a slow-but-sure process, as in Virginia. Some of them had realized in 1776 that centralization was their protection: a central government to suppress internal rebellions, to regulate trade, and to control the actions of the state governments as the British had controlled the colonial governments.

The fight for centralization did not stop with the completion of the Articles of Confederation. Discontent with the document was expressed in the private correspondence of such conservative leaders as Washington, Dickinson, Charles Carroll, Robert Morris, Gouverneur Morris, James Wilson, and Alexander Hamilton. Even before they were finally ratified Hamilton proposed a revolutionary convention to create the kind of government the conservatives wanted. Once the Articles had been ratified, many serious attempts were made to amend them in such a way as to strengthen the central organization. These attempts at amendment failed, as did efforts to "interpret" into the Articles certain "nationalistic" ideas foreign to both the purpose and character of the document. Even if such amendments had been adopted, the constitution would not have been satisfactory to the conservative element, for it was impossible to change its nature by mere amendment. From the conservative point of view it was the wrong *kind* of government. Even if Congress had been given a limited income, as was proposed in various amendments, the central government would still have been a federal government and therefore inadequate in conservative opinion. The alterations proposed during the Confederation period were not fundamental, for they did not touch the vital question of the distribution of power between the states and the central government. The vast field of undefined and unenumerated powers lay with the states. Congress could function only within an area of precisely delegated and carefully limited authority. It was the creature of the state governments and thus, ultimately, of the electorate of the states.

Centralized government with a legal veto on state laws, the power to enact general and uniform legislation, and the power to use arms to subdue rebellious social groups within the states, had disappeared with the Declaration of Independence. The Articles of Confederation were designed to prevent its reappearance, and for this reason were not, and never could be, adequate from the point of view of the conservatives, who wanted the essence of the British imperial system restored in the American states.

John Dickinson and his conservative committee had sought to lay the legal foundation of such a system in their first draft of articles of confederation. The document was involved and legalistic to the point of obscurity, but it was an obscurity which would lend itself readily to multiple interpretation. Legally, ultimate authority lay with the central government, for only one conditional guarantee was given to the states, and only one specific restraint was placed on Congress. The states were guaranteed the control of their "internal police" in matters where such control did not interfere with the Articles of Confederation. Congress was restrained only from levying taxes other than those for support of the post office. This was a great but not insurmountable obstacle in the way of centralization. The important point is that the vital area of undefined and unenumerated powers fell within the domain of the central government, as Thomas Burke demonstrated to Congress in 1777.

The final draft of the Articles of Confederation was, as James Wilson said in the convention of 1787, "how different." Certain powers and no others were delegated to Congress. No phrase in the document could be construed as making the central government supreme over the states. Nothing remotely resembling such phrases as "obligation of contract," "supremacy of the laws," "necessary and proper" or "general welfare" were to be found in it. The control of war and foreign affairs was expressly granted to Congress, as was the power to regulate the trade with Indians who were not members of any of the states, but Congress might not infringe upon the right of any state to legislate upon matters within its own limits. Congress was given the power to regulate the value of both its own coinage and that of the states, but no control over the emission of paper money by the states. Congress was a court of last appeal, or rather a board of arbitration, in disputes between one state and another, and between private individuals claiming lands under different grants. Congress was given charge of the post office and the regulation of weights and measures. These were its "sole and exclusive" powers. In addition, it was given the authority to appoint a committee of the states to sit during the recesses of Congress and the power to control its own organization and sessions.

Eighteenth-century radicals looked upon the desire for office as a disease which fed upon office-holding. Hence they were careful to provide that Congress should never become an association of office holders. No one could be a member of Congress for more than three out of any six years. No one could be president of Congress for more than one year out of any three; thus no individual would be likely to acquire much prestige as head of the central government. The delegates were subject to recall at any time by the state governments which had selected them, and hence were usually responsive to the will of their electorates as expressed in the state legislatures. This serves to explain why so many votes in Congress were often inconsistent with a given delegate's political and economic views.

The Articles of Confederation placed few restraints upon the states, and even these tended to be qualified out of existence. No state could receive or send embassies or enter into alliances or treaties without the consent of Congress. No state could levy imposts or duties which might interfere with stipulations in treaties made by Congress. No treaty made by Congress, on the other hand, could interfere with the right of a state to subject foreigners to the same imposts and duties as were levied on its own citizens. The states were not to keep vessels of war in peacetime unless Congress deemed it to be necessary for purposes of defense. Neither could a state maintain troops unless Congress considered them necessary to garrison forts. States were forbidden to declare war without the consent of Congress except where sudden invasion would permit of no delay. Letters of marque and reprisal were to be granted only after a declaration of war by Congress and under conditions laid down by it. None of these restraints was a serious check upon the sovereignty of the states.

Between the states there was complete equality. Every state was required to have at least two representatives in Congress, and it might have as many as seven, though each delegation was to have only one vote. When more than two delegates from a state were present, the state's vote was decided by the majority of the delegation. If the vote was a tie, the state had no vote. Citizens of any state were allowed to emigrate freely to another. Extradition of criminals was provided for. The Articles declared that each state should give full faith to the judicial proceedings of every other state. Except in these things the states were not responsible to one another. The union that had been created was a federal union of equal states in which the central organization was carefully subordinated to the members of it.

The Articles of Confederation were designed to prevent the central government from infringing upon the rights of the states, whereas the Constitution of 1787 was designed as a check upon the power of the states and the democracy that found expression within their bounds. The character of the Articles of Confederation was the result of two realities: the reality of the psychological and legal independence of the states, and the reality of the belief that democracy was possible only within fairly small political units whose electorate had a direct check upon the officers of government. Such a check was impossible where the central government was far removed from the control of the people by distance and by law. The independence of the states was a product of colonial history. The distrust of centralization, of government spread over a great area, was the product of both political theory and practical experience. The rise of radicalism had been checked often enough to teach the radicals that central governments, however democratic in form, were fundamentally undemocratic in action.

This government, the product of the forces which brought about the American Revolution, failed not because it was inadequate but because the radicals failed to maintain the organization they had created to bring about the American Revolution. The radical movement was essentially a movement of parties within states, and their political and social aims were to a great extent local. To achieve their purpose, local independence, unity of all the states had been necessary. What the radicals failed to see was that they must continue their union if they were to maintain their local independence under the Articles of Confederation. Thomas Burke of North Carolina expressed the radical view admirably. Congress, he said, was a general council instituted for the purpose of opposing the usurpations of Great Britain and of conducting a war against her, of forming necessary foreign alliances, directing the army and navy, and making binding treaties. Since this was the nature of Congress and its power, it eliminated "all pretence for continuance of a Congress after the war is concluded, or of assuming a power to any other purposes."

Thus when the radicals had won their war, most of them were well content to go home and continue with the program of action they had started long before the war began. The thwarting of that program by the local conservatives and the British government had been one of the major causes of the Revolution. Needless to say, the motives of the radicals were not always the highest or the most disinterested, but their program was essentially democratic in tendency, for it widened the bases of political power and it declared that men should be bound only by those laws to which they had given their consent. Above all, when that program was idealized, as in the Declaration of Independence, it declared that the purpose of government was the protection of the life, liberty, and happiness of the individual, and when it did not fulfill this ideal it should be overthrown. Such a revolution was a practical possibility in a state unchecked by an outside and superior authority. Such an authority was rendered impossible by the Articles of Confederation.

What the radicals did not see was that the conservative elements in American society had learned a bitter lesson at the hands of the radicals. They too could call conventions. They too could paint dark pictures of the times and blame the supposed woes of the country on the Articles of Confederation, as the radicals had blamed the British government before 1776. They too could, and did, adopt the radical theory of the sovereignty of the people; in the name of the people they engineered a conservative counter-revolution and erected a nationalistic government whose purpose in part was to thwart the will of "the people" in whose name they acted. They too could use one name while pursuing a goal that was the opposite in fact. Thus, although the purpose of the conservatives was "nationalistic," they adopted the name "Federalist," for it served to disguise the extent of the changes they desired. True, the government they created had a good many "federal" features, but this was so because the conservatives were political realists and had to compromise with the political reality of actual state sovereignty.

What the conservatives in their turn failed to see was that the government they created might be captured by the radicals united on a national scale. Madison in *The Federalist* wrote that such a union was impossible, though he shortly helped to bring it about when faced with the workings of the government under the Constitution of 1787.

Wise old John Adams probably had the last word. Writing in 1808, he declared, "I have always called our Constitution a game at leap-frog."

Andrew C. McLaughlin

THE CONFEDERATE PERIOD AND THE FEDERAL CONVENTION

However much the Articles of Confederation may have lent themselves to the fulfillment of democratic aspiration towards the end of the Revolution and thereafter, there were serious difficulties of governance in the 1780s, most of which stemmed from the absence of a stronger central authority than the Articles provided. There were at least two major accomplishments of the Confederation government under the Articles, however, although each in its way was compromised in some respects by later events. The first was the negotiation of the Treaty of Paris in 1783 by which His Britannic Majesty recognized the independence of the United States and promised to withdraw troops from the territory of the new country, and by which the promise of the United States was pledged to the restoration of confiscated British properties in the several states. But the British did not fully honor the commitment to withdraw forces and the Confederation government had no power to force the states to permit legal proceedings in their own courts for the recovery of confiscated property. And of course such actions could not be pressed in federal courts since there were no federal courts.

The second of the two principal accomplishments was the enactment of the Northwest Ordinance of 1787 providing for the creation of not less than three states out of a vast domain covering what is now Ohio, Indiana, Illinois, Michigan, Wisconsin, and part of Minnesota. The Ordinance was a remarkably liberal document, both for its own time and ours. It provided for habeas corpus, trial by jury, religious freedom, the encouragement of education, and decency towards the Indians. And Article Six abolished slavery in the territory in language that was to be used again in the Thirteenth Amendment abolishing slavery throughout the United States.

The Articles of Confederation provided rules, formulas, passages, clauses, ideas and procedures for other parts of the United States Constitution also. For example, representation by states in the Confederation Congress was a feature of the New Jersey Plan in the Federal Convention of 1787, and became the basis for the organization of the United States Senate. The entitlement of all citizens to the privileges and immunities of citizens of the several states became a provision of Article IV of the Constitution, as did the full faith and credit clause, and the provision for the rendition of fugitives from justice among the several states. The protection of members of the Confederation Congress from arrest going to and from meetings of the Congress, and the immunity of members from accountability in any other place for "speech and debate" in Congress became Article I, Section 6 of

From Andrew C. McLaughlin, *A Constitutional History of the United States* (New York and London: D. Appleton-Century Co., Inc., 1935), pp. 137–150; 154–155; 192–197. Copyright © 1935 by D. Appleton-Century Company, Inc. Reprinted by permission of Irvington Publishers, Inc.

the Constitution. The denial to the states of any power to conduct foreign relations became Article I, Section 10. The prohibitions against the acceptance of titles of nobility or any emoluments from foreign governments appeared in Article I, Section 9. The prohibition to the states of any authority to grant letters of marque and reprisal appeared in Article I, Section 10. The power to regulate the value of coin and to fix the standards for weights and measures showed up in Article I, Section 8. The pledge for the payment of the public debt became part of Article VI. Even the well-known three-fifths provision in Article I, Section 2 of the Constitution for the calculation of election constituencies and the laying of direct taxes had been proposed in an amendment to the Articles, but failed of acceptance.

But these contributions of the Articles to the United States Constitution could occur only after the demise of the Confederation government, much as the best parts of an old structure may become incorporated into the new one that replaces it. During its seven years of existence, the Confederation operated with great difficulty. The next essay indicates what some of those difficulties were.

The vicissitudes of the years from the adoption of the Articles to the formation of the federal Constitution deserve more attention than can be given in these pages. Almost everything points in only one direction—toward the need of a competent central government and the necessity of finding a system of union which could maintain itself. Elaborate presentation of details is therefore for our purposes not required. The whole story is one of gradually increasing ineptitude; of a central government which could less and less function as it was supposed to function; of a general system which was creaking in every joint and beginning to hobble at every step. The men who came to Philadelphia in the spring of 1787 had learned the lessons taught by the failings of the Confederation.

One source of the difficulty was the Revolution itself. For the Revolution involved war; it started as a revolt against authority. It had deeply affected the old social order, and although, as we have pointed out, the philosophy on which the movement was founded had within it elements of stability and sobriety, the war left, as war always does, the combatants in a state of mental disquietude; social and economic foundations had been shaken; the full hopes of the conflict could not in the twinkling of an eye be gathered into reality. If a war is fought for liberty, why is it necessary to forge chains of perpetual union and obedience to government? Tom Paine's philosophy, which was permeated by the real spirit of real revolution, had gone beyond the limits of the older doctrines on which the social and political order was supposed to rest; for that ardent propagandist was not fond of picturing the state of nature as a place from which men had emerged for their own greater comfort and security; if his most widely trumpeted sayings are to be taken at their face value, all things which had grown up since the age of primeval bliss and serenity could have no real sanction for their existence, not even the sanction and support of time—"Government like dress, is the badge of lost innocence; the palaces of kings are built on the ruins of the bowers of paradise." Just how far this new state of nature and all the emanations of this tragic philosophy influenced the average man of those days, no one can say; but their presence is plain enough.

Furthermore, there was the age-old feeling that government is inevitably the enemy of man and not his servant. We cannot neglect the effect of the long struggle in history to curb government lest it act the tyrant. Government in America was not as yet securely in the hands of the people-at-large (if there be any such security anywhere at any time), but a long step forward had been taken. "It takes time," however, as John Jay remarked, "to make sovereigns of subjects"—a wise saying. It took time for the people to realize that the government was their own.

Interstate jealousy did not fail to add to the complexities of the situation.[1] The contest for local rights under the old imperial system had strengthened the sense of state reality; men were conscious of their states; the states were in a sense their own creation. It was difficult, after the strain of the war had gone, to feel acutely the reality of America and the dependence of its members one upon another; and as the days went by disorganization rather than integration seemed to be gathering headway, until the more serious patriots and watchers of the night feared for the safety of their country. States with commodious harbors had an advantage over their neighbors, and they did not shrink from using it. Madison, speaking of this condition, declared that at one time "New Jersey, placed between Phil[a]. & N. York, was likened to a Cask tapped at both ends: and N. Carolina between Virg[a]. & S. Carolina to a patient bleeding at

[1] "Il règne dans la formation de ces Etats un vice radical qui s'opposera toujours à une union parfaite, c'est que les Etats n'ont ré-ellement aucun intérêt pressant d'être sous un seul chef." ["There is a radical flaw in the makeup of these States that will always work against perfect union, that is, that the States really have no interest in being under a single head."—Ed.] Otto, French chargé d'affaires, to comte de Montmorin, April 10, 1787. See *The Records of the Federal Convention of 1787* (Max Farrand, ed.), III, p. 16.

both Arms."[2] The experience of those years brought clearly home to thinking men the need of some general regulation of commerce.

The industrial and commercial conditions after the war were in considerable confusion. Readjustments were necessary, especially for the resuscitation of the New England shipping industry. Some improvement came fairly quickly, and there is evidence that by 1786 the clouds of depression were beginning to lift. But it was hard to make much headway, especially as Britain was not ready to treat her former colonies as if they deserved particular favors or consideration; they had made their own beds, now let them lie there—a condition of retirement not suited to the restless spirit of the New England skippers whose ships were soon plowing the seas, even on to the Orient as well as to the ports of continental Europe. Commercial treaties were desirable, and some steps were taken in that direction; but it was hard to do anything effectively as long as the individual states could not be relied on to fulfill their obligations. Foreign nations naturally queried whether America was one or many, or, perhaps, one today and thirteen tomorrow.

The treaty of peace was not carried out. Britain still held the western posts from Lake Champlain to Mackinaw and thus retained control of the northern fur trade and influence over the Indians. Spain holding the mouth of the Mississippi was unwilling to allow free navigation through her territory. Trouble was brewing because of American treatment of the loyalists and because the stipulation in the treaty, that there should be no lawful impediment to the collection of debts due British creditors, received no particular attention. John Jay declared in 1786 that the treaty had been constantly violated by one state or another from the time of its signing and ratification. The Barbary powers, eager to take advantage of a helpless country, to seize American seamen, and to hold them for ransom, entered upon the game with lusty vigor. A nation which was not yet a nation in terms of law and political authority could do nothing to resist scorn and humiliation.

The pivotal problem, the immediate and unrelenting problem, was how to get revenue for the pressing needs of the Confederation.

[2] See Madison's preface to the debates in the Federal Convention, *Documentary History of the Constitution,* III, p. 7. The preface was written at a later time but Madison's general description of conditions is valuable. See also a letter from Madison to Jefferson, March 18, 1786, in Charles Warren, *The Making of the Constitution,* p. 16.

Financial affairs were in a pitiful shape and conditions daily grew worse. At the end of active hostilities the situation was bad enough. "Imagine," wrote Robert Morris who had charge of the newly-created office of superintendent of finance, "the situation of a man who is to direct the finances of a country almost without revenue (for such you will perceive this to be) surrounded by creditors whose distresses, while they increase their clamors, render it more difficult to appease them; an army ready to disband or mutiny; a government whose sole authority consists in the power of framing recommendations."[3] Conditions did not improve; gloom deepened into darkness. The continental paper money ere long became a joke; and the returns from requisitions upon the states soon were lamentably inadequate. A committee of Congress reported in 1786 that the amount received in fourteen months was not sufficient for the "bare maintenance of the federal government on the most economical establishment, and in time of profound peace."[4] The sums due for interest on the domestic and foreign debts were piling up to staggering heights and even the principal of the debts—for, strange as it may seem, Congress had succeeded in borrowing—was increasing ominously. Morris had by this time resigned; he did not wish to be a "minister of injustice." Congress was at its wit's end. "The crisis has arrived," a committee announced, "when the people of these United States, by whose will, and for whose benefit the federal government was instituted, must decide whether they will support their rank as a nation, by maintaining the public faith at home and abroad; or whether, for want of a timely exertion in establishing a general revenue, and thereby giving strength to the confederacy, they will hazard not only the existence of the union, but of those great and invaluable privileges for which they have so arduously and so honourably contended."[5]

At the very beginning, indeed before the Articles had been signed by the delegates from Maryland, Congress submitted to the states an amendment (February 3, 1781) vesting in Congress a power to levy a duty of 5 percent on imported goods, with a few exceptions, and a like duty on "prizes and prize goods." The monies arising from the duties were to be used for discharging the principal and interest of the public debts. The amendment was not adopted, one state, Rhode

[3] Letter from Morris to Franklin, January 11, 1783, in *The Revolutionary Diplomatic Correspondence of the United States* (Francis Wharton, ed.), VI, p. 203.
[4] February 15, 1786. *Journals of Congress* (1823 ed.), IV, pp. 619–20.
[5] February 15, 1786. Ibid., IV, p. 620.

Island, failing to ratify. Two years later a similar attempt to obtain revenue was made. In an amendment proposed at this time, certain commodities were designated with various rates of duties; on all other goods a 5 percent duty was provided for; the proceeds were to be applied to the discharge of the debts, but the duties were not to be continued for more than twenty-five years. The states were also recommended to take steps for appropriating annually for a like term of years the sum of $1 million, the amount to be apportioned among the states. This amendment met the same fate as its predecessor.

In 1784, an amendment was submitted to the states which, if it had been ratified, would have given Congress certain powers over the regulation or restraint of foreign commerce. "Unless the United States in Congress assembled," it was declared, "shall be vested with powers competent to the protection of commerce, they can never command reciprocal advantages in trade; and without these our foreign commerce must decline & eventually be annihilated. . . . " The amendment was ratified by only two states.

Within the individual states, paper money added to the confusion and made recovery of economic stability difficult. Some of the states refused to be drawn down into the whirlpool; but seven of the thirteen had entered upon the scheme. The wise and proper way to get out of debt was to resort to the printing-press; for what forsooth did free government exist? "Choose such men," said one voice crying from the wilderness of poverty and debt, "as will make a bank of paper money, big enough to pay all our debts, which will sink itself (that will be so much clear gain to the state)."[6] Without question, the debtor was in a bad way; but associated with this sort of appeal for relief were all the uneasy spirits whose attitudes of mind, when minds they used, were inimical to steady economic well-being and to stable and competent government. Whether one approves or disapproves the content and the agitation of the whole controversy, the fact remains that conditions were fraught with peril, a peril enchanced by the poverty of debtors and by the mental and spiritual disquietude which, as we all know, are the fruits of war and the companions of the ensuing peace.

Social unrest passed beyond the grumbling stage in Mas-

[6] *New Haven Gazette,* March 22, 1787. Quoted in O. G. Libby, *Geographical Distribution of the Vote of the Thirteen States on the Federal Constitution, 1787–8* (*Bulletin* of the University of Wisconsin, Economics, Political Science, and History Series, I, no. 1), p. 58.

sachusetts where Shays' rebellion broke out and aroused the anxieties of the conservatives from one end of the continent to the other. Its chiefest interest to us lies in the fact that it unquestionably had the effect of prompting men of mind as well as men of property to strengthen the union and to create self-respecting government. "There are combustibles in every State," Washington wrote in 1786, "which a spark might set fire to." "Good God!" he exclaimed, lamenting the disorder, "Who besides a Tory, could have foreseen, or a Briton predicted them?" John Marshall, writing to James Wilkinson early in 1787, said, "I fear, and there is no opinion more degrading to the dignity of man, that these have truth on their side who say that man is incapable of governing himself. I fear we may live to see another revolution."[7]

After this hurried view of the conditions during the so-called "critical period," we may now turn to a consideration of the political system to discover what the leaders of the time believed to be the trouble and especially to see what remedies they proposed. We have already seen that Congress had proposed amendments to the Articles authorizing the collection of customs duties to be used by Congress for defraying the debts of the union, and we have seen that in each case the amendment failed of ratification. These proposals showed the necessity of congressional income, not dependent on state caprice; a conspicuous defect in the Articles was the absence of congressional authority to obtain necessary funds; the old trouble of the taxing power in an imperial system remained. At sundry times the rights and authority of Congress and the character of the Confederation were discussed in Congress and beyond its doors. The proposals and announcements disclose the compelling nature of a serious problem and they bring before us the question of national existence as that question appeared to leading statesmen of the time.[8]

Almost immediately after Maryland's delegates had signed the Articles, a committee of Congress reported that by article thirteen a general and implied power was vested in Congress to carry all the Articles into effect against any state refusing or neglecting to abide

[7] Letter from Marshall to Wilkinson, January 5, 1787, in *Am. Hist. Rev.*, XII, p. 348. This coincidence of Washington's and Marshall's sentiments is instructive, if one would understand the later career of each. Marshall seems never to have forgotten the privations of Valley Forge or the menace of Shays' rebellion.

[8] A very useful collection of proposals of this kind is *Proposals to Amend the Articles of Confederation, 1781–1789* (*American History Leaflets,* A. B. Hart and Edward Channing, eds., no. 28).

by them; that no particular provision had been made for that purpose, and that therefore an amendment should be added fully authorizing Congress to use "the force of the United States" to compel a "State or States to fulfill their federal engagements. . . . " At that early date the need of compulsion was seen by a congressional committee including James Madison who presented the report. This report, sent to a grand committee, resulted in a full presentation (August 22, 1781) of what were believed to be requisites for "execution" of the Confederation; it was also recommended that certain additional powers should be given to Congress, notably the authority "To distrain the property of a state delinquent in its assigned proportion of men and money." Thus again, the central problem of imperial organization—how to secure supplies for the maintenance of the system—came up for solution, and the proposed solution was the use of force, or at least the seizure of property. These proposed amendents were not presented to the states for ratification.

Men interested in public affairs were actively discussing the nature and the defects of the union. Pelatiah Webster, an able publicist, issued *A Dissertation on the Political Union and Constitution of the Thirteen United States* in which he pointed out the necessity of vesting the power of taxation in what he called "The supreme authority"; this authority should have sufficient power to enforce obedience to treaties and alliances. "No laws of any State whatever," he declared, "which do not carry in them a force which extends to their effectual and final execution, can afford a certain or sufficient security to the subject." With this in mind, he proposed naively that every person, "whether in public or private character, who shall, by public vote or other overt act, disobey the supreme authority, shall be amendable [*sic*] to Congress," and shall be haled before that body to be fined or imprisoned, "on due conviction."[9] Hamilton in 1783 drafted resolutions "Intended to be submitted to Congress, but abandoned for want of support." He enumerated at length the defects of the Confederation, and made a severe arraignment of the system. The first defect consisted in "confining the power of the Federal Government within too narrow limits." The whole discussion or criticism is extremely interesting to anyone wishing to study the nature of Hamilton's political thinking as well as the critical problem

[9] This plan of Webster contained much more than is indicated in the text above; but the declaration concerning the necessity of force is the thing I wish to stand out clearly. . . .

of the time. He plainly objected not only to the inconsistencies of the Articles, but to the impracticability of their effective operation. In 1785, Noah Webster, in his *Sketches of American Policy,* announced a doctrine which by that time must have been fairly familiar, at least to those willing to think: " . . . in all the affairs that respect the whole, Congress must have the same power to enact laws and compel obedience throughout the continent, as the legislatures of the several states have in their respective jurisdictions."[10]

Of most significance, however, is the report (August 1786) of a grand committee of Congress of which Charles Pinckney of South Carolina was chairman.[11] It is important because Pinckney was an influential member of the Convention which met a few months later and drew up the Constitution of the United States. Early in 1786 Congress, in the manifesto mentioned on a previous page, had in a most solemn manner exposed the deplorable and perilous condition of the union. "Oh! my country!" said Jeremy Belknap, "To what an alarming situation are we reduced, that Congress must say to us, as Joshua did to Israel, 'Behold, I set before you life and death.' "[12]

The report of the committee is a sad commentary on the moribund Confederation, for if the proposed remedies had been administered, the result might well have been sudden demise in the place of lingering death. Congress was to be given the power to regulate interstate and foreign trade, with the consent of nine states, and the power of levying additional requisitions in the way of punishment upon any state not promptly complying with requisitions for men or money. If the delinquent and disobedient state should persist in its conduct, while the majority had lived up to their obligations, then Congress should have power to levy and collect taxes and in the last extremity compel the local officers in the delinquent state to do their

[10] A sentiment of almost exactly the same character came from Washington—one of those indications of the clearness with which he could sum up a situation without mincing phrases: "I do not conceive we can exist long as a nation without having lodged some where a power, which will pervade the whole Union in as energetic a manner as the authority of the State governments extends over the several States." George Washington, *Writings* (W. C. Ford, ed.), XI, pp. 53–54. The emphasis of Webster's document was on the need of effective power. To each State, in his opinion, might be left its "sovereign right of directing its own internal affairs; but give to Congress the sole right of conducting the general affairs of the continent." He thus advocated by the division of sovereignty an organization with effective force at the center.

[11] George Bancroft, *History of the Formation of the Constitution,* II, pp. 373–77.

[12] Letter of March 9, 1786, in Mass. Hist. Society *Collections,* fifth series, II, part 1, p. 431.

duty; should such a step prove ineffective, then Congress might itself appoint assessors and collectors. If there were further opposition to congressional authority, the conduct on the part of the state should be considered "an open violation of the federal compact." All this is an exposition of a desperate condition, for the ultimate remedy must be no remedy at all, but only a solemn declaration that a disobedient state had broken its promises; and yet the amendments contained provisions for compulsion upon the states by using every conceivable means of coercion short of sending troops into the state—if perchance the troops could be found ready to seize the property of citizens. The committee also proposed as amendments to the Articles that Congress be granted the power to institute a federal judiciary and to provide for securing the attendance of delegates in Congress; if such delegates did not attend, or if they withdrew, they should under certain circumstances be "proceeded against," provided punishment should extend no further than disqualifications to be delegates or to hold any office under the United States or any state.

Nothing could more amply demonstrate the feebleness and distraction of Congress and the necessity for energetic reform, if the union was to last many days. The cumbersome methods proposed for getting money, the practical admission of a continuing and probably inescapable refusal of the states to comply with reasonable requests to defray the absolutely necessary common expenses, and above all, the more pitiful suggestion of measures which might induce members from the states to come to Congress and attend to business, were a confession of masterly incapacity.

Another source of anxiety was the light-hearted way in which treaties were regarded by the states. John Jay, the Secretary for Foreign Affairs, on whose shoulders rested much of the wearying responsibility of the time, persuaded himself, or tried to, that treaties, when once made, were binding on the states and were part of the "laws of the land"—a significant expression. "Your secretary considers the thirteen independent sovereign states as having, by express delegation of power, formed and vested in Congress a perfect though limited sovereignty for the general and national purposes specified in the confederation. In this sovereignty they cannot severally participate (except by their delegates) or have concurrent jurisdiction. . . . When therefore a treaty is constitutionally made, ratified and published by Congress, it immediately becomes binding on the whole nation, and superadded to the laws of the land, without the intervention, consent or fiat of state legislatures."[13] In March, 1787, resolutions were passed by Congress declaring treaties "constitutionally made" were "part of the law of the land"; the states were called upon to repeal acts violating the treaty with Britain and to direct the state courts to adjudge cases in accord with the treaty, "any thing in the . . . acts to the contrary . . . notwithstanding."[14]

But what was the very center of the difficulty? What was the chief problem of the time? The trouble and confusion were manifestly caused by the failure of the states to abide by their obligations. The problem was to find a method, if union was to subsist at all, for overcoming the difficulty, to find therefore some arrangement, some scheme or plan of organization wherein there would be reasonable assurance that the states would fulfill their obligations and play their part under established articles of union and not make mockery of union by willful disregard or negligent delay. That was the *chief problem* of the day. The need of granting certain powers to Congress was plain; in other words, the distribution of powers between the center and the parts was imperfectly provided for in the Confederation. The distribution of powers, however, did not constitute the radical difficulty. If additional "powers" were granted Congress, could there be any assurance that the old trouble would not immediately arise? To the men of 1786—such men as were anxious for national stability—the real remedy appeared to be some application of force, the coercion of recalcitrant states, something more than the grant of naked authority to the central organ of union. The problem of imperial order had been reduced in some respects to fairly simple terms; if the task of distinguishing between powers was no longer especially troublesome, the question remaining was perplexing: could the states be held together in a firm and effective union and what arrangement could be made for securing or assuring obedience to their obligations as members of the union? Plainly enough the

[13] *Secret Journals of the Acts and Proceedings of Congress,* IV, pp. 203–204. Cf. Constitution, Art. VI, para. 2. A committee report to the Congress of the Confederation, discussed March 26, 1784, contained the following provision: " 'That these United States be considered in all such treaties, and in every case arising under them, as one nation, upon the principles of the federal constitution.' " A motion was made to strike out this instruction. On the question, shall it stand, the vote stood: New Hampshire, Massachusetts, New York, New Jersey, Pennsylvania, Maryland, Virginia, North Carolina, South Carolina, aye; Rhode Island, Connecticut, no. *Secret Journals of the Acts and Proceedings of Congress,* III, pp. 452–54.
[14] *Journals of Congress* (1823 ed.), IV, pp. 730, 737.

men of the time—the men of course who really thought—were troubled and perplexed; but few of them could even then see much further than the need of compulsion—the use of force against disobedient states.[15]

But the year of gloom was not allowed to pass utterly without hope or light. Virginia and Maryland had been discussing troublesome questions concerning the navigation of the Potomac. But if two states could consult upon matters of mutual interest, why not more than two? Out of these conferences, therefore, came the Annapolis convention in the autumn of 1786. Five states were represented, and a report was drawn up proposing a convention "to meet at Philadelphia on the second Monday in May next, to take into consideration the situation of the United States, to devise such further provisions as shall appear to them necessary to render the constitution of the federal government adequate to the exigencies of the Union. . . ." The proposal, submitted to the states, was sent to Congress which (February 21, 1787) passed a resolution in substantial accord with the recommendation from the Annapolis gathering. A method was thus found for stabilizing the union and for saving it from complete disintegration, saving the new-born United States from becoming "one of the most contemptible nations on the face of the earth."[16] Eager nationalists were anxiously at work during the months that followed; and when May came, the prospect of effective results appeared bright; at least there was ground for hope.

Seventy-four delegates were appointed to the Convention;[17] nine-

[15] Perhaps some of them did. Washington's statement quoted in note 10 (*ante*) may possibly be so interpreted. Noah Webster appears to me to have been nearest a grasp of a solution of the problem. But the way in which that solution was finally found is a most interesting study; and the study awaits us on the succeeding pages of this work. If the rule of apportioning requisitions were made "plain and easy," and if "refusal were then to follow demand," Richard Henry Lee declared, "I see clearly, that no form of government whatever, short of force, will answer. . . ." "Do you not think, sir, that it ought to be declared, by the new system, that any State act of legislation that shall contravene, or oppose, the authorized acts of Congress, or interfere with the expressed rights of that body, shall be *ipso facto* void, and of no force whatso ever?" Letter from Lee to George Mason, May 15, 1787, in K. M. Rowland, *The Life of George Mason,* II, pp. 105, 107. Jefferson wrote to Madison from Paris, June 20, 1787, suggesting appeals from state courts to a federal court. Jefferson, *Works* (federal ed.), V, p. 285. See also a letter from Richard Henry Lee to Madison, November 26, 1784, in *The Letters of Richard Henry Lee* (J. C. Ballagh, ed.), II, p. 307.

[16] Letter from William Grayson to Madison, March 22, 1786. Quoted in George Bancroft, *History of the Formation of the Constitution,* I, p. 258.

[17] This number includes those who declined to serve and the substitutes who in some cases took their places. *Records of the Federal Convention,* Max Farrand, ed., III, p. 557 ff. . . .

teen for one reason or another did not attend; thirty nine signed the document which resulted from nearly four months of discussion. Rhode Island did not deign to participate, and the delegates from New Hampshire did not come until July 23, after the Convention had decided some of its most difficult problems. The early and, indeed, the conspicuously troublesome questions were therefore passed upon by delegations from eleven states. Many of the members had had political experience. Even at that time, when men were not affected as we are likely to be by tradition, there was a general acknowledgment of the ability and rectitude of the delegates. America, in a crisis, had chosen her best.

One fact is very evident in the Convention's work—results were reached by debate, by interchange of opinion, by deliberate but earnest consideration of problems. There was little or no declamation for its own sake. Conclusions were the product of discussion; and the reader of the debates can today see the gradual unfolding of principles and institutional forms as the weeks went by. This means, of course, that no faction worked its will and no leader dominated the rest. Not one delegate envisaged in advance the whole system and all the fundamental principles on which it rested. For once at least in the course of history, opinions were formed and changed as the result of argument. . . .

Probably no one found every portion of the Constitution to his liking; but the work was finished, the result of patient toil and amicable accommodation. Refusal to accept the document with hopes for the future could mean nothing but folly; the choice lay between the hopeful chance of a national system and reversion to a confusion which might be little less than disaster.[18] Of the fifty-five delegates who had taken part in the Convention, thirty-nine signed the finished instrument; three, Mason, Gerry, and Randolph refused to sign. Martin left a few days before the end of the Convention and did not sign. Of the remaining twelve regular members who were not in attendance at the end and did not sign, seven are known to have approved and three are known to have disapproved of the Constitution.[19]

[18] Hamilton asked: "Is it possible to deliberate between anarchy and Convulsion on one side, and the chance of good to be expected from the plan on the other." Gouverneur Morris said, "The moment this plan goes forth all other considerations will be laid aside—and the great question will be, shall there be a national Government or not?"
[19] Jameson, "Studies in the History of the Federal Convention of 1787," op. cit., p. 157.

The Constitution was turned over to Washington to be sent to the Congress, with recommendations that it be submitted to the states. A letter to Congress was prepared by the Convention: "the consolidation of our Union," the letter declared, "the greatest interest of every true American," had been kept steadily in view and the Constitution was "the result of a spirit of amity. . . . " There is in the letter one especially significant statement: "It is obviously impracticable in the federal government of these States, to secure all rights of independent sovereignty to each, and yet provide for the interest and safety of all—Individuals entering into society, must give up a share of liberty to preserve the rest." In other words, the old philosophy of natural rights and of contract was here made to apply to the organization of the new system; the sovereignty of the states was to be diminished; a portion was to be surrendered.

The federal state which these men succeeded in formulating had the following salient features: (1) sovereign powers were distributed between the states and the national government; (2) the national government had only the powers granted it explicitly or by implication; the states individually retained the residue; (3) each government within its sphere of authority operated immediately over the individual citizen; (4) neither government was to be inferior to the other or in ordinary operation to come into contact with the other; (5) the constitutional system was established as law enforceable in courts and was superior to the authority of every state acting either through its government or by convention of its citizens; (6) the national government recognized and made applicable the principle of the separation of powers with certain modifications.

When we remember that the Convention met before the shadow of the Shays' rebellion had been lifted, and that conservatives had been distressed by the tribulations of the Confederate period, the liberality of the Constitution and the broad-mindedness of the delegates are particularly impressive. There was no decision to limit the suffrage or to prescribe property or religious qualifications for office. In these respects the delegates were more liberal than the makers of the state constitutions ten years before. Many of the members appear to have been holders of public securities;[20] but had they been penniless, they

---

Dickinson was absent, but at his request his name was put down by his colleague, Read. Farrand, *Records,* III, p. 81.

[20] I say "appear," because, though Professor C. A. Beard in his *An Economic Interpretation of the Constitution,* a product of toilsome research, has shown that a large number of the delegates presented bonds in 1791, in accordance with Hamilton's funding plan,

could scarcely have shown less interest in the obligation of the new government to pay the debts of the old—unless they had been quite without respect for public faith. An amendment declaring that the legislature "*shall* fulfill the engagements and discharge the debts of the United States," was objected to by Butler, "lest it should compel payment as well to the Bloodsuckers who had speculated on the distresses of others, as to those who had fought and bled for their country." Mason objected to the term "*shall*" as too strong, declaring "There was a great distinction between original creditors and those who purchased fraudulently of the ignorant and distressed." Randolph moved that "All debts contracted and engagements entered into, by or under the authority of Congress shall be as valid against the United States under this constitution as under the Confederation." The motion was adopted by a vote of ten to one, Pennsylvania alone voting in the negative.[21]

Two provisions in the Constitution were, in a way, directed toward the protection of property: no state shall emit bills of credit, and no state shall pass a law impairing the obligation of contracts. Both of these prohibitions resulted from the experiences of the Confederate period. Forty years later, John Marshall, who had lived through the critical years and had taken great interest in the adoption of the Constitution, said of the impairment of contracts: "The mischief had become so great, so alarming, as not only to impair commercial intercourse, and threaten the existence of credit, but to sap the morals of the people, and destroy the sanctity of private faith."[22]

Some of the delegates feared the rise of classes or, indeed, believed the stratification of society to be inevitable. Gouverneur Morris was ready on all occasions to inculcate the political depravity of men, and he pointed to the necessity of checking one vice or interest by

---

we cannot be entirely certain that these men owned the certificates in 1787. Furthermore, it is more than likely that in some cases the former members of the Convention acted, when they presented their certificates, as agents of other persons. An incomplete examination of the data, carried on at my suggestion by the Department of Historical Research of the Carnegie Institution at Washington, appears to justify this statement. A number of the more influential delegates presented no certificates in 1791. The fact remains that many of the delegates in all probability were creditors of the states and of the Congress.

[21] The Constitution says "All debts contracted and engagements entered into before the adoption of this Constitution shall be as valid against the United States under this Constitution as under the Confederation." Art. VI, para. 1. This statement leaves out the words "under the authority of Congress" of the Randolph resolution, and may indicate a purpose to allow the assumption of state debts.

[22] Dissenting opinion in *Ogden* v. *Saunders,* 12 Wheaton 213, 355 (1827).

an opposing vice or interest.[23] Madison, himself, though impatient with the cynicism of Morris, feared lest in the long run, as the numbers of the unpropertied classes increased, they might combine to endanger property and public liberty, or would become the tools of opulence and ambition. But, though the members of the Convention were rich men according to the standards of the time, there was practically no inclination to give special protection to wealth. There was not then, it is true, confidence in the wisdom of the common people (the confidence characteristic of the professed democracy of the next century); but on the other hand, the grievous influences of the rich and the rise of a plutocratic aristocracy were especially feared.[24] The men of those days believed in liberty; liberty and property were not considered mutually opposed. We may have forgotten for how many decades the word "liberty" was the chosen symbol of American life. A government with powers of ruthless interference with property would not have been considered a government to be endured by a free people.

Liberty was to be assured by a government so checked and balanced as to curb the sway of malign influences and to prevent the exercise of tyrannical authority. Just how much the delegates were affected by writings of John Adams, the supreme advocate of checks and balances, we do know. But the main desire of men, realizing as these men did the need of an effective national government, was to have a government so organized as to make liberty secure and to make difficult or impossible the despotism of faction or of passion.[25]

But on the whole the Convention was not ruled by abstract theories—doctrines quite abstracted from the teachings of history and from the facts well known to the Convention's members. Refer-

[23] Morris's philosophy is illustrated by his speech on July 2; see also, his remarks on August 7. He said on July 6: "As to the alarm sounded, of an aristocracy, his creed was that there never was, nor ever will be a civilized Society without an Aristocracy. His endeavor was to keep it as much as possible from doing mischief." Note Madison's comments, August 7 and 10. Madison in general desired proper protection for minorities. Mason's position is stated August 8 and 14 and September 15; Gerry's, August 14; Williamson's, September 5; Randolph's, September 5; Wilson's, September 6.

[24] Various announcements indicate this. Dickinson "doubted the policy of interweaving into a Republican constitution a veneration for wealth. He had always understood that a veneration for poverty and virtue, were the objects of republican encouragement." Franklin declared, "Some of the greatest rogues he was ever acquainted with, were the richest rogues."

[25] For Adams's philosophy, see his *Defence of the Constitutions of Government of the United States;* "Three Letters to Roger Sherman, on the Constitution of the United States," *Works* (C. F. Adams, ed.) VI, p. 427 ff. See especially C. M. Walsh, *The Political Science of John Adams.*

ences to the ancient world were occasionally indulged in; lessons from the failures of other nations were mentioned; the fundamental principles of constitutional rights and the elements of English liberty were in the minds of the men who made the Constitution. That generation, of which these men were the flower, had been steeped in the discussion of political principles and had been engaged in the actual construction of governments and constitutions. The greatest single teacher was experience, and the state constitutions were the chief source of governmental forms. The framers were now giving institutional reality to the ideas which the course of colonial history, the practices of the old empire, their own struggle for independence, and their earlier attempts to establish union had inculcated. All through the Revolutionary struggle, until the Revolution was made complete by the adoption of the Constitution, the men of that generation—though some engaged in the vaporings of self-created philosophy—did not bring many absolutely new ideas to birth. They were in fact tremendous realists. Had they set forth to create a new system free from the shackles of history, they must have failed. To call into being a constitutional system which has lasted for over a century, a system which has withstood perplexing diversities and conflicting sectional interests, the development of democracy, the increase of population from four million to thirty times that number, is a notable achievement.

Robert L. Schuyler

THE FRAMING AND ADOPTION OF THE CONSTITUTION

Under the Articles of Confederation, the states were the real centers of power and some orators in the states tended to view the Confederation government as an alien regime. In fact it was occasionally referred to as a "foreign government." Many of the men who had been prominent in the councils of the Revolution and the Confederation became alarmed by the course that events were taking under the Articles, including such national figures as Washington, Hamilton, Madison, and Jay. They and financial and merchant groups became convinced that the Confederation was too weak to endure, and that drastic change was necessary, change that would accomplish two goals—create a stronger central government and protect private property—although not all of the Patriots were of the same persuasion. Jefferson felt that the states should be as one in dealing with foreign affairs but that they should be several with respect to everything domestic. Of the Confederation government he wrote that with all of its imperfections "it is without comparison the best existing or that ever did exist." He told one of his French friends that the Confederation "is a wonderfully perfect instrument."

By 1789, however, it had been replaced by a new government under the Constitution of the United States, an instrument that was to be described a century later by William Gladstone, the British prime minister, as "the most wonderful work ever struck off at a given time by the brain and purpose of man." When one considers other wonderful works struck off at a given time by the brain and purpose of man—Magna Carta, for example, or the works of Isaac Newton, Sigmund Freud, Charles Darwin, and Karl Marx, all of which changed the course of civilization—Gladstone's statement may seem to some to be excessive. But it is true that the men of the Convention of 1787 were an assemblage of able and brilliant men, learned in the study of the politics and the constitutions of historical states, and widely experienced in the practice of politics in their own, a gifted group working in secrecy for the purpose of producing by debate and compromise what has become the oldest living national constitution.

It is nevertheless a wonder that America still operates under basically the same instrument the Framers devised, for in the two hundred years since the adoption of the Constitution, France, which had a revolution shortly after the American Revolution, has had one Directory, three empires, and five republics, and Germany has had four reichs. The American Constitution has been amended twenty-six times but only one amendment—the Eighteenth—added new substantive power directly, and that was repealed by the Twenty-first.

From *The Constitution of the United States* by Robert L. Schuyler, copyright 1923 by The Macmillan Company. Reprinted by permission of the author.

The Framers wrote a constitution, then, that has, by interpretation, been the basic law for a country that grew from almost 4 million people to one of over 200 million, a country that was once supported by a simple pastoral economy and small-scale merchants and became an industrial giant, a corporate leviathan, spending the biggest budgets known to man, and concentrating the most powerful military force in the history of the world. Under the Constitution of 1787, the nation has survived seven major wars, one violent rebellion, at least six major depressions and numerous lesser recessions. The Framers built better than they could have imagined.

The movement for a reorganization of the basic national law that led to the drafting of the Constitution is discussed with precise scholarship in this essay by Robert L. Schuyler.

On February 21, 1787, Congress . . . [in response to the report of the Annapolis Convention of the year before] adopted the following resolution:

> *That in the opinion of Congress, it is expedient, that on the second Monday in May next, a convention of delegates, who shall have been appointed by the several states, be held at Philadelphia, for the sole and express purpose of revising the Articles of Confederation, and reporting to Congress and the several legislatures, such alterations and provisions therein, as shall, when agreed to in Congress, and confirmed by the states, render the federal constitution adequate to the exigencies of government, and the preservation of the union.*

It turned out that in sanctioning the Philadelphia Convention the old congress was in effect signing its own death warrant.

Before the close of 1786, without waiting for congressional action, six states appointed delegates to the convention to be held at Philadelphia, and Virginia made a master-stroke by placing at the head of its delegation the name of George Washington. By May, 1787, all of the other states had followed suit, except New Hampshire and Rhode Island. New Hampshire acted tardily, and its delegates did not arrive in Philadelphia until after the convention had been in session for some time. Rhode Island, under the influence of the paper money party, refused to appoint delegates at all. However, a committee, representing the mercantile interests of the state, sent a letter to the convention, expressing regret at Rhode Island's noncompliance with the recommendation of congress and promising to support the work of the convention.

Neither the Annapolis Convention nor congress had specified how the delegates should be chosen. Appointment by the state legislatures, the method followed in choosing representatives in congress, was the normal one and was adopted by every state. Thus the delegates were chosen indirectly by the people, or rather by so many of them as were permitted by state law to exercise the franchise. In no state had the principle of universal adult male suffrage been adopted at this time. Statistics regarding the proportion of the population unenfranchised in the several states are wanting, but restrictions on the suffrage were generally in force. The most customary qualification for the franchise was the "freehold" qualification. This did not, however, withhold the vote from as large a portion of the community as would be the case today, for the distribution of land-ownership was much wider than it is at present. For delegates it was natural that those who took most interest in the convention and were especially opposed to a continuance of existing conditions should put themselves forward. . . .

In all sixty-two delegates were appointed; fifty-five attended some of the sessions of the convention, and thirty-nine put their names to the Constitution which the convention framed. Though sober history cannot accept Jefferson's eulogy of the convention as an "assembly of demi-gods," it must be admitted that it contained a considerable number of able and a few remarkable men. The average age of the members was about forty-two. A large majority were lawyers, with experience in public life; only a few had seen military service in the Revolution. They were men of affairs, whose business interests and associations combined with their knowledge of practical politics to make them keenly sensitive to the defects of the existing regime.

On account of the failure of delegates to reach Philadelphia on time, the result partly of bad weather and partly of a tardiness characteristic of the public life of the day, the convention was unable to organize until May 25, nearly a fortnight after the date set for its meeting, when Washington was unanimously chosen president and a secretary was appointed. A few days later rules of procedure were adopted. It was determined that each state should have one vote in the convention, as was the case in the congress of the Confederation. The great political cleavage in the country at this time was not sectional—not between north and south, nor even between east and west—but between large and small states, and the rule of state equality in the convention was, of course, favorable to the latter. It was also decided that seven states should constitute a quorum, and that sessions should be secret. Nothing spoken in the convention was to be published or communicated without leave. Secrecy, it was hoped, would free the convention from outside influence and enable it to submit the results of its deliberations to the country without divulging knowledge of the processes by which conclusions had been reached or of the opinions expressed by individual members in the course of debate.

The Virginians, who had arrived in advance of most of the other delegations, met frequently in informal caucus and drafted a series of resolutions, largely the work of Madison, which were presented to the convention on May 29 by Governor Randolph. The Virginia Plan, as the resolutions are called, provided for a division of the central government into three departments, legislative, executive and judicial; a legislature of two houses with enlarged powers, in which the representation of states should be proportional either to quotas of contribution or to free population, the members of the lower house to be elected by the people and those of the upper house by the lower house out of persons nominated by the state legislatures; an executive to be chosen by the legislature and to be ineligible for a second term; and a judicial department to consist of a supreme court and inferior courts. The general or "national" legislature, as it was called, was to have power to pass on the constitutionality of state laws and to call forth the force of the union against any state that failed to fulfill its federal obligations; and acts of the national legislature were to be subject to review by a council of revision to consist of the executive and a part of the judiciary. The legislative, executive and judicial authorities of the states were to be bound by oath to support the federal Constitution. The Virginia Plan may be called the large-state plan. It will be observed that it proposed changes in the structure and character of the federal government so sweeping that they could scarcely be regarded merely as a series of amendments to the Articles of Confederation. How far the delegates were bound by their instructions was a subject of dispute in the convention, but had these been followed literally, the convention could have done no more than propose amendments to the Articles. The great historical importance of the Virginia Plan lies in the fact that from it, with many changes, the Constitution in its final form was evolved.

On May 29, the same day that the Virginia Plan was put before the convention, another set of proposals was presented by Charles Pinckney of South Carolina. Perhaps on account of his youth,

Pinckney's plan does not seem to have been taken very seriously. Like the Virginia Plan, it was referred to the committee of the whole, which took no action upon it, though some use of it was made later by a special committee. The Pinckney Plan has been the subject of considerable scholarly wrangling among the pundits of the American Historical Association and others, into which it is unnecessary to enter here. It is enough to say that the document which has been printed as the Pinckney Plan is spurious and that no authentic copy of the original has yet come to light.

Later, in the course of debate, on June 18, Hamilton read in the convention a sketch which he intended not as a plan to be acted upon but merely as an indication of his own ideas and a suggestion of amendments which he would probably propose to the Virginia Plan. It shows Hamilton in favor of a powerful central government, with the states reduced almost to the level of provinces. It had little if any influence; and on the last day of the convention Hamilton himself, in urging every member to sign the Constitution, said that "no man's ideas were more remote from the plan [i.e., the Constitution] than his were known to be." It was reserved for imaginative spirits of later days to represent Hamilton as the author of the Constitution.

The small-state party in the convention was rather slow in organizing, and it was not till June 15 that their proposals, embodied in what is called the New Jersey Plan, were presented by Paterson of New Jersey. Its supporters called it a "federal" plan in contrast with the "national" Virginia Plan. Unlike the latter it preserved the principle of state equality, and its proposals were made as amendments to the Articles of Confederation. Congress was to remain a single-chamber assembly, in which each state was to have one vote, though it was to be invested with additional powers, especially in the important matters of taxation and commerce. There was to be a separate executive chosen by congress, and a supreme federal tribunal. Acts of congress and treaties were to be the "supreme law of the respective states" and it was provided that "the judiciary of the several states shall be bound thereby in their decisions, anything in the respective laws of individual states to the contrary notwithstanding." The federal executive was to be authorized to use force if necessary to execute such acts or treaties.

In the consideration of the work of the convention that follows, chronology will, for the most part, be disregarded, but it will make for clarity if we have in mind in advance the consecutive stages in the drafting of the Constitution. The convention, in committee of the whole, debated the Virginia Plan from May 30 to June 13, when it reported a series of 19 resolutions based on that plan with some modifications. On June 19 the committee of the whole, to which the New Jersey Plan had meanwhile been referred, reported in favor of its former resolutions as against that Plan, and debate on these resolutions began. It lasted till July 26 when twenty-three resolutions agreed upon by the convention were referred to a committee of detail, charged with preparing a draft Constitution, and the convention adjourned to August 6, to give the committee time to do its work. From August 6 to September 10 the convention debated, clause by clause, the Constitution reported by the committee of detail. On September 10 the Constitution, as agreed upon, was referred to a committee of style, which made its report two days later. From September 13 to 15 the convention compared the Constitution as reported by the committee of style with the draft which had been referred to that committee. On September 15 the completed Constitution was agreed to by the convention, and on September 17 the convention adjourned *sine die.*

It has always been understood that the Federal Convention met to improve the government of the United States, but the spirit in which its members went to their work has not so generally been apprehended. The Fathers were practical men. They lived at a time when a decent respect for the proprieties of political discussion required at least occasional reference to Locke and Montesquieu, and if an impression of familiarity with Grotius or Vattel could be conveyed by an apposite quotation, so much the better; but one who goes through the debates of the convention is likely to feel that such excursions into political philosophy as were made are to be regarded rather as purple patches than as integral parts of the proceedings. The scholarly Madison had gone extensively into the subject of Greek federalism, and he gave the convention the benefit of some of his researches in that field; but it was his experience in public life and his wide knowledge of the conditions of his day, not his classical lucubrations, that bore fruit at Philadelphia. In a diffuse harangue extending over two days—hot days, too—Luther Martin ranged freely over the history of political theory, but he seems to have bewildered and fatigued rather than enlightened or influenced his hearers. This is not to say that political theory did not count in the work that the convention did. Theories, political and other, that win general acceptance become a part of social heritage, and the influence over men exercised by their social heritage is not to be questioned. In this sense the Americans of 1787 were all disciples of John Locke, even those who had never read a page of Locke. The state of nature, the social compact, inherent individual rights, limitations on government, the right of revolution, were axiomatic in the thought of the time. But the debate at Philadelphia did not proceed along theoretical lines. John Dickinson expressed the prevailing point of view when he said in the convention: "Experience must be our only guide. Reason may mislead us."

> *God has conceded two sights to a man–*
> *One, of men's whole work, time's completed plan,*
> *The other of the minute's work, man's first*
> *Step to the plan's completeness.*

The thought expressed in these words of Browning's must have come now and then to a mind in the convention, given to speculating, in off hours, on "larger meanings" and "ultimate purposes." But while the convention was in session it was "the minute's work" that claimed attention. Another constitution was soon to be brought forth in another land. No doubt the doctrinaire character of the French National Assembly of 1789 has been greatly exaggerated, but when all is said the fact remains that the document which it produced breathes a spirit one does not catch in reading the American Constitution. Philadelphia yielded nothing comparable to the Declaration of the Rights of Man.

Professor Max Farrand, the editor of the *Records of the Federal Convention*, has compiled from the writings of the members of the convention, prior to its meeting a list of what they regarded as the defects of the Articles of Confederation, and his opinion, based on a detailed knowledge of the proceedings of the convention, is that there is little of importance in the Constitution that did not arise from the effort to correct these specific defects. In a document written toward the close of his life Madison, after enumerating the principal weaknesses of the Confederation, uttered this caution: "Such were the defects, the deformities, the diseases and the ominous prospects, for which the Convention were to provide a remedy, and which ought never to be overlooked in expounding and appreciating the Constitutional Charter, the remedy that was provided." These words of the

"Father of the Constitution" sound like a protest against judicial interpretation of the Constitution by judges ignorant of its historical setting and, therefore, unable to fathom the original intent of its provisions. Unfortunately, a knowledge of American history has not yet been made a prerequisite for admission to the Supreme Court.

An exhaustive investigation conducted on the line suggested by Madison's injunction would be nothing less than an historical commentary on the Constitution, and this is not the place for such an ambitious undertaking. But we must inquire, at least briefly, into the therapy which the diagnosticians at Philadelphia prescribed for the ailing body politic.

The vital defect in the Articles of Confederation, as has been pointed out, was state sovereignty. It was not that congress lacked this or that specific power, but that it could not in practice exercise effectively the powers that it nominally possessed; it was not that sufficient limitations were not placed on the states, but that they could not, in fact, be compelled to observe the limitations that were placed upon them. This, I take it, was what Madison meant when he wrote in *The Federalist*, shortly after the Constitution had been framed:

> *The truth is, that the great principles of the Constitution proposed by the Convention may be considered less as absolutely new, than as the expansion of principles which are found in the Articles of Confederation. . . . If the new Constitution be examined with accuracy and candor, it will be found that the change which it proposes consists much less in the addition of* New Powers *to the Union, than in the invigoration of its* Original Powers.

State sovereignty, there was the enemy. How did the convention go about to curb it?

In the first place, in the all-important matters of taxation and defense, it put the federal government in direct relations with the people of the United States. "The Congress," says the Constitution, "shall have Power to lay and collect Taxes, Duties, Imports and Excises," and "to raise and support Armies." The new congress, provided for in the Constitution, would not have to depend, like the congress of the Confederation, on requisitions on the states for revenue and for soldiers. This new, direct relationship between the federal government and the people involved a new conception of federalism, which was clearly perceived and pointed out in the convention. In opposing the election of members of the upper house of the proposed federal legislature by the state legislatures, James Wilson, as reported by Madison, said:

> *. . . it was necessary to observe the two-fold relation in which the people would stand. 1. as Citizens of the Genl. Govt. 2. as Citizens of their particular State. The Genl. Govt. was meant for them in the first capacity: the State Govts. in the second. Both Govts. were derived from the people—both meant for the people—both therefore ought to be regulated on the same principles. The same train of ideas which belonged to the relation of the Citizens to their State Govts. were applicable to their relation to the Genl. Govt. and in forming the latter, we ought to proceed by abstracting as much as possible from the idea of State Govts. With respect to the province & objects of the Genl. Govt. they should be considered as having no existence. . . . The Genl. Govt. is not an assembly of States, but of individuals for certain political purposes—it is not meant for the States, but for the individuals composing them; the* individuals *therefore not the States, ought to be represented in it.*

Wilson clearly grasped the principle of that dualism of government which is the essence of American federalism.

But it was not sufficient to empower the federal government to act directly on individuals. How were the states to be prevented from exercising powers denied to them, from treating the new Constitution, as they had treated the old Articles, as a "scrap of paper"? The Virginia Plan proposed to give the national legislature power "to negative all laws passed by the several States, contravening in the opinion of the National Legislature the articles of Union." The New Jersey Plan which, it will be recalled, was proposed as a series of amendments to the Articles of Confederation, provided that all acts of congress

> *made by virtue and in pursuance of the powers hereby and by the Articles of Confederation vested in them, and all treaties made and ratified under the authority of the United States shall be the supreme law of the respective States so far forth as those acts or treaties shall relate to the said States or their Citizens, and that the judiciary of the several States shall be bound thereby in their decisions, any thing in the respective laws of the individual States to the contrary notwithstanding; and that if any State, or any body of men in any State shall oppose or prevent the carrying into execution such acts or treaties, the federal Executive shall*

> *be authorized to call forth the power of the Confederated States, or so much thereof as may be necessary to enforce and compel an obedience to such acts, or an observance of such treaties.*

The committee of the whole, in the resolutions which it drafted, approved of the method provided for in the Virginia Plan, but this was subsequently rejected, and a resolution, moved by Luther Martin and almost identical with the provision of the New Jersey Plan that has been quoted, was unanimously adopted. As phrased by the committee of style, the substance of this resolution appears as Article VI, clause 2, of the Constitution:

> *This Constitution, and the Laws of the United States which shall be made in pursuance thereof; and all Treaties made, or which shall be made, under the Authority of the United States, shall be the supreme Law of the Land; and the Judges in every State shall be bound thereby, anything in the Constitution or Laws of any State to the contrary notwithstanding.*

Already, on a few occasions, state courts had held state statutes to be void on the ground that they were in conflict with state constitutions; we have noticed the Rhode Island case of *Trevett* v. *Weeden*, where, it will be recalled, the court's decision had proved comforting to the creditor and propertied classes. Henceforth it would be the duty of state courts to declare null and void all acts of state legislatures if they were in conflict with this new "supreme law of the land," assuming, of course, that the question of conflict was raised in a case before the court. But suppose a state court sustained a state law whose constitutionality had been called in question—a not improbable contingency. The members of the convention were too wise to leave the ultimate safeguarding of the Constitution to state judges. There is another provision of the Constitution, found in Article III, Section 2, which ordains that the judicial power of the United States "shall extend to all Cases, in Law and Equity, arising under this Constitution, the Laws of the United States, and Treaties made, or which shall be made, under their Authority." It was the intention of the framers that in such a case as has been supposed, where rights claimed under the federal Constitution, laws of Congress or treaties, and alleged to have been violated by state law, were denied by a state court and the constitutionality of the state law in question sustained, an appeal should lie from the court of the state to the supreme court of the United States, to which, in last resort, the duty of protecting the Constitution from violation by the states would thus be entrusted. The Judiciary Act of 1789, passed by the first congress under the new Constitution, many of whose members had sat in the Federal Convention, provided specifically for the taking of such appeals. More than forty years after the Constitution had gone into operation, when the state sovereignty which had been scotched by its adoption was again showing signs of vigor, Daniel Webster, in one of his most famous and powerful orations, declared that the two provisions of the Constitution that have been quoted were the keystone of the federal arch. "With these it is a constitution; without them it is a confederacy."

Mention may be made of a few of the other clauses of the Constitution that were intended as specific remedies. Much had been said and written before the meeting of the convention about the defective organization of the federal government. The combination of legislative, executive and judicial powers in congress had been widely condemned and the need for separate executive and judicial departments repeatedly urged. On this question in general the members of the convention were in agreement, and all of the plans presented provided for separate departments; differences of opinion were confined to matters of detail. The first three articles of the Constitution provide for the establishment, organization and powers of the three departments—legislative, executive and judicial—into which the federal government was to be divided.

Much fault had been found, also, with the organization and procedure of the old congress—especially with the lack of a second chamber, the representation of states rather than of people, the method of voting by states, and the rule requiring the assent of nine states for the enactment of all important measures. All these objections were met by the Constitution. A bicameral congress was provided for; the lower house was to be composed of representatives chosen directly by the people and voting as individuals; and in the upper house, though the states were to be equally represented, members were to vote as individuals, not by states. Instead of requiring an extraordinary majority of congress for all important legislation, as under the Articles, a bare majority of both houses was made sufficient, except for overriding a veto of the executive, in which case a two-thirds vote was required.

The Articles of Confederation, it will be remembered, could be amended only with the consent of all the state legislatures, and such unanimity it had been found impossible to secure for a single amendment, though many had been proposed. Indeed, it was the practical impossibility of amending the Articles by the procedure for which they provided that had led to the meeting of the convention. The Constitution provides for a less difficult method of amendment. In fact it provides for four possible methods, but only one of these has been resorted to so far. By this, amendments are initiated by a two-thirds vote of both houses of congress and become effective if ratified by the legislatures of three-fourths of the states.

Every American schoolboy has heard of the compromises of the Constitution, but what he has heard is not altogether correct. The traditional view is that there are three "great" compromises. These, as set forth in the textbooks, are: (1) a compromise between the large and the small states whereby states were to be represented according to population in the lower house of congress, which would give the advantage to the large states, and to have equal representation in the upper house, which would be favorable to the small states; (2) a compromise between the North and the South, whereby three-fifths of the slaves were to be counted in reckoning population for purposes of apportioning representation and direct taxes among the states; (3) a compromise between the North and the South that gave congress power to pass navigation acts, which was desired by the North, but prohibited interference by it with the foreign slave trade for a period of twenty years, which was in the interest of the South.

It will be noticed that of these three compromises two have to do with slavery, from which one would infer that in the framing of the Constitution slavery was a burning question. This, however, was not the case. Slavery was not the transcendent issue in 1787 that it came to be fifty years later. It was not yet a sectional question properly so called; and it is an interesting fact that the bitterest attack on the slave trade in the convention was made by a Virginia delegate. The line of cleavage in the convention, as has been said, was between large and small states, not between north and south. For more than fifty years after the adoption of the Constitution, however, the people of the United States knew scarcely anything about how it had been framed. The rule of secrecy agreed to by the delegates at Philadelphia was surprisingly well observed. When the convention adjourned, the official journal, together with other papers, were delivered to Washington and in 1796 were deposited by him in the department of state. In 1818 congress ordered them printed, and the work of editorship was undertaken by John Quincy Adams, then secretary of state. In 1819 there was published the *Journal, Acts and Proceedings of the Convention.* But the official journal proved very disappointing; it contained little more than a record of votes, and it threw no light upon the problems that confronted the convention or how they were met. But fortunately for history, Madison had appointed himself an unofficial reporter of the convention and with infinite pains had taken copious notes of the debates. He was unwilling to have them published during his lifetime, but when he died, in 1836, his papers were purchased by congress and his convention notes were published in 1840. They are our chief source of information for the drafting of the Constitution. Not until 1840, then, was it possible to know what had transpired in the Philadelphia conclave. Now by that time slavery had become a great sectional issue, the great public question of the day; it had been the subject of memorable compromises between North and South, and compromise, as the only means of preserving the union, was in the air. No one can reflect much upon history without perceiving how the conditions of the day have always colored historical interpretation. Here is a striking example of it. Hildreth, in the third volume of his *History of the United States*, published in 1849, devoted one-third of his chapter on "The Formation of the Federal Constitution" to the slavery debates in the convention and represented slavery as the subject of two of the three "great" compromises of the Constitution. The anachronism is intelligible enough, but it has seriously misled Americans about the making of their Constitution.

If one examines Madison's *Notes* and the other records of the convention that are now accessible—with a minimum of bias, as a student of history should—he will find it necessary to revise time-honored notions about the compromises of the Constitution. The so-called "three-fifths" compromise turns out to be mythical. Counting a slave as equivalent to three-fifths of a person does, on the face of it, seem like a compromise between counting him at par and not counting him at all. But the three-fifths ratio is found in an amendment proposed to the Articles of Confederation in 1783, which had been ratified by eleven states before the Federal Convention met. It appears in the New Jersey Plan in a provision for changing the basis of requisitions on the states from land value to population. There was nothing new about it, and it was not the result of compromise in the convention. The provisions that authorized congress to pass navigation acts and prevented it from abolishing the foreign slave trade for twenty years were reached through compromise, but they were not, and were not regarded as being, one of the "great" compromises of the Constitution.

The conventional view is most nearly correct with respect to the compromise on representation, though this too has been the subject of misinterpretation. Briefly, the compromise was reached in this way. The Virginia Plan proposed that the states should be represented *proportionally* in both houses of a two-house legislature; the New Jersey Plan proposed that they should be represented *equally* in a one-house legislature. The convention having voted in favor of a two-house legislature, the large states won a victory by carrying a resolution against equal representation in the lower house. Then the Connecticut delegates proposed equal representation in the lower house. Then the Connecticut delegates proposed equal representation in the upper house, their motion resulting in a tie vote. A special committee, made up of one member from each state, decidedly favorable in its personnel to the small-state party, recommended in effect, as parts of a single proposal, that in the lower house each state should be represented in proportion to population, counting three-fifths of the slaves, and that in the upper house each should have an equal vote. After much debate these propositions were adopted by a vote of five states to four, with the small states of Connecticut, New Jersey, Delaware, Maryland, and North Carolina in the affirmative, Pennsylvania, Virginia, South Carolina and Georgia in the negative, Massachusetts divided, and New York absent; Yates and Lansing had left the convention in disgust at the way things were going, and Hamilton was not in attendance at the time. The small states had been beaten on the question of representation in the lower house, but here they won a great though a narrow victory, which would have been impossible had the voting strength of the states in the convention been in proportion to their population. It was the most critical vote that was taken, for if it had gone the other way the small states would probably have withdrawn. How threatening the situation was may be inferred from the fact that it elicited from Franklin, who was not exactly orthodox in religion, a motion that divine guidance should be invoked and that the daily sessions of the convention should thereafter begin with prayer. A number of members objected to this on the ground that it might lead to "disagreeable animadversions" and create the impression that the convention was torn by dissensions; and there is a story that Hamilton observed that the convention was not in need of "foreign aid."

The most serious error that has been made about the compromises of the Constitution, however, is the error of omission. If one reads the Constitution in the light of the debates in the convention, he will detect compromises on all sides. Professor Farrand, in his excellent volume, *The Framing of the Constitution*, goes so far as to call the Constitution a "bundle of compromises." Take, for example, Article III, Section 1: "The judicial Power of the United States shall be vested in one Supreme Court, and in such inferior Courts as the Congress may from time to time ordain and establish." What could seem more direct and artless? Yet this *may* register a compromise—a compromise between those who desired and those who were opposed to the establishment of such courts. Or take this: "The House of Representatives shall be composed of Members chosen every second year. . . ." Behind that provision lurks a compromise: some members of the convention wanted a one-year term, others, a three-year term; they compromised on two years.

The method finally agreed upon for choosing the president embodies an important compromise. It was recognized as such by Bancroft in his *History of the Constitution*, and in recent years a few historians have described it correctly; but it has not yet made its way into the textbooks, where the "three great compromises" still reign supreme. The problem of how to choose the president, while not so critical as the question of representation, was even more perplexing. It led to a compromise between the large and the small states second in importance only to the great compromise over representation. Appointment by the federal legislature, by the state executives, direct election by the people, election by the state legislatures—each of these proposals found advocates and opponents. Wilson of Pennsylvania was the foremost of those who ventured to speak in favor of direct popular election. But the convention was suspicious and fearful of too much direct democracy, and its opinion was probably pretty well summed up by Mason of Virginia, who "conceived it would be as unnatural to refer the choice of a proper character for chief Magistrate to the people, as it would, to refer a trial of colors to a blind man. The extent of the Country renders it impossible that the people can have the requisite capacity to judge of the respective pretensions of the Candidates." The question of the president's term of office also gave rise to much debate. Periods ranging from four to fifteen years were suggested, while advocates of tenure during good behavior were not wanting. Toward the close of the convention this whole question, together with certain others upon which agreement had not been reached, was referred to a special committee, which recommended the following method for electing the president: Each state should choose, in such manner as its legislature might direct, a number of electors equal to the total number of representatives and senators to which it was entitled. The electors were to meet in their respective states and vote by ballot for two persons, at least one of whom should not be an inhabitant of their own state. This method of choosing the electors was favorable to the large states, since a large state would have more electors than a small state. But the vote of a majority of all the electors was made necessary to elect the president, and since it was expected that they would normally give their first ballots for citizens of their own states, it seemed probable that as a rule no one would receive the necessary number. In that event the senate was to choose the president from among the five persons who stood highest on the list, and in the senate each state would have equal representation. That is to say, and this was the essence of the compromise, the large states would have the advantage in the preliminary election, the small states in the final election. The plan recommended by the committee was adopted by the convention, except that the house of representatives was substituted for the senate as the body to make the eventual choice; but it was provided that when the house acted in this capacity each state should have one vote. The framers of the Constitution could not foresee that the development of national parties would destroy their carefully worked-out compromise. It was the party system that made possible the concentration of electoral votes on party candidates and also took from the electors the personal discretion in casting their ballots which the Fathers intended them to exercise. Only twice in American history has the election of the president been thrown into the house of representatives: in 1801, when a majority of the electors gave a tie vote for Jefferson and Burr, and in 1825, when the electoral votes were so scattered that no candidate received a majority. In all other presidential elections the electoral vote has been decisive. This is the most striking example in our political system of what is so conspicuous in the English Constitution, the virtual nullification of legal powers by constitutional custom. The electors have still the legal power to vote for whomsoever they please, but in fact they must cast their ballots for their party candidates.

> *The process of election* [*wrote Hamilton in* The Federalist *(No. 68)*] *affords a moral certainty that the office of President will never fall to the lot of any man who is not in an eminent degree endowed with the requisite qualifications. Talents for low intrigue and the little acts of popularity may alone suffice to elevate a man to the first honors in a single State; but it will require other talents, and a different kind of merit, to establish him in the esteem and confidence of the whole Union, or of so considerable a portion of it as would be necessary to make him a successful candidate for the distinguished office of President of the United States.*

The history of the presidency suggests that if Hamilton's opinion was correct, the method of electing the president devised by the Fathers had merits over that which now prevails.

The Constitution is in truth full of compromises. But this fact should not be permitted to obscure another, which is perhaps of equal importance, the fact, namely, that on many questions the convention was in agreement and did not need to resort to compromise. In the past the Constitution has been discussed and interpreted mainly by students of constitutional and political history, of government and of law. They have been naturally interested primarily in such matters as the structure and powers of the federal government, its relations to the state governments, sovereignty, checks and balances, separation of powers, guarantees of private rights and immunities, and kindred subjects. But we live in an industrial age, and this fact is more and more influencing our interpretation of the past. The signs are many and plain that Clio has grown weary of that trite dictum of a distinguished votary that "history is past politics." No doubt the "economic interpretation" of history, passing at times into the doctrine of economic determinism, has been overworked in some cases, but its claim has been securely established and must be recognized by all sober-minded historical students. A beginning has been made in the study of the "economics" of the Constitution, with the result that the older historical treatment of its formation has come to seem almost pitifully unsatisfying. No longer can we accept the view of John Fiske that the contest over the ratification of the Constitution was waged between the intelligent and the good on the one hand and the ignorant and the vicious on the other. No one can read much of the correspondence or pamphlet literature of the day without perceiving that powerful economic factors underlay the movement which resulted in the framing and adoption of the Constitution. Indeed these appear to have been the dynamic forces at work.

When the convention met, the people of the United States were divided into two factions or parties, with the division drawn along economic lines. The antagonism of rich and poor, creditor and debtor, merchant and small farmer, which was a commonplace of contemporary discussion, was a fact so portentous as to arouse in the minds of intelligent observers the most serious apprehensions for the stability of American institutions and the future of American society. In several states the advocates of paper money and debtor relief were in control of the legislatures. Radical measures in the interest of debtors, interfering with the rights of property and contract, had thoroughly alarmed the wealthier classes throughout the union and done much to convince them of the desirability of a change in the system of government. Madison is authority for the statement that "the mutability of the laws of the States" was the principal cause of the meeting of the Federal Convention. Of these laws he wrote:

> *The injustice of them has been so frequent and so flagrant as to alarm the most steadfast friends of Republicanism. I am persuaded I do not err in saying that the evils issuing from these sources contributed more to that uneasiness which produced the Convention, and prepared the public mind for a general reform, than those which occurred to our national character and interest from the inadequacy of the Confederation to its immediate objects.*

In other states the party of paper money and debtor relief had been beaten at the polls. In all there were large and discontented minorities, defeated for the moment but cherishing a sense of injustice and oppression. At the very moment when the delegates to the convention were assembling, Massachusetts was just recovering from the convulsion of a desperate debtors' insurrection. Nevertheless this cleavage of American society along economic lines was scarcely at all reflected in the convention. The large majority of the delegates were lawyers, closely allied with the business interests of the country. The bondholder, the money lender, the merchant, the manufacturer, the land speculator, were generously represented at Philadelphia. The small farmer, the debtor, the advocate of cheap money, were conspicuous by their absence. The convention technically represented the whole American people, but it actually reflected the opinions of one of the two parties into which the people were at that crisis divided. The disputes in the convention, the occasions for compromise, were many, but most of them arose over questions essentially political. If one approaches the work of the convention from the point of view of government and political science, he will naturally be impressed by its compromises. But on the great economic questions at issue between debtor and creditor, farmer and merchant, there was little need for compromise, for there was little disagreement among the delegates.

For the student of the Constitution as an economic document no clauses are more significant than those which give to congress the power to raise revenue by taxation, to borrow money on the credit of the United States and to regulate foreign and interstate commerce; that which declares that "all debts contracted and engagements entered into before the adoption of the Constitution shall be as valid against the United States under this Constitution, as under the Confederation"; and that which prohibits the emission of bills of credit and the impairment of the obligation of contract by the states. It is scarcely an exaggeration to say, with a recent student of the Constitution, that in these last two prohibitions "the economic history of the states between the Revolution and the adoption of the Constitution is compressed." Let us examine the evolution in the convention of these highly important economic clauses with a view to determining the nature of their origin.

Each of the "plans" presented in the convention proposed expressly or by implication to vest the power to raise a revenue by taxation in the federal legislature. It is true that the Virginia Plan contained no positive provision on this subject, but it made a sweeping grant of legislative power to the proposed legislature. The sixth resolution provided

> *that the National Legislature ought to be impowered to enjoy the Legislative Rights vested in Congress by the Confederation and moreover to legislate in all cases to which the separate States are incompetent, or in which the harmony of the United States may be interrupted by the exercise of individual Legislation.*

In view of the general recognition of the breakdown of the former system of federal requisitions upon the states, it seems certain that it was the intention of the framers of the Virginia Plan to include in this clause the power of taxation. The New Jersey Plan was explicit. The second resolution provided that congress

> *be authorized to pass acts for raising a revenue, by levying a duty or duties on all goods or merchandizes of foreign growth or manufacture, imported into any part of the United States, by Stamps on paper, vellum or parchment, and by a postage on all letters or packages passing through the general post-office, to be applied to such federal purposes as they shall deem proper and expedient; to make rules and regulations for the collection thereof; and the same from time to time, to alter and amend in such manner as they shall think proper.*

Though the text of the plan presented by Charles Pinckney has not been preserved, it is practically certain that it, too, proposed to confer the power of taxation upon the federal legislature. The plan put before the convention by Hamilton authorized the national legislature "to pass all laws whatsoever subject to the negative" of the executive. The draft constitution reported to the convention by the committee of detail on August 6 contained this provision: "The Legislature of the United States shall have the power to levy and collect taxes, duties, imports and excises." On August 16, this momentous clause was agreed to by the convention, Gerry alone voting in the negative. On September 4, the committee on unfinished parts recommended that the following words be added to the clause: "To pay the debts and provide for the common defence & general welfare of the U. S." This addition was agreed to unanimously. In the report of the committee of style, presented on September 13, this clause appeared as Article I, Section 8, Clause 1. Thus it is clear that this vital provision, so necessary for the restoration of public credit, was the result of agreement, not of compromise. Ezra Stiles, then president of Yale College, who had received some information of the proceedings of the convention from one of the delegates, recorded in his diary under date of December 21, 1787: "It appeared that they were pretty unanimous in the following ideas," and enumerated among them "that a certain Portion or Deg. of Dominion as to *Laws* and *Revenue* . . . was necessary to be ceded by individual States to the Authority of the National Council."

Turning to the regulations of commerce we find that all the plans advocated the vesting of this power in the federal legislature. It was clearly implied in the sixth resolution of the Virginia Plan, quoted above. The New Jersey Plan provided that in addition to the powers conferred upon Congress by the Articles of Confederation it should be authorized "to pass acts for the regulation of trade and commerce as well with foreign nations as with each other." The Pinckney Plan undoubtedly proposed to confer exclusive power over foreign and interstate trade upon the federal legislature. The Hamilton Plan, as already shown, contained an unlimited grant of legislative power to the national government. The seventh article of the report of the committee of detail made provision that the legislature of the United States should have power "to regulate commerce with foreign nations, and among the several States"; and this was unanimously agreed to on August 16. It thus appears that there was nowhere in the convention any opposition to this grant of authority to the federal government. Indeed, it was the lack of this power which had created a state of affairs that was largely responsible for the meeting of the convention.

In its report, the committee of detail inserted a provision giving the legislature of the United States power "to borrow money, and emit bills on the credit of the United States." This clause had been taken directly from the Articles of Confederation, and there was no opposition in the convention to the first part of it, which was agreed to unanimously on August 16. But the convention as a whole was vehemently opposed to paper money. Some of the delegates were in favor of inserting in the Constitution a clause expressly prohibiting the emission of bills of credit by the federal legislature, notably Gouverneur Morris, Ellsworth and Wilson. Others were content merely to omit from the clause in the report the words "and emit bills." None of the members of the convention was in favor of the exercise of the power in question, and Langdon, the merchant prince of New Hampshire, went so far as to declare that he would rather reject the whole Constitution than accept it with those three words retained. It was pointed out that a positive prohibition would antagonize the friends of paper money throughout the country, and the convention was content merely to strike out the obnoxious words "and emit bills." Had there been any party in the convention in favor of the emission of paper money by the federal government, this action might be regarded as in the nature of a compromise between them and those members who desired a positive prohibition. But as this was not the case, the omission cannot be viewed as a compromise.

The interests of the public creditors naturally engaged the attention of a convention one of whose primary objects was to restore public credit and many of whose members were holders of public securities. The Virginia Plan declared that provision ought to be made for the fulfillment of all the engagements of the congress of the Confederation. On August 21, a committee which had been appointed to consider the assumption of the state debts by the federal government reported as follows:

> *The Legislature of the United States shall have power to fulfill the engagements which have been entered into by Congress, and to discharge as well the debts of the United States as the debts incurred by the several States during the late war, for the common defense and general welfare.*

Only the first part of this recommendation, that relating to the debts of the United States, need be considered here. It was debated on August 22, and a substitute amendment proposed by Gouverneur Morris was unanimously adopted. "The Legislature," it ran, "*shall* discharge the debts and fulfill the engagements of the United States." In the debate on this amendment, on August 25, objection was taken to the mandatory form in which the amendment was framed. "The use of the word *shall*," said Mason, "will beget speculation and increase the pestilent practice of stock-jobbing." Doctor Johnson thought that no express provision need be made on the subject, for, as he observed, "changing the government cannot change the obligation of the U.S. which devolves of course on the New Government." His sentiments seem to have been those of the great majority, who adopted, by vote of ten states to one, a substitute clause moved by Randolph, declaring that "all debts contracted and engagements entered into, by or under the authority of Congress, shall be as valid against the United States under this Constitution as under the Confederation." This was submitted to the committee of style which substituted the words "before the adoption of the Constitution" for "by or under the authority of Congress," and in this form it was finally accepted by the convention as Article VI, Clause 1, of the Constitution. This clause has been called a compromise. But since there was no sentiment worthy of mention in the convention in favor of repudiating or scaling down the existing federal debt, it cannot, it seems to me, properly be viewed in that light.

The Constitution expressly prohibits the states from emitting bills of credit or enacting laws impairing the obligation of contract. Neither prohibition appeared in any of the plans presented in the convention. In the report of the committee of detail, however, it was provided that no state, without the consent of the United States, should emit bills of credit. On August 28, when the convention in its consideration of the report had reached this clause, it was moved by Wilson and seconded by Sherman to make this restriction absolute, instead of permitting the states to exercise this power if they received the consent of the United States. Sherman was an especially bitter opponent of fiat money. "Mr. Sherman," Madison tells us in his *Notes,* "thought this a favorable crisis for crushing paper money. If the consent of the Legislature could authorize emissions of it, the friends of paper money would make every exertion to get into the Legislature in order to license it." Gorham of Massachusetts, whose state had just passed through the throes of Shays's Rebellion, was fully aware of the strength of the paper-money party, and he thought that "an absolute prohibition of paper money would rouse the most desperate opposition from its partisans." Nevertheless, the convention was so resolute in its determination to destroy paper money that Wilson's motion, making the prohibition absolute, was adopted by vote of eight states to one, with one divided. King of Massachusetts now moved, in the words of the Ordinance of 1787, which had just been passed by the congress of the Confederation for the government of the Northwest Territory, that a prohibition be added restraining the states from interfering in private contracts. The provision of the Ordinance in question enacted that

> *in the just preservation of rights and property, it is understood and declared, that no law ought ever to be made or have force in the said territory, that shall, in any manner whatever, interfere with or affect private contracts, or engagements,* bona fide, *and without fraud previously formed.*

There was considerable discussion of King's motion. Even Gouverneur Morris, stalwart champion of the rights of property and contract though he was, thought this was going too far. "There are," he said, "a thousand laws relating to bringing actions—limitations of actions . . . which affect contracts—the Judicial power of the U.S. will be a protection in cases within their jurisdiction; and within the State itself a majority must rule, whatever may be the mischief done among themselves." This view found some support in the convention, and King's motion was not voted on at that time.

The draft constitution referred to the committee of style provided as an absolute prohibition that no state should emit bills of credit. It contained, however, no provision respecting the impairment of the obligation of contracts by the states. Nevertheless, in the report of the committee of style this prohibition was included in Article I, Section 10, Clause 1. Additions having been made to this clause, it was adopted by the convention *without debate* on September 14. Chief credit for the work of the committee of style is by general consent given to Gouverneur Morris, its chairman, but in the inclusion of this particular restriction on the states it is impossible not to suspect the influence of King, who was one of its members.

James McHenry, one of Maryland's delegates to the convention, being later called upon to explain to the house of delegates of Maryland the principles upon which the Constitution had been based, informed that body that it had been argued that the power to emit bills of credit ought to be left to the states, but that "this was overruled by a vast majority as the best Security that could be given for the Public faith at home and the extension of commerce with Foreigners." Luther Martin, also of Maryland, was one of the very few members of the convention to say a good word for paper money, and the restraints placed by the Constitution upon the states in this and other matters formed one of his reasons for opposing its adoption. In his *Genuine Information* he wrote:

> *By the tenth section every State is* prohibited from emitting bills of credit. *As it was reported by the committee of detail, the States were* only *prohibited from emitting them* without the consent of Congress; *but the convention was so* smitten *with the* paper money dread, *that they insisted the prohibition should be* absolute.

The provisions of the Constitution whose origins have been examined were undoubtedly of fundamental economic importance, and it has been shown that they were not the result of compromise, if by that word we mean adjustment of divergent views and interests, reached by mutual concession. The great struggle in the Federal Convention was between the representatives of the large and the small states, and to harmonize their conflicting political interests compromise had to be invoked; concessions had to be made by each party to secure a *modus vivendi* which would be reasonably satisfactory to both. But the battle was not fought on economic lines. Had the contests in the convention turned upon the questions at issue throughout the country between rich and poor, had Daniel Shays and Patrick Henry stood as leaders opposed to Madison and Gouverneur Morris, the struggle would surely have been no less bitter, but the compromises, it may be conjectured, would have been different.

Though the spirit that prevailed in the convention was intensely practical, though its members adhered closely to the business in hand, refraining from oratorical appeals to imagination and emotion which the presence of outsiders would no doubt have encouraged, the larger significance of what was done during those momentous summer weeks at Philadelphia was not wholly unperceived. "We are making Experiments in Politicks," observed Franklin. And Jefferson, watching with eager interest in Paris the oncoming of the French Revolution, wrote:

> *The example of changing a constitution by assembling the wise men of the state, instead of assembling armies, will be worth as much to the world as the former examples we have given them.*

Viewed in retrospect, from the somber background of the late war and its aftermath, the making of the Constitution takes on heightened meaning. A comparison between the American states of 1787 and the European states of 1914 may seem fanciful, yet it is not wholly so. It is true that there were no such historic rivalries and deep-seated animosities between the sovereign states of America as there were between the sovereign states of Europe, but—and this goes to the root of the matter—there was state sovereignty in both cases. In the former, as in the latter, there were many causes of war-breeding friction. There were small states, suspicious and fearful of more powerful neighbors; there were commercial jealousies and tariff discriminations; there were vexatious boundary disputes; there were injuries inflicted by states upon citizens of other states. Indeed, actual hostilities between states, albeit on a petty scale, had taken place. When the Constitution was before the people a popular Federalist argument was that its rejection would lead to the dissolution of the Union and to chronic strife between the individual states or between such partial confederacies as might be formed. "To look for a continuation of harmony between a number of independent, unconnected sovereignties in the same neighborhood," wrote Hamilton in *The Federalist,* "would be to disregard the uniform course of human events, and to set at defiance the accumulated experience of ages." I am anxious not to do violence to facts or to indulge in far-fetched historical interpretation. No member of the convention, so far as I know, professed himself a pacifist, the convention did not think of itself as a peace conference or of the document which it drafted as a covenant of a league of nations. Interstate warfare had not assumed such proportions as to seem one of the major evils to be remedied. But in their effort to form "a more perfect union" the framers of the Constitution removed to a considerable extent the causes of interstate strife, and they provided means for the settlement of future disputes. No one can tell how many were prevented from arising by the provisions in the Constitution which abolished interstate tariffs and forbade states to pass laws in violation of contract. We do know, however, that the supreme court, to which the Constitution gives jurisdiction in controversies between the states, has rendered decisions in more than eighty interstate controversies, controversies over boundaries, contracts, riparian rights and other questions. It has been suggested that the interstate jurisdiction of the supreme court might well serve as an example for internationalists to follow; and in this connection a letter written by Franklin to a friend in Europe, shortly after the close of the convention, deserves to be quoted:

> *I send you enclos'd the propos'd new Federal Constitution for these States. I was engag'd 4 Months of the last Summer in the Convention that form'd it. It is now sent by Congress to the several States for their Confirmation. If it succeeds, I do not see why you might not in Europe carry the Project of good Henry the 4th into Execution, by forming a Federal Union and One Grand Republick of all its different States & Kingdoms; by means of a like Convention; for we had many Interests to reconcile.*

The history of the intervening years lends something of pathos to Franklin's benevolent hopes.

Though the Constitution was agreed to unanimously by the states represented in the convention, unanimity did not extend to individual members. Several delegates who disapproved of the Constitution withdrew from the convention before its close, and three dissentients who remained to the end, Randolph, Mason and Gerry, refused for various reasons to put their signatures to the new instrument. The last two actively opposed ratification, and all of them considered the Constitution seriously defective and favored a subsequent convention to improve it.

It contributes to an appreciation of the human aspects of the convention to learn from Washington's Diary that after the last session the members "adjourned to the City Tavern, dined together and took a cordial leave of each other." The precise nature of this leave-taking in which the Fathers indulged may be left to the imagination—it was at any rate unmarred by premonitions of an eighteenth amendment to the document they had just drafted.

The old congress, as we have seen, had had nothing to do with the movement that had led to the meeting of the convention; it had merely sanctioned it at the eleventh hour, after several states had already appointed delegates. Nor did it now exert any influence. Its feebleness is shown by the fact that during the summer of 1787 its membership was reduced to six states—less than a quorum—"although," as its president despairingly wrote, "matters of the highest importance are pressing for a decision." The convention took matters into its own hands. It directed that the Constitution be laid before congress and advised that it be then submitted to conventions in the several states, chosen by the people thereof on the recommendation of their respective legislatures, for their approval. Ratification by popular conventions was preferred to ratification by state legislatures for several reasons. It was thought that it would give the new system a broader popular basis than the old had possessed; conventions, moreover, might prove less attached to state sovereignty than legislatures, and therefore less unwilling to accept an instrument diminishing the powers of the states; perhaps, too, it would be easier to secure adoption from single-chamber conventions than from double-chamber legislatures. In accordance with what was virtually the instruction given by the convention, congress, without expressing any opinion on the Constitution, voted unanimously to transmit it to the state legislatures, to be submitted by them to conventions in the states.

Here ends the first act of a constitutional revolution. The Federal Convention, called solely to propose amendments to the Articles of Confederation, which could legally become effective only if ratified by all the states, had disregarded its instructions. None of the delegates had been authorized to go further than was proposed in the report of the Annapolis Convention and the call issued by congress. In fact, the legislature of Delaware, in its act appointing the state's delegates to the Federal Convention, expressly stipulated that no amendment proposed to the Articles of Confederation should extend to the provision guaranteeing each state an equal vote in congress. Yet the convention not only drafted a wholly new plan of government, but—and this most decisively marks its revolutionary character—it inserted in the Constitution the provision that it should go into effect when ratified by nine states. Professor J. W. Burgess, in his *Political Science and Comparative Constitutional Law*, has forcefully pointed out that what the convention "actually did, stripped of all fiction and verbiage, was to assume constituent powers, ordain a constitution of government and liberty and demand a *plébiscite* thereon over the heads of all existing legally organized powers. Had Julius or Napoleon committed these acts, they would have been pronounced *coups d'état.*"

The submission of the Constitution to the states was the signal for the alignment of the American people into two opposing political factions. For the next year the adoption or rejection of the Constitution was the principal topic of political interest. Those who favored the new system called themselves Federalists and gave to their opponents the name of Antifederalists. It should be understood that the adoption of the Constitution was the work of a party. In every state it had friends and enemies, and unfortunately the party passions of the day have left their mark deeply engraved in the writings of American historians who have treated of this great epoch in our development. The formation of the Constitution has been dealt with almost exclusively from the Federalist point of view, and the judgments of partisans, inspired by the heat of conflict, have been perpetuated in what purports to be sober history. Thus the struggle has been generally represented as one between the good and the wise, on the one hand, and the foolish and the ignorant on the other. Federalist orators have been represented as wise and far-seeing patriots. Antifederalists as "demagogues." This view is unhistorical and unfair. Neither party possessed a monopoly of wisdom and virtue or of folly and vice. Victory, it is true, crowned the efforts of the Federalists; and conjectures as to what would have followed their defeat lie outside the scope of history. But the time has surely come when we can be fair to the men of 1787, to whichever party they belonged. In some of the states the Antifederalists were in an undoubted majority, and, so far as can be determined, they constituted nearly if not quite one-half of the American people. We should be careful about indicting even half a nation.

Contemporary evidence makes it clear that the Federal and Antifederal parties were composed of groups based principally upon economic interests, though this fact has not in general received adequate recognition. A few quotations from contemporary writings will put the truth in a clear light. According to Hamilton, surveying the situation at the close of the convention, the new Constitution had in its favor, among other factors,

> *the good will of the commercial interest throughout the states which will give all its efforts to the establishment of a government capable of regulating, protecting and extending the commerce of the Union . . . the good will of most men of property in the several states who wish a government of the Union able to protect them against domestic violence and the depredations which the democratic spirit is apt to make on property;—and who are besides anxious for the respectability of the nation—the hopes of the creditors of the United States that a general government possessing the means of doing it will pay the debt of the Union. A strong belief in the people at large of the insufficiency of the present confederation to preserve the existence of the Union and of the necessity of the Union to their safety and prosperity. . . . Against its success is to be put . . . the influence of many* inconsiderable *men in possession of considerable offices under the state governments who will fear a diminution of their consequence, power and emolument by the establishment of the general government and who can hope for nothing there—the influence of some* considerable *men in office possessed of talents and popularity who partly from the same motives and partly from a desire of* playing a part *in a convulsion for their own aggrandisement will oppose the quiet adoption of the new government— . . . add to these causes the disinclination of the people to taxes and of course to a strong government—the opposition of all men much in debt who will not wish to see a government established one object of which is to restrain the means of cheating Creditors—the democratical jealousy of the people which may be alarmed at the appearance of institutions that may seem calculated to place the power of the community in few hands and to raise a few individuals to stations of great preeminence.*

A correspondent, writing to Washington from New Haven at about the same time, said:

> *All the different Classes in the liberal professions will be in favor of the proposed Constitution. The Clergy, Lawyers, Physicians & Merchants will have considerable influence on Society. Nor will the Officers of the late Army be backward in expressing their approbation.*

"The new constitution," General Knox informed Washington early in October, 1787, "is received with great joy by all the commercial part of the community." Madison wrote to Jefferson in December, 1787, that in New England "the men of letters, the principal Officers of Government, the judges and lawyers and clergy and men of property furnish only here and there an adversary."

In January, 1788, Rufus King, a member of the Massachusetts ratifying convention, wrote to Madison:

> *An apprehension that the liberties of the people are in danger, and a distrust of men of property or Education have a more powerful Effect upon the minds of our Opponents than any Specific Objections against the constitution.*

And shortly after this he said that the opposition arose chiefly

> *from an opinion that is immovable, that some injury is plotted against them—that the system is the production of the rich and ambitious, that they discover its operations and that the consequences will be the establishment of two orders in the Society, one comprehending the opulent and great, the other the poor and illiterate. The extraordinary Union in favor of the Constitution in this State of the Wealthy and sensible part of it is in confirmation of these opinions and every exertion hitherto made to eradicate it, has been in vain.*

In February, 1788, Madison wrote that in New York "the weight of abilities and of property is on the side of the Constitution."

In June, 1788, a citizen of New Hampshire assured Washington that three-fourths of the property and a larger proportion of the ability of his state were friendly to the Constitution. He added:

> *The opposition here (as has generally been the case) was composed of men who were involved in debt, and of consequence would be averse to any government which was likely to abolish their tender Laws and cut off every hope of accomplishing their favorite plan of introducing a paper currency.*

An examination of the make-up of the state ratifying conventions shows that in the main the commercial, financial and maritime sections sent Federalist delegates, while the distinctively rural communities sent Antifederalists. In a monograph entitled *The Geographical Distribution of the Vote of the Thirteen States on the Federal Constitution,* one of the most significant contributions that has been made to the social and economic history of the United States, Dr. O. G. Libby, on the basis of a careful study of the votes of the delegates in the state ratifying conventions, supplemented and corrected as far as possible by other data, shows the areas that supported and those that opposed the Constitution. His conclusion is that

> *the Constitution was carried in the original thirteen states by the influence of those classes along the great highways of commerce, the seacoast, the Connecticut river, the Shenandoah valley and the Ohio river; and in proportion as the material interests along these arteries of intercourse were advanced and strengthened, the Constitution was most readily received and most heartily supported.*

Of course, other than purely economic influences operated on both sides. The patriotic desire to establish a strong government under which the United States could play a dignified part in international affairs, a larger conception of nationality and a perception of the possibilities awaiting the United States if welded together by a vigorous general government, and a fear that only by adopting the Constitution could the union be preserved—all these were factors favoring the proposed system. On the other hand, there was a widespread feeling that the new Constitution, which contained no bill of rights, would prove injurious to liberty; persons whose interests were centered in their localities and who were devoted to state sovereignty were naturally loath to see the states shorn of any of their powers; men who deprecated a radical change of government condemned the whole movement for the Constitution as illegal—as, strictly speaking, it was. Sectional elements, too, entered into the complex of influences. In the South, especially in Virginia and its western counties, there was widespread suspicion of New England and the middle states; the desire for the North to win commercial advantages for itself at the expense of the Southwest was still fresh in men's minds, and the fear was entertained that the adoption of the Constitution would make easier the aggrandizement of the commercial section at the expense of the agricultural. And then, too, the politicians on both sides, made great use of the Constitution as a political issue with which to enlist support and build up their own power. A good deal of emphasis should be placed upon the canny remark of Franklin at the time that the United States was a "Nation of Politicians."

The Federalists unquestionably enjoyed great advantages over their opponents in the struggle. In most of the states the majority of the natural leaders of public opinion were on their side. The New England clergy, the professional classes, the newspaper proprietors, the financial and mercantile interests, the great planters of the South, and men of superior education in general, were supporters of the Constitution. The name of Washington lent it powerful aid not only in Virginia but throughout the country. The Federalists conducted a strenuous "campaign of education." Handbills composed by ardent friends of the Constitution were circulated [and] broadcast throughout the remote communities. Articles dwelling upon the advantages to be expected from the adoption of the Constitution were printed and reprinted in the local newspapers, and appeals were freely made to local and class interests. Of course, the Antifederalists were not idle. Their orators and pamphleteers pointed out some real and many imaginary defects in the Constitution. But in this campaign of education the advantage lay with the Federalists, who were better organized, who had more money to spend, whose leaders in general came from the upper classes, and whose arguments were based upon wider knowledge. Of the mass of literature begotten of this crisis little is read nowadays except by historical students or antiquarians. One of these partisan productions, however, has earned the reputation of a truly great treatise in political science. This was a series of 85 essays, printed in various New York newspapers over the signature of "Publius" and now famous as *The Federalist*. Most of the papers were written by Hamilton and Madison, and a few were from the pen of Jay. The purpose of the writers was to win support for the Constitution in New York, but the essays were widely reprinted and at once attracted attention. Washington wrote that they would "merit the Notice of Posterity," and Jefferson, then United States minister in Paris, went so far as to say that they constituted "the best commentary on the principles of government which ever was written." It has remained the most authoritative, as it was the earliest, commentary on the Constitution.

Of the greatest advantage to the Federalists was the argument that rejection of the Constitution would result in disunion and disaster. Washington's correspondence is full of assertions that the defeat of the Constitution would lead to anarchy. "I have for some time been persuaded," wrote Madison in February, 1788, "that the question on which the proposed Constitution must turn, is the simple one whether the Union shall or shall not be continued." This was a most telling argument, and the skillful Federalist politicians made full use of it.

And the Federalists were united in support of a constructive program. From New Hampshire to Georgia they stood on the same platform. It should be remarked in this connection that the meaning of the words "federal" and "federalist" had undergone a metamorphosis. In the early days of the convention "federal" had been applied to the proposals of the small-state party, which opposed the abandonment of the Articles of Confederation and objected to the Virginia Plan on the ground that it was not "federal." On June 14, Paterson of New Jersey said that "it was the wish of several deputations, particularly that of N. Jersey, that further time might be allowed them to contemplate the plan reported from the Committee of the Whole, and to digest one purely federal, and contradistinguished from the reported plan," and the New Jersey Plan, which he presented on the next day, was offered as a "federal" plan, in contrast with the "national" Virginia Plan. After the New Jersey Plan had been rejected, the large-state party, in a spirit of conciliation, agreed to drop the word "national," and eventually all supporters of the Constitution came to call themselves "Federalists." None of the Federalist leaders claimed perfection for the Constitution, but they pointed out that it could be improved by amendment after adoption. The Antifederalists, on the other hand, with no constructive plan of their own to offer, were united only in opposing the Constitution. The very name "Antifederalist" was a liability, for it suggested mere opposition and obstruction.

> *Events have demonstrated* [said Madison] *that no coalition can ever take place in favor of a new Plan among the adversaries to the proposed one. The grounds of objection among the non-signing members of the Convention are by no means the same. The disapproving members who were absent but who have since published their objections differ irreconcilably from each of them. The writers against the Constitution are as little agreed with one another; and the principles which have been disclosed by the several minorities where the Constitution has not been unanimously adopted, are as heterogeneous as can be imagined.*

In all of the states except Rhode Island the legislatures called conventions to pass upon the new Constitution. Those qualified by state law to vote for members of the lower house of the state legislature were permitted to vote for delegates to the conventions, but at this time, as we have seen, the suffrage was restricted in all of the states, in most cases by a free-hold qualification. The legislature of New York, however, made an exception and allowed all adult males to vote for delegates to the convention. Thus in every state but New York an appreciable proportion of the adult male population was not represented in the ratifying conventions, precisely what proportion cannot be ascertained. In spite of the momentous character of the decision to be made by the conventions it appears that in all of the states indifference or ignorance kept large numbers of qualified voters from exercising their privilege. It has been conjectured that not more than 160,000 persons, or about 5 percent of the total population of the United States, expressed any opinion on the new instrument of government.

The great compromise of the Constitution had won support for it in the small states, and it was Delaware that first ratified, on December 7, 1787. There was no serious opposition in the state, and the vote of the convention was unanimous.

In Pennsylvania the state legislature was in session in Philadelphia when the Federal Convention adjourned. Without waiting for action by congress, which was then sitting in New York, the Federalists in the Pennsylvania assembly voted to call a state convention, despite a protest by a minority at this unseemly haste. To prevent further action nineteen members of the minority by agreement absented themselves from the sessions of the assembly, leaving less than a quorum in attendance. Efforts by the majority to induce the absentees to return failed, and the assembly was unable to pass legislation necessary to provide for the election of delegates to the state convention. Presently, the resolution of congress recommending the submission of the Constitution to a convention was received. A Federalist mob now intervened and dragged two of the absentees, the worse for rough handling, to the assembly room. One of the unfortunates tried to escape from his seat, but friends of the Constitution barred his exit. Thanks to these applications of "direct action," the assembly, now having a quorum, proceeded to provide for the election of delegates to meet in convention at Philadelphia. Sixteen members of the minority issued an address to the people, which recited that violence had been used to secure a quorum, declared that the Federal Convention had had no authority to frame a new Constitution, and called attention, among other things, to the facts that the proposed Constitution contained no bill of rights, no provision for annual elections and no guarantee against standing armies in time of peace. This at once elicited rejoinders from the Federalists, and the contest over the Constitution in Pennsylvania was soon in full swing. The convention met on November 21. The delegates from Philadelphia and the other commercial communities were strongly Federalist, while those from the purely agricultural areas, and especially the western counties, were as decidedly Antifederalist. The Antifederalist delegates proposed several reasonable amendments and attempted to secure an adjournment in order to give time for more deliberate consideration, but they were voted down. The Federalist majority was determined to reap the full advantage of its present strength, and the Constitution was ratified on December 12 by a vote of 46 to 23. In an address to the people 21 members of the minority protested bitterly against the haste and violence by which ratification had been secured.

> *The convention* [*they declared*] *was called by a legislature made up in part of members who had been dragged to their seats and kept there against their wills, and so early a day was set for the election of delegates that many a voter did not know of it until it was passed . . . Of the seventy thousand freemen entitled to vote but thirteen thousand voted.*

The discomfited Antifederalists of western Pennsylvania continued to cherish a hostility toward the Constitution that flared up in rebellion in 1794.

The New Jersey convention spent only one week in debate and ratified the Constitution unanimously on December 18. On January 2, 1788, Georgia followed suit with a unanimous ratification, and on January 9 Connecticut gave its approval by a vote of 128 to 40.

It was in the large and important state of Massachusetts that the Federalists met their first check. In no commonwealth were the people more politically-minded than in Massachusetts—the nursery of that institution of direct democracy, the New England town meeting—and in none was there more widespread distrust and suspicion of delegated power. Nowhere, furthermore, was there a sharper division between the mercantile and financial interests, on the one side, and agrarianism, on the other. The embers of Shays's Rebellion were still smoldering. In a letter written to Washington in January, 1788, General Knox thus clearly described the situation in Massachusetts.

There are three parties existing in that state at present, differing in their numbers and greatly differing in their wealth and talents.

The 1st is the commercial part of the state to which are added all the men of considerable property, the clergy, the lawyers—including all the judges of all the courts, and all the officers of the late army, and also the neighborhood of all the great towns—its numbers may include 3/7ths of the state. This party are for vigorous government, perhaps many of them would have been still more pleased with the new Constitution had it been more analogous to the British Constitution.

The 2d party are the eastern part of the state lying beyond New Hampshire forming the province of Main[e]*—This party are chiefly looking towards the erection of a new state and the majority of them will adopt or reject the new Constitution as it may facilitate or retard their designs—this party 2/7ths.*

The 3d party are the Insurgents or their favorers, the great majority of whom are for an annihilation of debts, public and private, and therefore they will not approve the new Constitution—this party 2/7ths.

When the Constitution was first received in Massachusetts, it was greeted with general approval, but the enthusiastic support given it by merchants, money-lenders, lawyers and clergymen—the "aristocracy"—aroused the suspicions of the farmers and mechanics—the "democracy." The Massachusetts convention met on January 9, 1788, and it is the opinion of Professor S. B. Harding, who has made a careful study of ratification in Massachusetts, that if a vote had been taken at once the Constitution would have been defeated overwhelmingly. The Federalist leaders in the convention, however, were far more skillful than their opponents. Among them were Rufus King, Gorham and Strong, all of whom had been members of the Federal Convention, ex-Governor Bowdoin, the champion of law and order in Shays's Rebellion, and General Lincoln, who had routed the Shaysites. There were two politicians in the state whose attitude toward the Constitution was of especial importance on account of their great personal influence and following. These were Samuel Adams, the old Revolutionary patriot, the "man of town meeting," as he has been called, and John Hancock, also of Revolutionary fame and at the time governor of the commonwealth. At first Adams was opposed to the Constitution, and Hancock was noncommittal. The astute Federalist leaders, knowing how sensitive both men were to the opinion of the masses, instigated the mechanics of Boston to hold a meeting just before the opening of the state convention, at which resolutions warmly endorsing the Constitution were carried. This fact undoubtedly had great influence with Adams, who never spoke against any feature of the Constitution in the convention. For several weeks, however, Hancock, though elected chairman of the convention, absented himself from its sessions. Gout was the reason alleged for his nonattendance, but some who knew the governor well diagnosed the malady as political in character. He did not take his place in the convention until the Federalists had won him a plan of ratifying the Constitution and at the same time proposing amendments to it by pledging him their support in the coming gubernatorial election in Massachusetts and holding before him the prospect of becoming the first vice-president, perhaps the first president, of the United States. The plan of ratifying with amendments won over some of the Antifederalists in the convention, though there was no assurance that the amendments to be proposed would ever be adopted. Seeing the tide turning against them, the Antifederalists tried to adjourn, believing that public discussion of the Constitution and the proposed amendments would be favorable to them, but their attempt failed, and on February 7 the Constitution was ratified by the close vote of 187–168. Of the nine amendments recommended the most important was one explicitly declaring that "all powers not expressly delegated by the aforesaid Constitution are reserved to the several States to be by them exercised." The precedent set by Massachusetts of recommending amendments was followed by several other states and materially facilitated the process of ratification. The economic basis of the contest in Massachusetts is clearly indicated by the fact that the four coast counties, comprising the commercial section of the state, gave 100 votes in the convention for the Constitution and only 19 against it, while the interior counties, like Worcester and Berkshire, gave majorities as strongly Antifederalist.

The Maryland convention met at Annapolis on April 21, 1788. Though the opponents of the Constitution were ably led by Luther Martin, the large Federalist majority resolved on speedy action, believing that this would have a good effect on the states which had not yet ratified, especially Virginia, and refused to permit votes to be taken on the separate parts of the Constitution. Within a week the instrument was ratified by a vote of 63 to 11. The Virginia Federalists were jubilant over Maryland's action.

In South Carolina a good deal of opposition to the Constitution was manifested in the legislature, but the convention was strongly Federalist and ratified by a large majority on May 23. Eight states had now come under the "new roof," and according to the Constitution itself only one more ratification was needed to insure the inauguration of the new system.

The Federalists throughout the country anticipated an easy victory in New Hampshire. Sullivan, the governor of the state, and Langdon, its wealthiest and most influential citizen, were, in the words of a contemporary, "uniting their whole interest in favor of the Constitution." But when the delegates to the convention assembled at Exeter on February 13, 1788, the Federalists found to their dismay that a very large proportion of them had received positive instructions from their constituents to vote against the Constitution. Several of the delegates so instructed were "converted" to the Federalist side but dared not violate their instructions. In the words of a contemporary,

> *It was therefore thought advisable by the Gentlemen in favor, and those Converted, that they had best adjourn and Return to their Constituents, and give up their Instructions, and if they would not Consent for them to act according to the dictates of their own reason, they would resign & they may choose new Delegates to meet in June at Exeter. It is thought this measure will have its desired effect, for before June the Illiberal and Ignorant will be brought in to what is right and Just.*

Thus the New Hampshire Federalists saved themselves from defeat only by persuading some of the "converted" Antifederalists to disregard their instructions and concur in a policy of delay. Active influences must have been at work in the state during the next few months, for when the convention met again in June the Constitution was adopted after a debate of only four days by a vote of 57 to 47.

Nine states had now ratified the new Constitution, but the important commonwealths of Virginia and New York were still to be heard from. In Virginia the contest was bitter and close. The Antifederalists enjoyed unusually good leadership, for their forces were marshalled by Patrick Henry, Richard Henry Lee and George Mason. Without the weight of Washington's name the Federalists would probably have been defeated, though they were ably led in the convention by Madison and the young John Marshall, the future chief-justice of the supreme court. Jefferson, then United States minister in France, was watching with intense interest the course of events in America, of which he was informed by correspondents, and his views were a factor of importance in Virginia. At first Jefferson was afraid of the Constitution. He thought that all the good in it might have been secured by a few amendments to the Articles of Confederation. Always apprehensive of strong government, he did not share the Federalist opinion of the utter insufficiency of the Articles of Confederation. He feared that the proposed government would be too "energetic" and believed that the Federalists had been unduly alarmed by such experiences as Shays's Rebellion. Jefferson carried Locke's theory of government to the limit of logic. He not only argued that the original social compact should be renewed periodically, since he held that one generation had no right to bind its successors, but he looked upon occasional rebellion as the manifestation of a healthy spirit of liberty. Since the thirteen United States had undergone only one insurrection in eleven years he calculated an average for each state of only one in a century and a half, and gravely observed: "No country should be so long without one." Upon reflection, however, he came to the conclusion that the wisest course would be for nine states to ratify the Constitution (which would insure its adoption) and for the rest to reject it until essential amendments had been secured. In particular, he deemed a bill of rights, guaranteeing individual liberty, a necessary safeguard against tyranny, and he was also afraid that the reeligibility of the president would make possible the establishment of a virtual monarchy. But his opinion grew more favorable as a result of additional reflection and correspondence, and he approved of the Massachusetts plan of ratifying and proposing amendments.

Virginia was divided into several clearly marked areas. The eastern or "tidewater" section was strongly in favor of the Constitution. Here were located the larger towns and the estates of the great planters. Farther west, extending to the Blue Ridge, the chief element in the population were the small farmers, who were as strongly opposed to the Constitution. In the Shenandoah Valley, peopled principally by Scotch-Irish and Germans from Pennsylvania, sentiment appears to have been overwhelmingly Federalist, but in the Kentucky district the Antifederalists were in a large majority. On June 25, after stirring and exciting debates in the convention, the Constitution was ratified by the close margin of 89 to 79. The Massachusetts precedent was followed, and a series of amendments were recommended. Ten states had now ratified, and the Federalists throughout the country celebrated the Fourth of July, 1788, both as the anniversary of Independence and as the birth of the new Constitution.

The anxiety of the friends of the Constitution, however, was not yet entirely allayed. True, the requisite number of states had ratified, but New York had not yet given its decision, and if that commonwealth held aloof, it was doubtful if the new system could be successfully inaugurated. The situation in New York gave ground for the gravest apprehension.

The city of New York and the surrounding territory, the commercial section of the state, was strongly Federalist, but the interior was almost solidly opposed to the Constitution, and Governor Clinton's powerful political machine was working hard to secure its defeat. The publication of a letter written by Yates and Lansing to the governor, stating that they had withdrawn from the Federal Convention because it had violated its instructions and exceeded its authority, had no little effect. Scarcely had the Constitution been published when Clinton, over the *nomme de guerre* of "Cato," began a series of articles, which elicited replies from Hamilton, disguised as "Caesar." It was "Cato's" attacks on the Constitution that induced Hamilton, Madison and Jay to collaborate in the publication of the series of papers that became famous as *The Federalist.* Many other lesser champions entered the lists, and the war of words became spirited. Governor Clinton, without comment, submitted the Constitution with accompanying papers to the state legislature, which met in January, 1788, and early in February the legislature called a convention. When it was clear that the elections had gone against the Federalists there was some talk that New York City and the neighboring region might separate from the rest of the state and cast in its lot with the new union, if the New York convention refused to ratify.

The convention met in June at Poughkeepsie, with the Antifederalists in a majority of two-thirds. The commercial counties—New York, Kings, Queens, Richmond and Westchester—sent Federalist delegations; Albany, Clinton, Columbia, Montgomery, Ulster and Washington sent Antifederalists; Dutchess and Suffolk were divided. For more than a month the Constitution was debated, clause by clause. The Federalists were well led by Hamilton, Jay and Robert R. Livingston, while Melancton Smith, Lansing and Yates, supported by Clinton, marshalled the opposition. News that New Hampshire, the ninth state, had ratified encouraged the Federalists, who argued that the question now was clearly one of union or disunion; and even more helpful to them was the news of Virginia's ratification. The ranks of the opposition were wavering when Lansing introduced a series of explanatory, recommendatory and conditional amendments. The Federalists were prepared to accept amendments, so long as ratification was not much contingent on their adoption, but contingent ratification, they held, was not ratification in the sense in which that word was used in the Constitution, and would not make the state a member of the new Union. Madison, then in New York, gave it as his opinion that the Constitution required ratification "in toto and forever," adding, "It has been so adopted by the other states." A motion to authorize the state to withdraw from the Union if amendments were not made within a certain period was defeated, and on July 26 the convention ratified by a vote of 30 to 27. The principal credit for this achievement is correctly given to Hamilton. The convention, however, not only recommended a number of amendments and directed the representatives of the state in congress to use all reasonable means to secure their adoption, but by unanimous vote it issued a circular letter to the other states urging that a second general convention be called to consider the numerous amendments proposed by the various state conventions. Some of the Federalists were all the more willing to make this apparent concession to their opponents because they believed that the agitation for a second convention would evaporate in talk; and events proved their surmise correct.

Two states failed to adopt the Constitution until after the new government had gone into operation. In Rhode Island, where the government was dominated by the paper money party, a unique course of action was pursued. Copies of the Constitution were distributed among the towns of the state, to give the people full opportunity to study it, and the legislature voted to submit the question of ratification directly to the people in their town meetings. When the vote was taken, late in March, 1788, it was seen that only a small part of the qualified voters had taken the trouble to register an opinion. 237 votes were cast in favor of the Constitution and 2,708 against it. The Federalists, who objected to this method of ascertaining the will of the people of the state, seem to have generally refrained from voting. In Newport only one vote was cast in favor of the Constitution. In North Carolina the Federalists had expected a victory, but the convention turned out to be strongly Antifederalist and adjourned without having either ratified or rejected the Constitution. A contemporary probably stated the case correctly when he said: "Whatever ostensible reasons may be offered by these two States for the rejection of this Constitution, from what I can learn the true one is the inhibition of paper money. . . . "

The ratification of the Constitution marked the consummation of the revolution which the Federal Convention had begun. Supporters of the Constitution attempted at the time and have attempted since to give it the color of legality, but their arguments are not convincing. Candor must recognize that the establishment of the Constitution can be justified only by the right of a people to change their form of government without legal authority, the right which had been invoked in 1776, the right of revolution.

Vernon L. Parrington

THE GREAT DEBATE

In one sense it can be said that in the adoption of the new Constitution, eleven states seceded from thirteen, for the Framers met in Philadelphia ostensibly to propose amendments to the Articles of Confederation, wrote an entirely new instrument of government instead, and managed to have it submitted for ratification, not to the state legislatures, which would have been customary, but to conventions called in each of the states for the specific purpose of considering ratification. It then went into effect after eleven states had ratified, leaving only two states, Rhode Island and North Carolina, as continuing members of the Confederation. The maneuver was an appeal to the "people" over the heads of the established governments, or, perhaps, around established procedures, and although it may seem to a modern reader as more "democratic" inasmuch as the "people" were directly engaged in the ratification process, it was irregular procedure in the context of the day. Why were the Framers so insistent upon change that they engaged in what, even in their day, was regarded by critics of the Constitution as sharp practice? This question raises an issue with which the rest of this book is concerned, namely, how is one to interpret the work of the Founding Fathers?

The following essays present various interpretations of the nature of the Constitution of 1787. This first is from Vernon L. Parrington's Main Currents in American Thought, *and it supplies a statement of the view that the Framers of the Constitution did not intend to promote democracy but rather to avoid it and its consequences; and he illustrates his theme from the writings of men of the times, especially James Madison among the supporters of the Constitution and Richard Henry Lee among its critics.*

When one considers the bulk of commentary that has grown up about the Constitution, it is surprising how little abstract political speculation accompanied its making and adoption. It was the first response to the current liberal demand for written constitutions as a safeguard against tyranny, but it was aimed at the encroachments of agrarian majorities rather than at Tory minorities. It was the work of able lawyers and men of affairs confronting a definite situation, rather than of political philosophers; and it was accompanied by none of that searching examination of fundamental rights and principles which made the earlier Puritan and later French debate over

From *Main Currents in American Thought* by Vernon L. Parrington, copyright 1927, 1930, by Harcourt, Brace and Company, Inc. Reprinted by permission of Harcourt, Brace and Company, Inc.

constitutional principles so rich in creative speculation. Not a single political thinker comparable to the great English and French philosophers emerged from the struggle. The debate drew freely upon the materials supplied by those thinkers, but it added little that was new.

The Constitution was a venture in republicanism, on a scale and under conditions without historical precedent. It was inevitable, therefore, that the debate should concern itself greatly with the nature of republicanism and its adaptability to American conditions. As the argument developed, two major questions assumed critical importance: the question of the powers of the Federal state, and the question of the sovereign rights of the majority; and in dealing with both the debaters were on ground inadequately surveyed. Of definite republican theory little was available except the writings of a small group of seventeenth-century republicans. Of democratic theory, on the other hand, even less was available. American democratic aspiration had far outrun old-world liberalism, and had produced no independent speculation of its own. French democratic theory still awaited the rise of Jacobinism to clarify its principles. The party of Commonwealth Levelers, to be sure, with their doctrines of a "paramount law," manhood suffrage, and annual parliaments, offered much that might have proved suggestive; but the literature of the Levelers was buried too deep under Tory obloquy to be resurrected, and nowhere else was to be found any considerable body of democratic theory. It was inevitable, therefore, that the debaters should go back to the English liberals of the preceding century.

Consider for a moment the authorities bandied to and fro in the great debate. With such exceptions as Machiavelli, Vattel, Pufendorf, Montesquieu, they were the well-known English theorists, Hobbes, Harrington, Milton, Sidney, Halifax, Hume, and Blackstone. Unhappily for the democrats every one of these great names counted against their aspirations. Hobbes was a state absolutist whose *Leviathan* provided sharp weapons for those who wished to tone the government high; Hume was a Tory who accepted the traditional interpretation of human nature in the light of which democracy was the open door to anarchy; Blackstone was a Tory lawyer, who interpreted the British constitution by a narrow legalism that was obsolete before the *Commentaries* came from the press. Harrington, Milton, and perhaps Sidney, were republicans of strong aristocratic bias, and Halifax and Locke—the latter by much the most influential of all—were constitutional monarchists.[1] Every one of these great authorities either distrusted or violently condemned democracy, yet they provided the major body of theory made use of by the Federalists.

On the other hand, the slowly accumulating democratic theory was unknown to the members of the convention. In 1761 Robert Wallace had advanced an Owenite theory of property, attacking the principle of economic individualism as responsible for the current evils of government by landed property; but his book, *Various Prospects*, made no ripple on the placid waters of English liberalism.[2] In 1768 Joseph Priestley, a thinker who later was to exercise great influence in America, who lived here for a number of years and was intimate with Jefferson, published his essay, *First Principles of Government*, a work embodying the first English interpretation of the perfectibility of man, the rule of reason, the theory of the diminished state, and the Benthamite principle of utilitarianism or expediency in statecraft, which struck at the principle of coercive sovereignty. But the ideas of Priestley were probably little known in America in 1787, and his influence was undermined further by a theological attack which sought to fasten upon him the stigma of atheism. In short, in this war of ideas the democrats were provided with little ammunition and fought at a great disadvantage. If the debate had taken place five years later, after the French Revolution had provided new democratic theory, the disparity of intellectual equipment would have been far less marked.

One other fact must be kept in mind, namely, that the great debate was in reality two debates, one carried on in the quiet of the convention hall, the other in the open. Each interprets the other, and taken together they reveal the conflict of forces and ideas that determined the form of the Constitution. In the privacy of the convention the speakers were free to express their views frankly, and in consequence a loose rein was given to the play of ideas; fundamental principles were examined critically and economic motives and class interests openly acknowledged. But in arguing the case before the generality of voters without doors a more cautious approach was necessary; arguments must be tempered to well-known prejudices, and circumspection must take the place of frankness. In the earlier

[1] These English liberals have been often regarded as democrats. Thus Merriam says of Locke, "He was the most famous of seventeenth-century democratic thinkers." *American Political Theories*, p. 90.
[2] See Laski, *Political Thought from Locke to Bentham*, p. 188.

debate, among innumerable lesser problems, two main questions dominated the argument: the question of the form of the centralized state—whether it should be aristocratic or republican; and if republican—as was inevitable—the question of what should be done about the majority will—how representation should be so refined as to guarantee stability to the government and security to the minority. In the second debate the appeal was to expediency rather than to principles, and turned on three chief points: the need of adoption in view of the desperate condition of the country; the adaptation of the proposed republican form to the vast extent of territory and diversity of interests; and the necessity of providing checks upon political parties if anarchy were to be avoided.

In the convention the need of a strong state, with powers beyond local legislatures, was not so much debated as assumed. By common consent it was agreed that the present lack of a centralized, coercive sovereignty was the source of all current evils. How many members preferred monarchy to republicanism, in principle, it is impossible to determine; but they all realized the inexpediency of attempting to set it up; even Hamilton yielded to the logic of Colonel Mason's argument: "Notwithstanding the oppression and injustice experienced among us from democracy, the genius of the people is in favor of it, and the genius of the people must be consulted." Accepting then the principle of republicanism as a compromise between the extremes of monarchy and democracy, the practical problem remained of erecting a system that should secure the minority against the aggressions of political faction. If the danger lay in an uncontrolled majority will, the way of safety lay in imposing restraints upon that will. In elaborating a system of checks and balances the members of the convention were influenced by the practical considerations of economic determinism more than by the theories of Montesquieu. They were realists who followed the teachings of the greatest political thinkers from Aristotle to Locke in asserting that the problem of government lay in arranging a stable balance between the economic interests of the major classes. The revolutionary conception of equalitarianism, that asserted the rights of man apart from property and superior to property, did not enter into their thinking as a workable hypothesis. The very conditions of the unsettled times were an argument against it. Property, they argued, is the stabilizing force in society; it is conservative and cautious; having everything to lose by social upheavals, it is a restraining force upon factional unrest. The propertyless, on the other hand, having nothing to lose, easily become the victims of demagogues and embroil society with foolish experiments. The republican experiment might work in America because property was widely distributed, but in the course of time a propertyless majority would arise, whose fickle and subversive will must be held in check. The problem, therefore, was to provide in time against such an eventuality. Certain members of the convention did not go so far in their fear of the propertyless, but relied upon the ability of property to protect itself by extralegal means. "Give the votes to people who have no property," argued Gouverneur Morris, "and they will sell them to the rich, who will be able to buy them."[3] But the more general view was expressed by Madison:

> *The landed interest, at present, is prevalent, but in process of time . . . when the number of landholders shall be comparatively small . . . will not the landed interests be overbalanced in future elections? and, unless wisely provided against, what will become of our government? In England, at this day, if elections were open to all classes of people, the property of landed proprietors would be insecure. An agrarian law would take place. If these observations be just, our government ought to secure the permanent interests of the country against innovation. Landholders ought to have a share in the government, to support these invaluable interests, and to balance and check the other. They ought to be so constituted as to protect the minority of the opulent against the majority.*[4]

This conception of the natural sovereignty of the landed interest with its stake-in-society theory of political rights, America inherited from England; and although the new Constitution professed to rest on the sovereignty of the people, the men who framed it refused to interpret the term, sovereignty of the people, in an equalitarian sense. They did not profess to be, in the words of John Quincy Adams, "slavish adorers of our sovereign lords the people." Every principle of their social and political philosophy taught them the desirability of limiting the majority will in order that the wiser minority will might rule. Paul Leicester Ford has asserted that "the Federal compact was the first deliberate attempt and assent of a majority to tie its own hands; to give to the minority guarantees of fair and equal treatment, without which democratic government is well-nigh impossible, save when developed along the lines of socialism."[5] Such partisan misin-

[3] *Elliot's Debates*, Vol. I, p. 386.
[4] Ibid., Vol. I, pp. 449–50.
[5] *The Federalist*, Introduction, p. viii.

terpretation of plain historical fact is characteristic of our Federalist historians. If the hands of the disfranchised majority were tied by the voting minority, it is a bit absurd to attribute the resulting guarantees to an altruistic sense of justice, deliberately expressed by the former. Very possibly in a world so aristocratic as was America in 1787, no other course would have succeeded; but there is not a single historical fact to justify so naive an interpretation, and the bitter partisan warfare which followed is sufficient to disprove it.

We are too prone to forget the wide popular disfavor with which the new Constitution was received. No sooner did the second debate open than it became evident that the majority opinion held quite a different conception of the sovereignty of the people than was expressed by the convention. It had no desire to tie its own hands; it did not take kindly to the proposal to transfer power from the several states to the Federal government. The villagers and small men were afraid of the new instrument; they asserted that it had been prepared by aristocrats and moneyed men, and they repudiated the stake-in-society principle. "The Constitution," said General Thompson in the Massachusetts Convention, "and the reasons which induced gentlemen to frame it, ought to have been sent to the several towns to be considered by them. My town considered it seven hours, and after this there was not one in favor of it." In Rhode Island, where it was thus submitted, it was rejected "by a very great majority." The state of mind of the agrarian majority was thus expressed by Amos Singletary, of Sutton, Massachusetts:

> *These lawyers, and men of learning, and moneyed men, that talk so finely, and gloss over matters so smoothly, to make us, poor illiterate people, swallow down the pill, expect to get into Congress themselves; they expect to be the managers of this Constitution, and get all the power and all the money into their own hands, and then they will swallow up all us little folks, like the great leviathan.*[6]

Among the host of pamphlets and newspaper articles that quickly appeared, *The Federalist* written by Hamilton and Madison with some help from Jay, and *Letters from the Federal Farmer to the Republican*, by Richard Henry Lee, fairly adequately present the opposing arguments. By common consent *The Federalist* was at once accepted by its party as an unanswerable defense of the Constitution; and its

[6] Quoted in Harding, *The Federal Constitution in Massachusetts.*

fame has grown greater with the passing years. No other work on political theory in the American library has been rated so high, or been more frequently cited. From the mass of contemporary pamphlets it emerges like a colossus. It "has been seriously and reverently called the Bible of Republicanism," says a legal historian, which "for comprehensiveness of design, strength, clearness, and simplicity . . . has no parallel among the writings of men, not even excepting or overlooking those of Montesquieu and Aristotle";[7] and a literary historian pronounces authoritatively, "it is so wisely thoughtful that one may almost declare it the permanent basis of sound thinking concerning American constitutional law."[8]

The Federalist was the work of able lawyers, with whom was joined a notable political thinker. In very large part it is of interest only to students of early constitutional theory and practice. It was designed as a frankly partisan argument to appeal to an influential group in New York, many members of which had followed George Clinton and Robert Yates in opposition to the Constitution. On the political side it develops four main theses: the necessity for taking effective action in view of the self-confessed failure of the Articles of Confederation; the urgent need of a sovereign, unitary state, to avoid the horrors which must follow from "the political monster of an *imperium in imperio*"; the necessity of providing that justice shall prevail over the majority will; and the adaptability of the republican form to a great extent of territory and divergent interests. Of these the second and third lay bare the heart of Federalist political theory; and in the treatment of them there is no shrinking from the conclusions of the earlier debate, although the tone is conciliatory.

The argument for a unitary, sovereign state, developed by Hamilton, and the argument for justice, developed by Madison, rest upon the same basis and are regarded as the twin problems of government. The true sanction of government is found, not in good will, as Bentham and later democratic thinkers have urged, but in coercion;[9] and coercion is accepted as necessary because of universal selfishness. "Why has government been instituted at all? Because the passions of men will not conform to the dictates of reason and justice, without restraint."[10] Granted coercive sovereignty, govern-

[7] Carson, *History of the Supreme Court*, quoted by Ford, *The Federalist*, p. xxix.
[8] Wendell, *Literary History of America*, p. 118.
[9] Number 15.
[10] Ibid.

ment must guarantee justice to all; and justice demands that the majority shall suffer needful restraint equally with the minority. The great and insidious danger to good government has always been faction, the argument runs, and a chief merit of the Constitution lay in its provisions to lessen the disasters of factional ambition. "Complaints are everywhere heard from our most considerate and virtuous citizens, equally the friends of public and private faith, and of public and personal liberty, that our governments are too unstable, that the public good is disregarded in the conflict of rival parties, and that measures are too often decided, not according to the rules of justice and the rights of the minor party, but by the superior force of an interested and overbearing majority."[11]

No theory is more representative of the time than the theory of faction. It was a first line of defense thrown up against the advancing democratic movement. The term had long served conveniently to stigmatize any popular unrest, the "factious multitude" having been held synonymous in earlier usage with mob; but in the eighteenth century the word was applied generally to political parties. In a world moving inevitably towards manhood suffrage, a sharp alignment of parties with definite platforms was greatly feared by the minority, for the organization of the rank and file of voters must end in majority control. An honest appeal to the people was the last thing desired by the Federalists, and the democratic machinery of recalls and referendums and rotation in office, which had developed during the war, was stigmatized as factional devices which in the end must destroy good government. "As every appeal to the people would carry an implication of some defect in the government," argued Madison,[12] "frequent appeals would in a great measure deprive the government of that veneration which time bestows on everything, and without which the wisest and freest governments would not possess the requisite stability." "The danger of disturbing the public tranquillity by interesting too strongly the public passions is a still more serious objection against a frequent reference of constitutional questions to the decisions of the whole society."

In the remarkable tenth number, which compresses within a few pages pretty much the whole Federalist theory of political science,

[11] Number 10.
[12] Number 49.

Madison has explained the Federalist objections to political parties and party government.

> *By a faction, I understand a number of citizens, whether amounting to a majority or minority of the whole, who are united and actuated by some common impulse of passion, or of interest, adverse to the rights of other citizens, or to the permanent and aggregate interests of the community. . . . If a faction consists of less than a majority, relief is supplied by the republican principle, which enables the majority to defeat its sinister views, by regular vote. . . . When a majority is included in a faction, the form of popular government, on the other hand, enables it to sacrifice to its ruling passion or interest, both the public good and the rights of other citizens. To secure the public good and private rights, against the danger of such a faction, is then the great object to which our inquiries are directed. . . . By what means is this great object attainable? Evidently by one of two only. Either the existence of the same passion or interest in a majority at the same time must be prevented; or the majority, having such coexistent passion or interest, must be rendered by their number and local situations, unable to concert and carry into effect schemes of oppression. If the impulse and the opportunity be suffered to coincide, we well know, that neither moral nor religious motives can be relied on as an adequate control.*

In full agreement with the greater political thinkers of the past, Madison then traces political parties to economic sources. Since in every society the diversity of economic groups creates diversity of political programs, party divisions and party alignments are inevitable in the ordinary course of events. The unequal distribution of property is the realistic basis of all politics, and the "*sentiments* and *views* which arise from the possession of different degrees and kinds of property form the stuff of so-called 'political psychology.' "[13]

> *The diversity in the faculties of men, from which the rights of property originate, is . . . an insuperable obstacle to a uniformity of interests. The protection of these faculties is the first object of government. From the protection of different and unequal faculties of acquiring property, the possession of different degrees and kinds of property immediately results; and from the influence of these on the sentiments and views of the respective proprietors, ensues a division of the society into different interests and parties.*
>
> *The latent causes of faction are thus sown in the nature of man; and we see them everywhere brought into different degrees of activity, ac-*

[13] Beard, *The Economic Basis of Politics*, pp. 29–32.

> *cording to the different circumstances of civil society. A zeal for different opinions . . . [has] divided mankind into parties, inflamed them with mutual animosity, and rendered them much more disposed to vex and oppress each other than to cooperate for their common good. . . . But the most common and durable source of factions has been the various and unequal distribution of property. Those who hold and those who are without property have ever formed distinct interests of society. Those who are creditors, and those who are debtors, fall under a like discrimination. A landed interest, a manufacturing interest, a mercantile interest, a moneyed interest, with many lesser interests, grow up of necessity in civilized nations, and divide them into different classes actuated by different sentiments and views. The regulation of these various and interfering interests, forms the principal task of modern legislation, and involves the spirit of party and faction in the necessary and ordinary operations of the government.*

As a means of securing a necessary balance between rival interests, Madison approved a republican rather than a democratic form of government:

> *The two great points of difference, between a democracy and a republic, are, first, the delegation of the government, in the latter, to a small number of citizens elected by the rest; secondly, the greater number of citizens, and greater sphere of country, over which the latter may be extended. The effect of the first difference is, on the one hand, to refine or enlarge the public views, by passing them through the medium of a chosen body of citizens, whose wisdom may best discern the true interests of their country, and whose patriotism and love of justice, will be least likely to sacrifice it to temporary or partial considerations. Under such a regulation, it may well happen, that the public voice, pronounced by the representatives of the people, will be more consonant to the public good, than if pronounced by the people themselves, convened for the purpose. . . . The other point of difference is, the greater number of citizens, and extent of territory, which may be brought within the compass of republican, than of democratic government; and it is this circumstance principally which renders factious combinations less to be dreaded in the former, than in the latter. . . . Extend the sphere, and you take in a greater variety of parties and interests; you make it less probable that a majority of the whole will have a common motive to invade the rights of other citizens; or if such a common motive exists, it will be more difficult for all who feel it to discover their strength, and act in unison with each other.*[14]

In such argument Madison was adapting to his purpose the views of Milton and other seventeenth-century republicans, to whom in the

[14] Number 10.

dangerous days when the Puritan Commonwealth was breaking up, the "noise and shouting of the rude multitude," the drunken ribaldry of the London rabble, was prophetic of "new injunctions to manacle the native libertie of mankinde." But it has long since become a commonplace of political observation that the minority and not the majority is the more dangerous to the common well-being, for it is the minority that most frequently uses government to its own ends.

The contrast in temper and argument between *The Federalist* and Richard Henry Lee's *Letters from the Federal Farmer*[15] is striking. The calmness and fair-mindedness of the work persuade one that it ill deserves the name partisan; it comes near to being a frank and disinterested examination of the proposed instrument of government. Its sharpest strictures are tempered by ready acknowledgment of excellent features. The burden of Lee's accusation is that the instrument is undemocratic; that it must result in placing the majority under control of the minority; and that it in no wise reflects the sober judgment of the body of the people. He is more restrained than Elbridge Gerry, who asserted that it was the outcome of a conspiracy hatched in secret, a work of "such motley mixture, that its enemies cannot trace a feature of Democratic or Republican extract." But the Farmer's restraint adds weight to the serious charges which he brings against the instrument, and the unseemly haste of its advocates in urging its speedy adoption. It was not to destroy the work of the Convention that he pleaded for delay; but that it should receive full and fair consideration, and be disposed of as its merits or defects should warrant.

His first concern is that the Constitution should not be adopted with the inconsiderate haste for which *The Federalist* was pressing. "The first principal question that occurs, is, Whether, considering our situation, we ought to precipitate the adoption of the proposed Constitution?" Hamilton had made much of the desperate state of affairs that admitted of no delay; Lee replied by denying, with Franklin and other competent observers, that the present state was desperate. Matters were improving daily, peace was restoring the ravages of war.

[15] The full title is: *Observations leading to a fair examination of the system of government, proposed by the late Convention; and to several essential and necessary alterations in it. In a number of Letters from the Federal Farmer to the Republican.* Reprinted in Ford's pamphlets.

> *I know uneasy men, who with very much to precipitate, do not admit all these facts; but they are facts well known to all men who are thoroughly informed in the affairs of this country. It must, however, be admitted, that our federal system is defective, and that some of the state governments are not well administered; but . . . we impute to the defects in our governments many evils and embarrassments which are most clearly the result of the late war. . . . When we want a man to change his condition, we describe it as wretched, miserable, and despised; and we draw a pleasing picture of that which we would have him assume. . . . It is too often the case in political concerns that men state facts not as they are, but as they wish them to be. . . . Men who feel easy in their circumstances, and such as are not sanguine in their expectations relative to the consequences of the proposed change, will remain quiet under the existing governments. Many commercial and monied men, who are uneasy, not without just cause, ought to be respected; and by no means, unreasonably disappointed in their expectations and hopes. . . . It is natural for men, who wish to hasten the adoption of a measure, to tell us, now is the crisis—now is the critical moment which must be seized or all will be lost; and to shut the door against free enquiry, whenever conscious the thing presented has defects in it, which time and investigation will probably discover. . . . If it is true, what has been so often said, that the people of this country cannot change their constitution for the worse, I presume it still behoves them to endeavor deliberately to change it for the better.*

Granted that experience has demonstrated the need of revising the Articles of Confederation in certain essential points, Lee maintains that the enemies of democracy have been making undue capital out of the shortcomings of an emergency government, in the hope of subverting the democratic state governments and substituting a more aristocratic form.

> *The confederation was formed when great confidence was placed in the voluntary exertions of individuals, and of the respective states; and the framers of it, to guard against usurpation, so limited, and checked the powers, that, in many respects, they are inadequate to the exigencies of the union. . . . During the war, the general confusion, and the introduction of paper money, infused in the minds of people vague ideas respecting government and credit. We expected too much from the return of peace, and of course we have been disappointed. Our governments have been new and unsettled; and several legislatures, by making tender, suspension, and paper money laws, have given just cause of uneasiness to creditors. By these and other causes, several orders of men in the community have been prepared by degrees, for a change of government; and this very abuse of power in the legislatures, which in some cases has been charged upon the democratic part of the community, has furnished*

aristocratical men with those very weapons, and those very means, with which, in great measure, they are rapidly effecting their favorite object.

The methods by which the convention was brought together at a time when the "idea of destroying ultimately, the state government, and forming one consolidated system, could not have been admitted," is traced briefly with penetrating comment, and the unfortunate decision of some excellent republicans to take no part in the work is regretted:

Here the favorable moment for changing the government was evidently discerned by a few men, who seized it with address. . . . Tho' they chose men principally connected with commerce and the judicial departments, yet they appointed many good republican characters—had they all attended we should see, I am persuaded, a better system presented. The non-attendance of eight or nine men, who were appointed members of the convention, I shall ever consider as a very unfortunate event to the United States.—Had they attended, I am pretty clear that the results . . . would not have had that strong tendency to aristocracy now discernible in every part of the plan . . . the young visionary men, and the consolidating aristocracy, would have been more restrained than they have been.

Lee frankly concedes that the instrument possesses many excellent features, but he considers it greatly vitiated by the "want of that one important factor in a free government, a representation of the people." "Because we have sometimes abused democracy, I am not among those who think a democratic branch a nuisance." "Every man of reflection must see, that the change now proposed, is a transfer of power from the many to the few." The present agitation may be traced to its source in "two very unprincipled parties," between whom stand the great mass of honest and substantial people:

One party is composed of little insurgents, men in debt, who want no law, and who want a share of the property of others; these are called levellers, Shaysites, &c. The other party is composed of a few, but more dangerous men, with their servile dependents; these avariciously grasp at all power and property; you may discover in all the actions of these men, an evident dislike to free and equal government, and they go systematically to work to change, essentially, the forms of government in this country; these are called aristocrats, m——ites, &c. Between these two parties is the weight of the community: the men of middling property, men not in debt on the one hand, and men, on the other, content with republican governments, and not aiming at immense fortunes, offices and

> *power. In 1786, the little insurgents, the levellers, came forth, invaded the rights of others, and attempted to establish governments according to their wills. Their movements evidently gave encouragement to the other party, which, in 1787, has taken the political field, and with its fashionable dependents, and the tongue and the pen, is endeavoring to establish in a great haste, a politer kind of government. These two parties . . . are really insignificant, compared with the solid, free, and independent part of the community.*

Calm voices such as Lee's were few in those strident days, and the Federalists fairly overwhelmed the silent majority with clamorous argument. Polite culture and professional learning joined forces to write down the agrarians. The Hartford Wits dedicated smart couplets to the cause; Francis Hopkinson made merry over their ways; Noah Webster confuted them with his economic interpretation of politics; lawyer-scholars like James Wilson and John Dickinson exposed their heresies, solid businessmen like Peletiah Webster contributed after the measure of their intelligence. In their ardor the Federalists went further. "What can be the views of those gentlemen in Boston," asked Lee pertinently, "who countenanced the printers in shutting up the press against a fair and free investigation?" From the strident debate emerged not only the Constitution, but political parties, no longer to be spoken of as factions, but eventually to be accepted as necessary agencies in republican government.

James Madison

THE FEDERALIST, NUMBER TEN

In the previous essay, Vernon L. Parrington supplied generously long quotations from Number Ten of The Federalist *by James Madison, but the purpose was to support the thesis that the men of the Convention were primarily interested in guarding against the advent of democracy, not in promoting it. But the analysis by Parrington, although sharp, is nevertheless somewhat incomplete, and the famous essay by James Madison deserves to be read in its entirety, as an important statement of political principles of broad application.*

The late Douglass Adair pointed out that interest in the tenth Federalist *has been almost exclusively a concern of the twentieth century. It was written in 1787 but it was not until 1913, he said, "one hundred twenty-five years later, that Charles A. Beard made this particular essay famous for students of the United States Constitution."*[1] *Before Beard, practically no commentators of the Constitution, and none of Madison's biographers, had thought that the tenth* Federalist *was of special importance to an understanding either of the American Constitution or of the political system that developed under it. After Beard, the essay, according to Adair, was most quoted as an explanation of the philosophy of the Framers and of the Constitution itself.*[2] *One of those using it so was, of course, Vernon L. Parrington.*

The tendency of Parrington and many others, however, was to center attention upon the economic elements that make for political division and to ignore the noneconomic elements. It is true that Madison said that the most durable cause of "faction" was the unequal distribution of property, but he also said that there were many other causes. Those like Beard and Parrington, with a penchant for economic interpretations of political behavior, perhaps gave economic factors more weight than Madison intended; for Madison, according to Adair, was writing, in succinct form, a whole political theory, much of which he derived from David Hume. It was the belief of Hume and of Madison that there were regular patterns in the behavior of men, that human nature did not change, and that politics was a science, that is to say, universal in its manifestations and predictable in its consequences.

If we assume that there are patterns of political behavior and that politics is a science capable of prediction, we see the tenth Federalist *in a some-*

From an 1826 edition of *The Federalist,* published by Glazier & Company, Hallowell, Maine. The title page states that Madison himself corrected his own essays in this edition.

[1] Trevor Colbourn, ed., *Fame and the Founding Fathers: Essays by Douglass Adair* (New York, 1974), p. 93. Two of the essays are titled, "The Tenth Federalist Revisited," (p. 75) and "That Politics May Be Reduced to a Science: David Hume, James Madison and the Tenth Federalist."

[2] Ibid., p. 76.

what different aspect from that presented by Beard and Parrington. First, as Adair points out, Madison argued (against the wisdom of his day) that the very size of the United States and the diversity of interests within it made a just republic possible. The prevailing view was that republics could prosper only in small domains and that large realms required monarchical government, a view entertained by Montesquieu. Hume thought otherwise and so did James Madison.

Second, the turbulence of small polities could be attributed to the close proximity of the people who fall into the easy tendency of separating into small parties along class lines, with the poor ever ready to exploit the rich and the latter too quick to use repression to protect themselves. If government could be designed to control and curb both these destructive tendencies, something like justice and stability would emerge. Such a design would be better secured in a large rather than a small political system.

Third, the tenth Federalist *was prescient in laying the foundation for what was later to be recognized as the concept of the group basis of politics, a conception of particular applicability to the United States in which a rich ethno-cultural variety came to characterize the population through immigration from abroad. For although Madison did acknowledge that the unequal distribution of property was the most durable source of "faction," he recognized that a zeal for different opinions, religion, and other elements were causes of faction also. Finally, the reader of the tenth* Federalist *cannot help being impressed by the concern of James Madison for* justice, *for which stability was a necessary condition. His famous essay is, on its face, a statement of principles of universal application; it is not special pleading for the rich. When he talks about the protection of minorities from the factionalism of majorities, he can be read, as economic interpretations have read him, as one bent upon saving men of property from pillage by the poor, but there are many minorities in a pluralistic system—ethnic, religious, social, and political—whose protection from arbitrary majorities is also embodied in the United States Constitution, under the protection of the Bill of Rights.*

To the People of the State of New York: Among the numerous advantages promised by a well-constructed union, none deserves to be more accurately developed than its tendency to break and control the violence of faction. The friend of popular governments, never finds himself so much alarmed for their character and fate, as when he contemplates their propensity to this dangerous vice. He will not fail, therefore, to set a due value on any plan which, without violating the principles to which he is attached, provides a proper cure for it. The instability, injustice, and confusion introduced into the public councils, have, in truth, been the mortal diseases under which popular governments have everywhere perished; as they continue to be the favourite and fruitful topics from which the adversaries to liberty derive their most specious declamations. The valuable improvements made by the American constitutions on the popular models, both ancient and modern, cannot certainly be too much admired; but it would be an unwarrantable partiality, to contend that they have as effectually obviated the danger on this side, as was wished and expected. Complaints are everywhere heard from our most considerate and virtuous citizens, equally the friends of public and private faith, and of public and personal liberty, that our governments are too unstable; that the public good is disregarded in the conflicts of rival parties; and that measures are too often decided, not according to the rules of justice, and the rights of the minor party, but by the superior force of an interested and overbearing majority. However anxiously we may wish that these complaints had no foundation, the evidence of known facts will not permit us to deny that they are in some degree true. It will be found, indeed, on a candid review of our situation, that some of the distresses under which we labour have been erroneously charged on the operation of our governments; but it will be found, at the same time, that other causes will not alone account for many of our heaviest misfortunes; and, particularly, for that prevailing and increasing distrust of public engagements, and alarm for private rights, which are echoed from one end of the continent to the other. These must be chiefly, if not wholly, effects of the unsteadiness and injustice, with which a factious spirit has tainted our public administrations.

By a faction, I understand a number of citizens, whether amounting to a majority or minority of the whole, who are united and actuated by some common impulse of passion, or of interest, adverse to the rights of other citizens, or to the permanent and aggregate interests of the community.

There are two methods of curing the mischiefs of faction: The one, by removing its causes; the other, by controling its effects.

There are again two methods of removing the causes of faction: The one, by destroying the liberty which is essential to its existence; the other, by giving to every citizen the same opinions, the same passions, and the same interests.

It could never be more truly said, than of the first remedy, that it was worse than the disease. Liberty is to faction what air is to fire, an aliment without which it instantly expires. But it could not be a less folly to abolish liberty, which is essential to political life, because it nourishes faction, than it would be to wish the annihilation of air, which is essential to animal life, because it imparts to fire its destructive agency.

The second expedient is as impracticable, as the first would be unwise. As long as the reason of man continues fallible, and he is at liberty to exercise it, different opinions will be formed. As long as the connection subsists between his reason and his self-love, his opinions and his passions will have a reciprocal influence on each other; and the former will be objects to which the latter will attach themselves. The diversity in the faculties of men, from which the rights of property originate, is not less an insuperable obstacle to an uniformity of interests. The protection of these faculties is the first object of government. From the protection of different and unequal faculties of acquiring property, the possession of different degrees and kinds of property immediately results; and from the influence of these on the sentiments and views of the respective proprietors, ensues a division of the society into different interests and parties.

The latent causes of faction are thus sown in the nature of man; and we see them everywhere brought into different degrees of activity, according to the different circumstances of civil society. A zeal for different opinions concerning religion, concerning government, and many other points, as well of speculation as of practice; an attachment to different leaders ambitiously contending for preeminence and power; or to persons of other descriptions whose fortunes have been interesting to the human passions, have, in turn, divided mankind into parties, inflamed them with mutual animosity, and rendered them much more disposed to vex and oppress each other, than to cooperate for their common good. So strong is this propensity of mankind, to fall into mutual animosities, that where no substantial occasion presents itself, the most frivolous and fanciful distinctions have been sufficient to kindle their unfriendly passions and excite their most violent conflicts. But the most common and durable source of factions, has been the various and unequal distribution of property. Those who hold, and those who are without property, have ever formed distinct interests in society. Those who are creditors, and those who are debtors, fall under a like discrimination. A landed interest, a manufacturing interest, a mercantile interest, a moneyed interest, with many lesser interests, grow up of necessity in civilized nations, and divide them into different classes, actuated by different sentiments and views. The regulation of these various and interfering interests forms the principal task of modern legislation, and involves the spirit of party and faction in the necessary and ordinary operations of the government.

No man is allowed to be a judge in his own cause; because his interest will certainly bias his judgment, and, not improbably, corrupt his integrity. With equal, nay, with greater reason, a body of men are unfit to be both judges and parties at the same time; yet what are many of the most important acts of legislation, but so many judicial determinations, not indeed concerning the rights of single persons, but concerning the rights of large bodies of citizens? And what are the different classes of legislators, but advocates and parties to the causes which they determine? Is a law proposed concerning private debts? It is a question to which the creditors are parties on one side, and the debtors on the other. Justice ought to hold the balance between them. Yet the parties are, and must be, themselves the judges; and the most numerous party, or, in other words, the most powerful faction, must be expected to prevail. Shall domestic manufactures be encouraged, and in what degree, by restrictions on foreign manufactures? are questions which would be differently decided by the landed and the manufacturing classes; and probably by neither with a sole regard to justice and the public good. The apportionment of taxes, on the various descriptions of property, is an act which seems to require the most exact impartiality; yet there is, perhaps, no legislative act, in which greater opportunity and temptation are given to a predominant party to trample on the rules of justice. Every shilling, with which they overburden the inferior number, is a shilling saved to their own pockets.

It is in vain to say, that enlightened statesmen will be able to adjust these clashing interests, and render them all subservient to the public good. Enlightened statesmen will not always be at the helm: nor, in many cases, can such an adjustment be made at all, without taking into view indirect and remote considerations, which will rarely prevail over the immediate interest which one party may find in disregarding the rights of another, or the good of the whole.

The inference to which we are brought is, that the *causes* of faction cannot be removed; and that relief is only to be sought in the means of controling its *effects.*

If a faction consists of less than a majority, relief is supplied by the republican principle, which enables the majority to defeat its sinister views, by regular vote. It may clog the administration, it may convulse the society; but it will be unable to execute and mask its violence under the forms of the constitution. When a majority is included in a faction, the form of popular government, on the other hand, enables it to sacrifice to its ruling passion or interest, both the public good and the rights of other citizens. To secure the public good, and private rights, against the danger of such a faction, and at the same time to preserve the spirit and the form of popular government, is then the great object to which our inquiries are directed. Let me add, that it is the great desideratum, by which alone this form of government can be rescued from the opprobrium under which it has so long laboured, and be recommended to the esteem and adoption of mankind.

By what means is this object attainable? Evidently by one of two only. Either the existence of the same passion or interest in a majority, at the same time, must be prevented; or the majority, having such coexistent passion or interest, must be rendered, by their number and local situation, unable to concert and carry into effect schemes of oppression. If the impulse and the opportunity be suffered to coincide, we well know that neither moral nor religious motives can be relied on as an adequate control. They are not found to be such on the injustice and violence of individuals, and lose their efficacy in proportion to the number combined together; that is, in proportion as their efficacy becomes needful.

From this view of the subject, it may be concluded, that a pure democracy, by which I mean a society consisting of a small number of citizens, who assemble and administer the government in person, can admit of no cure for the mischiefs of faction. A common passion or interest will, in almost every case, be felt by a majority of the whole; a communication and concert, results from the form of government itself; and there is nothing to check the inducements to sacrifice the weaker party, or an obnoxious individual. Hence it is, that such democracies have ever been spectacles of turbulence and contention; have ever been found incompatible with personal security, or the rights of property; and have in general been as short in their lives, as they have been violent in their deaths. Theoretic politicians, who have patronized this species of government, have erroneously supposed, that by reducing mankind to a perfect equality in their political rights, they would, at the same time, be perfectly equalized and assimilated in their possessions, their opinions, and their passions.

A republic, by which I mean a government in which the scheme of representation takes place, opens a different prospect, and promises the cure for which we are seeking. Let us examine the points in which it varies from pure democracy, and we shall comprehend both the nature of the cure and the efficacy which it must derive from the union.

The two great points of difference, between a democracy and a republic, are, first, the delegation of the government, in the latter, to a small number of citizens elected by the rest; secondly, the greater number of citizens, and greater sphere of country, over which the latter may be extended.

The effect of the first difference is, on the one hand, to refine and enlarge the public views, by passing them through the medium of a chosen body of citizens, whose wisdom may best discern the true interest of their country, and whose patriotism and love of justice, will be least likely to sacrifice it to temporary or partial considerations. Under such a regulation, it may well happen, that the public voice, pronounced by the representatives of the people, will be more consonant to the public good, than if pronounced by the people themselves, convened for the purpose. On the other hand the effect may be inverted. Men of factious tempers, of local prejudices, or of sinister designs, may by intrigue, by corruption, or by other means, first obtain the suffrages, and then betray the interests of the people. The question resulting is, whether small or extensive republics are most favourable to the election of proper guardians of the public weal; and it is clearly decided in favour of the latter by two obvious considerations.

In the first place, it is to be remarked that, however small the republic may be, the representatives must be raised to a certain number, in order to guard against the cabals of a few; and that however large it may be, they must be limited to a certain number, in order to guard against the confusion of a multitude. Hence, the number of representatives in the two cases not being in proportion to that of the constituents, and being proportionally greatest in the small republic, it follows, that if the proportion of fit characters be not less in the large than in the small republic, the former will present a greater option, and consequently a greater probability of a fit choice.

In the next place, as each representative will be chosen by a greater number of citizens in the large than in the small republic, it will be more difficult for unworthy candidates to practise with success the vicious arts, by which elections are too often carried; and the suffrages of the people being more free, will be more likely to centre in men who possess the most attractive merit, and the most diffusive and established characters.

It must be confessed, that in this, as in most other cases, there is a mean, on both sides of which inconveniences will be found to lie. By enlarging too much the number of electors, you render the representative too little acquainted with all their local circumstances and lesser interests; as by reducing it too much, you render him unduly attached to these, and too little fit to comprehend and pursue great and national objects. The federal constitution forms a happy combination in this respect; the great and aggregate interests being referred to the national, the local and particular to the state legislatures.

The other point of difference is, the greater number of citizens, and extent of territory, which may be brought within the compass of republican, than of democratic government; and it is this circumstance principally which renders factious combinations less to be dreaded in the former, than in the latter. The smaller the society, the fewer probably will be the distinct parties and interests composing it; the fewer the distinct parties and interests, the more frequently will a majority be found of the same party; and the smaller the number of individuals composing a majority, and the smaller the compass within which they are placed, the more easily will they concert and execute their plans of oppression. Extend the sphere, and you take in a greater variety of parties and interests; you make it less probable that a majority of the whole will have a common motive to invade the rights of other citizens; or if such a common motive exists, it will be more difficult for all who feel it to discover their own strength, and to act in unison with each other. Besides other impediments, it may be remarked, that where there is a consciousness of unjust or dishonourable purposes, communication is always checked by distrust, in proportion to the number whose concurrence is necessary.

Hence, it clearly appears, that the same advantage, which a republic has over a democracy, in controlling the effects of faction, is enjoyed by a large over a small republic,—is enjoyed by the union over the states composing it. Does this advantage consist in the substitution of representatives, whose enlightened views and virtuous sentiments render them superior to local prejudices, and to schemes of injustice? It will not be denied that the representation of the union will be most likely to possess these requisite endowments. Does it consist in the greater security afforded by a greater variety of parties, against the event of any one party being able to outnumber and oppress the rest? In an equal degree does the increased variety of parties, comprised within the union, increase the security? Does it, in fine, consist in the greater obstacles opposed to the concert and accomplishment of the secret wishes of an unjust and interested majority? Here, again, the extent of the union gives it the most palpable advantage.

The influence of factious leaders may kindle a flame within their particular states, but will be unable to spread a general conflagration through the other states: a religious sect may degenerate into a political faction in a part of the confederacy; but the variety of sects dispersed over the entire face of it, must secure the national councils against any danger from that source: a rage for paper money, for an abolition of debts, for an equal division of property, or for any other improper or wicked project, will be less apt to pervade the whole body of the union than a particular member of it; in the same proportion as such a malady is more likely to taint a particular county or district, than an entire state.

In the extent and proper structure of the union, therefore, we behold a republican remedy for the diseases most incident to republican government. And according to the degree of pleasure and pride we feel in being republicans, ought to be our zeal in cherishing the spirit, and supporting the character of federalists.

PUBLIUS

Earl Latham

PHILADELPHIENSIS: A CRITIC OF THE CONSTITUTION

The following is a brief essay introducing an unusual young man who for a short time engaged himself in the controversy over the ratification of the Constitution in Philadelphia. He was evidently without high social position, he lacked extensive means, and he was certainly without influence on the final outcome of the debate in Pennsylvania. But he is a reminder that the controversy over the Constitution was not always a debate among great men discussing philosophy at the highest and most dignified levels of noble and disinterested discourse. There is an anxious human quality in the engagement of Philadelphiensis *in the dialog, and his contribution illustrates the lengths to which some proponents of the Constitution were prepared to go in their zeal for ratification.*

Equally ardent but more sophisticated, by contrast, was the exchange in New York between Alexander Hamilton and the Antifederalist Governor George Clinton. With sarcasm scarcely concealing his antidemocratic sentiments, Hamilton, writing under the name of "Caesar," called the governor a demagog for proposing that the proffered constitution might be amended or substituted by a new one, and said of the suggestion, "O excellent thought, and happily advised! Be clamorous, my friends—be discontented—assert your prerogative—forever assert the power and majesty of the people." *Governor Clinton, in turn, writing under the classical pseudonym "Cato," told his readers that this "Caeser mocks your dignity and laughs at the majesty of the people," offers a take-it-or-leave-it Constitution, and threatens military force to impose it upon the people if they reject the new instrument of government. He then accused the Philadelphia convention of having exceeded its authority (which was only to propose amendments to the Articles of Confederation), deprived the states of their sovereignty, and failed to send the new Constitution to state legislatures in the manner prescribed for amending the Articles, all to the end that the "present national government" should be annihilated. Hamilton's answer was an intemperate attack on those (i.e., Clinton) "who gain influence by cajoling the unthinking mass (tho' I pity their delusions), and ringing in their ears the gracious sound of their* absolute Sovereignty." *He said, "For my part, I am not much attached to the* majesty of the multitude . . . ," *and he ventured the view that men of "good education and deep reflection, only, are judges of the* form of a *government." He concluded that everything Cato could say against the new Constitution had already been said "in a neighboring State by the glorious defenders of* Shaysism." *Hamilton's later contributions to what became known as* The Federalist Papers *were more temperate and less antidemocratic in tone.*

Philadelphiensis *was not a man of the world, as were Alexander Hamilton and Governor Clinton of New York. He was not working from a strong power base as were the two New York political rivals but, instead, was speaking for himself as a lone and vulnerable individual. It is because he was one of Hamilton's despised "multitude" that he deserves a hearing.*

In her collection of source materials on the views and opinions of Antifederalist writers and speakers when the Constitution was before the state conventions for ratification, Professor Cecilia Kenyon included four essays by an author who called himself *Philadelphiensis.*[1] The letters appeared in *The Independent Gazeteer, or The Chronicle of Freedom* from November 7, 1787 to April 11, 1788 and Professor Kenyon said they "represent some of the more flamboyant of the Antifederalist attacks on the Constitution."[2]

Emotions did run high in some of the agitation over the Constitution and an orotund and somewhat purple rhetoric, ringing and touched with bombast, characterized the style of some in the debate. But the champions as well as the critics of the Constitution had their excesses, and the controversy stirred by the letters of *Philadelphiensis* shows also the lengths that the Federalist champions were prepared to go in flamboyance and libel to counteract the opposition. The whole controversy of which *Philadelphiensis* was a part is instructive to those writers who tend to regard the colonials as a homogenized society of equals, all middle class, without serious social differences.

The series of letters started when *Philadelphiensis* on November 7, 1787 argued with *Galba* as to whether writers should use their true names. *Philadelphiensis* was against the idea on the ground that it was the value of the argument that counted, not the identity of the author.[3] Three weeks later he was back with a criticism of the proposed Constitution on the ground that it put religious liberty in danger, especially in Pennsylvania where many (e.g., Quakers) are "principled against fighting or bearing arms."[4] The military features of the proposed new government gave him special alarm throughout his correspondence of several months, and he strongly opposed the vesting of power in a central government to maintain a standing army. This concern, with an extension of his remarks on civil liberty,

[1] Cecilia M. Kenyon, ed., *The Antifederalists* (Indianapolis, 1966).
[2] Ibid., p. 69.
[3] *The Independent Gazeteer* (Philadelphia), November 7, 1787. *Philadelphiensis* numbered his contributions and this is Number 1.
[4] Ibid., November 28, 1787 (Number 2).

was voiced again within a week.[5] People oppressed will not fight for their governments if it should become necessary, he thought; and a standing army was both a symbol and an instrument of oppression.

By the time of his third letter, however (December 5, 1787), *Philadelphiensis* had increased the vigor and range of his denunciations. The Constitution was not the work of liberty-loving patriots, he said, but the work of wealthy men. It is true, he admitted, that they had fought to throw off a foreign tyranny, but they had done this only so that they could impose a tyranny of their own upon the people. These wealthy men tried to justify their new Constitution on the ground that "we want efficient government," but it was not the efficiency they offered that the people needed. The efficiency the people needed was efficiency in the protection of the "liberties, lives and property of the people governed," and this the proposed Constitution did not provide. Instead, it failed to protect the people in their most basic liberties among which he mentioned freedom of conscience, freedom of the press, and trial by jury. The argument of *Philadelphiensis* that the Constitution was defective in that it lacked a bill of rights was so forcefully and so often stated by other critics that the Federalists promised to make such a bill the first business of the new government, which it was, leading to the adoption of the first ten amendments to the Constitution.

Philadelphiensis published a letter every week in December 1787 in the *Independent Gazeteer.*[6] The last three of these letters adverted to a number of issues, on some of which he had touched in earlier correspondence, but they dealt also with the international aspects of the proposed Constitution. It had been argued in behalf of the new regime that it would make the country "eminent" in the world, that it would be strong against enemies because it would be unified under an effective government equipped with adequate powers. John Jay, under the name *Publius,* wrote four of his five essays in the series that came to be known as *The Federalist Papers* entirely on the advantages and benefits of the proposed government in the conduct of foreign affairs.[7]

A cordial union under an efficient national government, according to Jay, would afford the people the best security that could be

[5] Ibid., December 5, 1787 (Number 3).
[6] These were dated December 5, 12, 19 and 27, 1787.
[7] These were Numbers 2–5, and appeared originally in the *Independent Journal* (New York).

devised against hostilities from abroad. A united America would afford the world the fewest occasions for any wars, even just wars, such as would arise from the breaking of treaties or the commission of direct violence, because one united government would respect its treaty obligations more surely than thirteen separated states. And the reason for this (besides, presumably, the arithmetical aspect) would be that "once an efficient national government" was established, "the best men in the country" would not only consent to serve in it but would also "generally be appointed to manage it." The counsels of the new central authority would then be "more wise, systematical, and judicious than those of the individual states," would be more satisfactory with respect to other nations and would be more safe with respect to the American people. There would be greater security against unjust wars also, those that proceed from direct and unlawful violence, because such "violences are more frequently caused by the passions and interests of a part than of the whole," of "one or two states than of the Union." So, a strong union would secure the safety of the people by reducing the causes of both just and unjust wars. Such union would also protect the people from foreign hostility and insult and the wars of aggression that might follow. Our commerce is international, said Jay, and could excite the jealousies of foreign nations which might create hostilities out of pretended reasons. Seeing us strong and united, they would be much more disposed to court our friendship than risk our resentment.

Now there is no evidence that *Philadelphiensis* was answering, in Philadelphia, the specific arguments being made in New York by Jay to convince New Yorkers to accept the new Constitution, but the themes of the Federalist agitation were not confined to New York, and we have already seen that *Philadelphiensis* expressed opposition to several points that were in fact made by Jay, especially the supposed virtue of the "efficient national government" that was being proposed. In his December letters, however, *Philadelphiensis* did not confine himself to the question of "efficiency" but attacked on a broader front. Not only would the proposed government not make the country eminent in international affairs, discouraging other countries from provoking our resentments; it would have precisely the opposite effect, he said. The new regime would not be strong against foreign enemies but would be despised and contemptible. The standing army would not be a protection against foreign enemies but would be used against domestic ones. (In fact, Jay had indeed said that the new order would protect the safety of the people as well from foreign arms and influences "as from dangers of the *like kind* arising from domestic causes."[8]) That standing army would consist of the "purging of European prisons" and other "low ruffians." Although *Philadelphiensis* was vehemently opposed to a standing army, he had no objection to a navy. He took the position, rather, that a navy was all that was needed to protect the country from foreign aggression, a navy, that is to say, under the Confederation system, not one under the domination of the proposed new Congress.

The true strength of a political system, *Philadelphiensis* argued, lay in the combination of energy with freedom; national strength and liberty went hand in hand. Freedom and superiority were joined as one. The negative proof of this proposition was the example of the Turkish empire where despotism and slavery were joined. Since the proposed Constitution destroyed freedom, it would, therefore, also destroy national strength and energy, and reduce the population to Turkish slavery. He attacked Dr. Benjamin Rush, a Federalist member of the Pennsylvania ratifying convention and an advocate of the new Constitution, who had said that the adoption of the Constitution would "produce paleness and distress at the Court of St. James." In the estimation of *Philadelphiensis,* about half of the people of the country were against the proposed Constitution, and to impose it upon the dissenting half, if nine states should ratify, would, at the least, not be "prudent." This final destruction of the freedom of the people had been presaged by the actions of the Federalists in Pennsylvania in suppressing "dissent of the virtuous minority" in the Pennsylvania ratifying convention. (The Federalist managers of the Pennsylvania ratifying convention had ruled out of order, on the ground that it was too late, a petition by Antifederalists against the adoption of the new Constitution.)

The international theme was pursued further by *Philadelphiensis* in the first of the two letters he published in the *Gazeteer* in January 1788.[9] The issue was again the value of a navy and the relation between a navy and neutrality, but the discourse broadened into an attack upon the champions of the Constitution in class terms. *Philadelphiensis* said that a navy armed neutrality and protected it;

[8] *Federalist,* Number 3.
[9] The dates were January 10 and January 24, 1788.

and that if the United States were going to become a commercial power, it would certainly need a navy. Under the Confederation he admitted that the people had not delegated enough power to the Confederation Congress but he said, in extenuation, that the Confederation Congress had not even used the powers it had—it had never built a navy! Instead, the Confederation government had spent money on ambassadors and gifts and he asked, rhetorically, if the limited Confederation Congress had so acted, how much worse would things be under the proposed Constitution. All of this was said in a context of sardonic references to the "well born," and it concluded with the statement that under the new Constitution, "The poor working-man is not to be thought of except his work will add to the character and dignity of the lordling nobility."

By the end of January 1788, (if, indeed, not before) *Philadelphiensis* had aroused public curiosity about his identity. An attempt was made to provoke him into disclosing his identity by a writer using the name *Pennsylvania Mechanic* who said that *he* had left his real name with the printer, and urged others to do the same so that he could interview them. The *Mechanic* said that it was possible that they might convert him to the opposition against the Constitution, although it is doubtful that he believed this, or thought that his readers would. *Philadelphiensis* referred the *Pennsylvania Mechanic* (whom he suspected of being a blacksmith in the service of the "well born") to his first letter in the *Gazeteer.* He refused the *Mechanic*'s suggestion that he disclose his identity, said that the proposal was a trap, and that to comply with it would be to expose one's interest, property, and even life to the opposition. He repeated his earlier statement on the subject of voluntary disclosure; he was against it because it is only the argument that counts, and not its source.

By February 1788 the decibel level of the protest by *Philadelphiensis* had risen sharply and in that month he hammered at two major themes—the first, a familiar one, and the second, one that he had not agitated quite so vigorously, although, perhaps the more important of the two. The first was the danger of a military establishment, and the second was the nature of the presidency under the proposed system of government. His letter dated February 7, 1788 happened to be printed the day after Massachusetts had ratified the Constitution, following a hard debate in which the Antifederalist opposition had been promised that a bill of rights would be added to the Constitution, Massachusetts thereby becoming the sixth state to ratify.[10] (This news was obviously not available when the letter was written.) *Philadelphiensis* attacked the "aristocratics" as an "infernal junto of demagogues" who had perpetrated a conspiracy against the American people, the concert of "a few tyrants" whose "views are to lord it over the rest of their fellow citizens, to trample the poorer part of the people under their feet, that they may be rendered their servants and slaves."

But his hardest blows were laid on the presidency under the proposed Constitution. "Who can deny," he asked, "but the president general will be king to all intents and purposes, and one of the most dangerous kind too; a king elected to command a standing army?" The president he thought would be master of the Congress through the veto power if he were a man of spirit, and the Congress would thus be no check upon him. But if it were otherwise and the president should not be a man of enterprising spirit, he would become "the minion of the aristocratics, doing according to their will and pleasure, and confirming every law they may think proper to make, without any regard to their public utility." The idea of unlimited powers "lodged in so small a number of the well born, elevated so far above the rest of their fellow citizens, and supported by a king with a standing army" ought, he thought, to make the blood of a free citizen boil with indignation.

The Massachusetts vote, as has been indicated, took place after his letter was written, but he expressed some hope for rejection there that must have been sorely disappointed. He said,

> *If the state of Massachusetts should reject the proposed constitution, of which there is a strong probability, what a contemptible figure must its advocates make, who, after it made its appearance from the dark conclave, affirmed that there was* [sic] *but five men opposed to it in the United States. The convention of that state was chosen in the moment of blind enthusiasm, and yet we find it so much divided that the issue is doubtful. The sentiments of the people are changing every day, and were that convention to be elected now, I doubt not but four-fifths would be against it.*

He thought that the proposed system of government could never have been established over freemen except by surprise, and he rec-

[10] The others had been Delaware, December 7, 1787; Pennsylvania, December 12, 1787; New Jersey, December 18, 1787; Georgia, January 2, 1788; and Connecticut, January 9, 1788.

ommended that another general convention be called so that the grave questions of the fundamental distribution of power could be considered more deliberately and in full knowledge of all the issues.

The new theme of surprise and the need for greater deliberation was developed further in the second letter of *Philadelphiensis* in February 1788.[11] He asked, "If the proposed plan be a good one on the whole, why should its friends endeavour to prevent investigating its merits or defects? Why should they hurry it on us before we have even read it?" This was of course a little disingenuous since *Philadelphiensis* seemed to be quite familiar with the contents of the proposed Constitution, but he perhaps had good reason to protest the hurry-up tactics in Pennsylvania where, as he described it, the Federalists employed "bullies to drag some members of the Assembly per force to the House to make a quorum," in order to have it call a ratifying convention. But the major attack in the second letter of February 1788 centered again on the presidency and the flavor of the author's rhetoric may be appreciated in the following excerpt:

> *The President-general, who is to be our king after this government is established, is vested with powers exceeding those of the most despotic monarch we know of in modern times. What a handsome return have these men made to the people of America for their confidence! Through the misconduct of these bold conspirators we have lost the most glorious opportunity that any country ever had to establish a free system of government. America under one purely democratical, would be rendered the happiest and most powerful nation in the universe, but under the proposed one, composed of an elective king and a standing army, officered by his sycophants, the starvelings of the Cincinnati, and an aristocratical Congress of the well-born, an iota of happiness, freedom, or national strength cannot exist. What a pitiful figure these ungrateful men will make in history; who, for the hopes of obtaining some lucrative employment, or of receiving a little more homage from the rest of their fellow creatures, framed a system of oppression that must involve in its consequences the misery of their own off-spring?*

The results in Massachusetts had become known by the time *Philadelphiensis* wrote his letter of February 21, 1788. He found some solace in the closeness of the vote and noted that ratification had passed by only a majority of 19 votes although "through the influence of the tyrants of Boston" very little information had reached the people. The press had been of small help because it was, gener-

[11] The date of the second letter was February 21, 1788.

ally speaking, "devoted to the well-born and their tools." Getting a 19-vote majority out of a convention of almost 400 members, he concluded, was little better than a rejection. He attacked John Hancock as one of those who hoped to find superior distinctions in the new system, and was doubtless correct in his estimation of his character since the Federalists had made the same low estimate and flattered Hancock cynically to line him up in support of the Constitution.

Philadelphiensis published his eleventh letter in the *Gazeteer* on March 8, 1788 and his final one on April 11, 1788, and the difference of tone between them is quite remarkable, the first still full of fire and fury and the second modest and defensive. Between the two missives, he had himself been violently attacked in the pages of the *Gazeteer* with some evident effect upon his ardor. The March letter is one of the most closely argued and coherent of the twelve that he published, an appeal to the pocketbooks of Pennsylvanians who under the new system of government, he said, would suffer economically. The commonwealth had never been delinquent in its contributions to the general government but under the new one would stand on an equal footing with the most delinquent state of the Union. The argument was not really very substantial, although it was earnestly pressed. Pennsylvania would receive no credit for its generosity, he said, although just what credit it should have received was not made clear. Pennsylvania's generosity might even penalize it doubly in that future levies on Pennsylvania citizens would be proportionate to the exertions heretofore made. This argument was evidently founded on the constitutional provision that taxes should be uniform throughout the states. He was on surer ground in predicting that the Congress would tax to the utmost. But he was wrong to predict that the promised amendments in the form of a bill of rights would not issue from the new government as soon as it was established.

Three days after this letter, on March 11, 1788, the *Gazeteer* published a letter from *A.B.* to the "People of the United States." *Philadelphiensis,* who had cherished his anonymity, was identified as Benjamin Workman, "one of the well born tutors in the University of Pennsylvania." *A.B.* said that it had been only three years since Benjamin Workman had left his "vast estate in Ireland," but that this "citizen almost three years old" who did not own a foot of land in America was nevertheless telling people that the authors of the proposed Constitution were "a parcel of fools, villains, traitors, conspirators, despots'' and so on. The "people of the United States" were asked whether they had more confidence in George Washington and Benjamin Franklin than in Benjamin Workman.

A.B. also said that Workman was not alone in his agitation against the Constitution but that he and another, identified as "Peter Vandegelder," had joined forces in publishing the correspondence in the *Gazeteer.* So that the "people of the United States" would be sure to appreciate the baseness of these two critics of the Constitution, *A.B.* said that Vandegelder's landlord had thrown him out of his lodgings. Not only did Vandegelder presumably not own a foot of land, like his friend Workman; the matter was even worse—Vandegelder had been released from jail only a year before "by virtue of the insolvent act." Debtors like Vandegelder and people like Workman who did not own a foot of land were obviously trashy people when compared with George Washington and Benjamin Franklin, and *A.B.* suggested that, since the University of Pennsylvania now knew who *Philadelphiensis* was, they might wish to discharge him from his employment there.

Three days after *A.B.*'s letter was printed, there was an answer from one "Peter Van Galder" (March 14, 1788). He identified *A.B.* as Francis Hopkinson,[12] and protested the malice evident in *A.B.*'s attack upon him. He did not say that Workman *was Philadelphiensis,* but he did say that he and Workman had indeed been working together. They had sat up together, he said, many nights "until ten or eleven o'clock" correcting a new edition of Gough's *Arithmetic,* and a new system of "Gauging," both of which were in press. He expressed strong resentment against Hopkinson's slurs upon his character and said that he himself had been a soldier in the Revolution. As to his economic status, he argued that "all freemen are equally dear to the commonwealth."

On March 21, 1788, fresh attack upon *Philadelphiensis* came from another quarter, this time from a writer who signed himself *Probus* and who had written in the *Federal Gazette* that *Philadelphiensis* had been an embezzler abroad who had been forced to flee to America. In the *Gazeteer* of March 21, he presented a dismaying list of the moral and other shortcomings of which the object of his malice was guilty. He accused him of spending £1,000 in a mead house, of stealing a dead ox, and of committing outrages (unnamed) on the

[12] Listed by Clinton Rossiter, *1787: The Grand Convention* (New York, 1966), p. 35, along with Thomas Jefferson, Noah Webster, and others as one of the "hopeful proofs of genius" of the period.

highway. He was accused also of having had a twenty-fifth wife while the first twenty-four were still alive, but said that he had been pardoned for this transgression because of his youth, he being sixteen years old at the time. *Probus* accused *Philadelphiensis* further of having attacked and robbed a regiment of footguards of a month's pay (presumably abroad), a deed that certainly puts to shame the puny accomplishments of the James boys and the Dalton brothers at a later time.

Philadelphiensis then went into banking in London, according to *Probus,* and had failed there, with coffers full (presumably fraudulent bankruptcy). When his fraud was discovered, he then went to Cork and set sail in an East India ship that he had seized in Cork harbor and went to France. He sold the ship to Jews in Bordeaux and set himself up as an Irish baronet, but his deception was uncovered, although it is not said how this was done. His pretensions exposed, he then went to the waterside, plundered the King's custom house of about £100,000 in dollars, and agreed with the captain of an Irish cutter to give him half of the loot to help him escape. The cutter, however, was wrecked on the Lizard and *Philadelphiensis* had to travel to London on foot with no money. However severe these straits, one surely could count on the resourcefulness of a man capable of attacking and robbing a regiment of footguards and plundering the King's custom house, and *Probus* did not disappoint the expectations of his readers. Penniless on the road to London, *Philadelphiensis,* said *Probus,* was "constrained" to make an attack on the King's carriage surrounded by 500 guards, wounding the King. His fantastic luck seems to have left him at this point, for *Probus* merely says that he was then thrown into limbo.

The answer of *Philadelphiensis* to this melodramatic account of his alleged delinquencies was that he could not answer until *Probus* had proved his charges. He did not admit that Benjamin Workman was *Philadelphiensis. Probus* never proved his charges. *Philadelphiensis* did attack Francis Hopkinson, however, in a letter dated March 26, 1788. Or, rather, "Benjamin Workman" attacked Hopkinson, still without admitting any connection with *Philadelphiensis.* He charged Hopkinson with making scurrilous accusations. The gravamen of Hopkinson's complaint, said Workman, amounted to this—that one in America scarcely four years, and a humble tutor at the University of Pennsylvania, should not be so above himself as to write about politics. "Benjamin Workman" thought that in so saying, Hopkinson showed that he did not really understand freedom.

In this answer to Francis Hopkinson the tone of "Benjamin Workman" was very moderate, not at all in the extravagant mode of the earlier arguments of *Philadelphiensis* against the Federalists, and he did not expatiate on the reasons that supported the conclusion that Hopkinson did not understand freedom, but one can surmise what they might have been. Freedom is a universal principle and at the level of principle, it is of no consequence that the speaker is poor or newly arrived, nor that he does not own a foot of land. Freedom is not the prerogative of the well-born and the landed, those with an economic stake in the outcome of public policies. Indeed it is of no consequence, as *Philadelphiensis* had said twice, that the speaker had any kind of personal identification at all; it was the merit of the argument that counted, and *ad hominem* attacks were rhetorical devices to invite the listener's allegiance on grounds having nothing to do with the merits of the argument.

That *Philadelphiensis* was thrown on the defensive by the oratorical fouls committed against him by Francis Hopkinson and *Probus* is evident in Benjamin Workman's last letter in the unhappy exchange. This appeared in the *Gazeteer* of April 1, 1788 and was an extension of his remarks in the letter of March 26. The letter appeared over the signature of Benjamin Workman (as had that of March 26) and it attacked Hopkinson again for scurrility. But by this time, the writer gave evidence that he had been deeply hurt by the vicious assault upon him in the previous three weeks. He said that he (Workman) had benefited America more than any other man in the profession he followed, that of teacher. He said that he taught navigation, lunar observations, and other maritime skills to scores of students (one hundred ten persons, he said).[13] Of this number, some seventy or so were already aboard sailing ships as officers, and among these were fifteen captains. There is something a little pathetic in this defense that he (Workman) was a worthwhile fellow even though he was newly arrived from abroad and did not own a foot of land in America. He pleaded merit against class, and valued contribution higher than status, surely two themes that were more prophetic of the America

[13] This is internal evidence that Workman and *Philadelphiensis* were the same. A tutor of navigation, lunar observations, and other maritime skills might have a professional interest in a navy for which *Philadelphiensis* had argued so passionately.

that was to become a place of opportunity for the penniless than the sour crabbedness of a Francis Hopkinson, who measured the quality of men by the property they held.

The following letter is the last that *Philadelphiensis* (he never did admit to being Benjamin Workman) published in the *Gazeteer* on the subject of the Constitution. It is obviously a summary statement, in which he renews his warning about the concentration of power that the Constitution placed in the presidency:

My Fellow Citizens,

The essays under the signature of Philadelphiensis are represented as without argument, and their prime object is said to be to involve this devoted country in a civil war. But time, the discoverer of future events, will certainly show that the calling another Federal Convention is the only rational way to prevent it. Heaven grant that these eyes may never behold that dreadful scene. The writer of these essays was actuated by the purest motives, namely, to defend the liberty and advance the happiness of his fellow citizens. These he conceived insecure, or rather destroyed, if the proposed constitution should be established, and hence he labored to procure another Convention. The expediency of this measure was demonstrated by illustrating the principal defects in the proposed system; —defects did I say—the expression is too soft—the ruin that must follow its adoption.

If pointing out the unlimited powers of the new Congress over the lives and property of their fellow citizens, which may and certainly would be abused, be not an argument against it, there remains no fixed determinate idea to be annexed to the term argument; indeed, on such principles right and wrong, freedom and slavery have no essential difference, and the human mind is a mere chaos.

Some feeble attempts have been made by the advocates of this system of tyranny, to answer the objections made to the smallness of the number of representatives and senators, and the improper powers delegated to them; but, as far as I recollect, no one has been found bold enough to stand forth in defense of that dangerous and uncontrouled officer, the President General, or more properly, our new KING.

A few pieces under the signature of an American Citizen *were published immediately after the Constitution broke the shell, and the hydra made its way from the dark conclave into the open light; in the first number of which the writer, in touching on the President, endeavoured to conceal his immense powers, by representing the King of Great-Britain as possessed of many hereditary prerogatives, rights and powers that he was not possessed of; that is, he shows what he is not, but neglects to show what he really is; but so flimsey a palliative could scarcely escape the censure of the most ignorant advocate for such an officer; and since we hear of no further attempts to prove the necessity of a King being set over the freemen of America.*

The writer of these essays has clearly proven, that the president is a King to all intents and purposes, and at the same time one of the most dangerous kind too—an elective King, the commander in chief of a standing army, etc., and to these add, that he has a negative over the proceedings of both branches of the legislature: and to complete his uncontrouled sway, he is neither restrained nor assisted by a privy council, which is a novelty in government. I challenge the politicians of the whole continent to find in any period of history a monarch more absolute.

Who is so base as not to burn with resentment against the conspirators, who have dared to establish such a tyrant over his life, his liberty and property? Is the flame of sacred liberty so entirely extinguished in the American breast as not to be kindled again? No; you mistaken despots, do not let such a preposterous thought madden you into perseverance, lest your persons fall sacrifices to the resentment of an injured country. Stop at once, and join the rest of your fellow citizens. Let another Convention be immediately called, and let a system of government fitted to the pure principles of the Revolution, be framed. Then a general amnesty among all ranks and degrees of your fellow citizens must succeed, and America become the seat of liberty, peace, friendship and happiness; and her government have ample energy and respectability among the nations of the earth; yes, she will thereby be rendered the great arbiter of the world.[14]

Philadelphiensis, No. XII

Philadelphiensis was obviously wrong to think that there would be a civil war in his time unless another Federal Convention were called, but he was right in feeling that there was a civil war potential in the ambiguities of the Constitution about the role of the states within the new Union, a potentiality that became four years of bloody war in 1861. Of all his previous arguments against the Constitution, the one to which he adverted in his last piece was the concentration of powers in the presidency and in this, in ways he could not have imagined, he was correct for several reasons, although some of his were wrong. The existence of the veto power and the absence of a privy council had nothing to do with the eventual concentration of presidential power—what later historians called "imperial presidency"—but the military power of the President as commander-in-

[14] *The Independent Gazeteer* or *The Chronicle of Freedom,* Volume VII, Number 727, April 11, 1788.

chief did. Despite the disclaimers of *An American Citizen* that the president had inherent powers—unlike the King of Great Britain—doctrines of inherent power in the presidency and the virtually uncontrolled use of the military justification, produced the American misadventure in Vietnam in the 1960s and the constitutional crisis connected with Watergate in the 1970s. *Philadelphiensis* would certainly have recognized in 1975 a close resemblance between the president-king he denounced in 1788 and the president-king who abdicated in August of 1974.

Charles A. Beard

AN ECONOMIC INTERPRETATION OF THE CONSTITUTION

Until the twentieth century, a Federalist conservative interpretation of the origins of the Constitution and its ratification had prevailed. But the work of Charles Beard, An Economic Interpretation of the Constitution, *published in 1913, radically changed the conventional view, and became the standard interpretation among American historians for over forty years. Beard's general thesis was that the men of the Convention had important economic interests to protect and that they met in Philadelphia to devise a system of government that would do so. His special thesis was that significant numbers of the Framers owned personalty in the form of public bonds and notes and that this interest explained their concern to replace the Confederation Government with one that would not only secure their investments but enhance them.*

The idea was a shocking one to the contemporaries of Charles Beard, although the notion that much political activity could be explained in terms of economic interest had been a familiar one at least since the time of James Harrington, the seventeenth-century Englishman, whose Oceana *had maintained that the real basis of political power was property, especially landed property; and, of course, James Madison, who had said that the most durable cause of faction was the unequal distribution of property. But Beard was not professing abstract principle; he was talking about sanctified figures of American history, men canonized by American historiography, invested by admiring writers with super-normal attributes of selflessness and dedication, free of ulteriority.*

Certain events had prepared the way for Beard's new and more critical appraisal, and made it plausible in his time. The Progressive movement in the early years of the twentieth century was a reaction to a business ethic that had come to dominate law and politics in the thirty-five years after the Civil War, an ethic that exalted self-interest as the principal agent of social change, celebrated it as the source of all material good in a remarkably productive new industrial system, and invested it with the authority of Natural Law. The new economic system did indeed lead to the enormous capital development of the country and then to a lavish production of an abundance of goods, but at a great social cost to workers, women and children in factories, small farmers, the frequently unemployed, and to decent government. The Progressive movement was a reform movement whose supporters were repelled by the grossness of greed, and who acted to lay legislative and other political curbs and restraints upon its most malign

From *An Economic Interpretation of the Constitution of the United States* by Charles A. Beard, copyright 1935 by The Macmillan Company. Reprinted by permission of The Macmillan Company, publishers.

effects. It was in the spirit of the Progressive movement that An Economic Interpretation of the Constitution *was written.*

The material that follows is taken from two sections of Beard's famous book. The section titled "The Economic Interests of the Members of the Convention" is to be found in Chapter 5 and the material titled "The Political Doctrines of the Members of the Convention" is taken from Chapter 7.

The Economic Interests of the Members of the Convention

A survey of the economic interests of the members of the Convention presents certain conclusions:

A majority of the members were lawyers by profession.

Most of the members came from towns, on or near the coast, that is, from the regions in which personalty was largely concentrated.

Not one member represented in his immediate personal economic interests the small farming or mechanic classes.

The overwhelming majority of members, at least five-sixths, were immediately, directly, and personally interested in the outcome of their labors at Philadelphia, and were to a greater or less extent economic beneficiaries from the adoption of the Constitution.

1. Public security interests were extensively represented in the Convention. Of the fifty-five members who attended no less than forty appear on the Records of the Treasury Department for sums varying from a few dollars up to more than one hundred thousand dollars. Among the minor holders were Bassett, Blount, Brearley, Broom, Butler, Carroll, Few, Hamilton, L. Martin, Mason, Mercer, Mifflin, Read, Spaight, Wilson, and Wythe. Among the larger holders (taking the sum of about $5,000 as the criterion) were Baldwin, Blair, Clymer, Dayton, Ellsworth, Fitzsimons, Gilman, Gerry, Gorham, Jenifer, Johnson, King, Langdon, Lansing, Livingston,[1] McClurg, R. Morris, C. C. Pinckney, C. Pinckney, Randolph, Sherman, Strong, Washington, and Williamson.

It is interesting to note that, with the exception of New York, and possibly Delaware, each state had one or more prominent representatives in the Convention who held more than a negligible amount of securities, and who could therefore speak with feeling and authority on the question of providing in the new Constitution for the full discharge of the public debt:

[1] Livingston's holdings are problematical.

Langdon and Gilman, of New Hampshire.

Gerry, Strong, and King, of Massachusetts.

Ellsworth, Sherman, and Johnson, of Connecticut.

Hamilton, of New York. Although he held no large amount personally, he was the special pleader for the holders of public securities and the maintenance of public faith.

Dayton, of New Jersey.

Robert Morris, Clymer, and Fitzsimons, of Pennsylvania.

Mercer and Carroll, of Maryland.

Blair, McClurg, and Randolph, of Virginia.

Williamson, of North Carolina.

The two Pinckneys, of South Carolina.

Few and Baldwin, of Georgia.

2. Personalty invested in lands for speculation was represented by at least fourteen members: Blount, Dayton, Few, Fitzsimons, Franklin, Gilman, Gerry, Gorham, Hamilton, Mason, R. Morris, Washington, Williamson, and Wilson.

3. Personalty in the form of money loaned at interest was represented by at least twenty-four members: Bassett, Broom, Butler, Carroll, Clymer, Davie, Dickinson, Ellsworth, Few, Fitzsimons, Franklin, Gilman, Ingersoll, Johnson, King, Langdon, Mason, McHenry, C. C. Pinckney, C. Pinckney, Randolph, Read, Washington, and Williamson.

4. Personalty in mercantile, manufacturing, and shipping lines was represented by at least eleven members: Broom, Clymer, Ellsworth, Fitzsimons, Gerry, King, Langdon, McHenry, Mifflin, G. Morris, and R. Morris.

5. Personalty in slaves was represented by at least fifteen members: Butler, Davie, Jenifer, A. Martin, L. Martin, Mason, Mercer, C. C. Pinckney, C. Pinckney, Randolph, Reed, Rutledge, Spaight, Washington, and Wythe.

It cannot be said, therefore, that the members of the Convention were "disinterested." On the contrary, we are forced to accept the profoundly significant conclusion that they knew through their personal experiences in economic affairs the precise results which the new government that they were setting up was designed to attain. As a group of doctrinaires, like the Frankfort assembly of 1848, they would have failed miserably; but as practical men they were able to build the new government upon the only foundations which could be stable: fundamental economic interests.[2]

The Political Doctrines of the Members of the Convention

It is now interesting to inquire whether the members of the Convention at large entertained substantially identical views as to the political science of the system. There are several difficulties in the way of such an investigation. Not all of the delegates, indeed not all of the most influential, were speech-makers or writers or philosophers. As intensely practical men they were concerned with tangible results, not with the manner in which political scientists might view the details of their operations. There is, accordingly, a considerable danger of attempting too much in making generalizations, and to obviate this as far as possible, the method of taking the members in alphabetical order is adopted, and the evidence of the views entertained by each is fully documented.[3]

The leaders in politics and political philosophy in the eighteenth century were not far removed from that frank recognition of class rights which characterized English society, and they were not under the necessity of obscuring—at least to the same extent as modern partisan writers—the essential economic antagonisms featuring in law and constitution-making. Their clarity of thought was greatly facilitated by the disfranchisement of the propertyless, which made it unnecessary for political writers to address themselves to the proletariat and to explain dominant group interests in such a manner as to make them appear in the garb of "public policy."

There does not appear, of course, in the writings of American political scientists in the eighteenth century, that sharp recognition of class rights which characterizes the feudal legists, because within the propertied interests politically represented in the government, there were divisions which had to be glossed over; and there were also mutterings of unrest on the part of the disfranchised which later broke out in the storm that swept away the property qualifications on voters and introduced political equalitarianism. Under these cir-

[2] The fact that a few members of the Convention, who had considerable economic interests at stake, refused to support the Constitution does not invalidate the general conclusions here presented. In the cases of Yates, Lansing, Luther Martin, and Mason, definite economic reasons for their action are forthcoming; but this is a minor detail.
[3] A few whose views were not ascertained are omitted.

cumstances the supporters of the Constitution had to be somewhat circumspect in the expression of their views; but, happily for science, the proceedings at Philadelphia during the drafting of the Constitution were secret, and they were able to discuss with utmost frankness the actual politico-economic results which they desired to reach. Fortunately, also, fragmentary reports of these proceedings have come down to us, and have been put in a definitive form by Professor Farrand.

Abraham Baldwin, of Georgia, did not indulge in any lengthy disquisitions on government in the Convention, and his literary remains are apparently very meager. However, his view that the Senate of the United States ought to represent property came out in the debate on June 29, over a motion by Ellsworth to the effect that the "rule of suffrage in the second branch be the same as that established by the Articles of Confederation." Baldwin immediately opposed the proposition, saying, "He thought the second branch ought to be the representation of property, and that in forming it therefore some reference ought to be had to the relative wealth of their constituents, and to the principles on which the senate of Massachusetts was constituted."[4] At the time the senate of that commonwealth rested upon special freehold and personalty qualifications, and the members were apportioned among the several districts on the basis of the amount of taxes paid by each. It is thus apparent that Baldwin wished the Senate of the new government to be based frankly upon property.

Gunning Bedford, of Delaware, did not participate extensively in the debates of the Convention, but it seems from the character of the few remarks that he made that he favored a more democratic form than was finally adopted, although he signed the Constitution. This inference is drawn from a brief notice of his objection to the establishment of a council of revision composed of the executive and a certain number of the judiciary to exercise a sort of censorship over the acts of Congress. Madison records as follows:

> *Mr. Bedford was opposed to every check on the Legislative, even the Council of Revision first proposed. He thought it would be sufficient to mark out in the Constitution the boundaries to the Legislative Authority, which would give all the requisite security to the rights of the other departments. The Representatives of the People were the best judges of what was for their interest, and ought to be under no external controul*

[4] Farrand, *Records,* Vol. I, p. 469.

> *whatever. The two branches would produce a sufficient controul within the Legislature itself.*[5]

Jacob Broom was among those who wished to "lessen the dependence of the general government on the people," to use Jefferson's phrase, by lengthening the terms of public officers. He seconded Read's motion to increase the term of Senators to nine years;[6] he opposed the election of the executive by popular vote, and supported Luther Martin's resolution in favor of election by electors appointed by the legislatures of the several states;[7] he wished to give life tenure to the executive, that is, during good behavior,[8] and he favored the suggestion that Congress should be given a negative over state legislatures.[9] Broom seldom spoke in the Convention, but there is no doubt that he believed in a restricted and well "balanced" democracy.

Pierce Butler, of South Carolina, on more than one occasion urged the desirability of making property at least one of the elements in the distribution of representation. On June 6, when Charles Pinckney moved that the lower house of the national legislature should be chosen by the state legislatures and not by the people, Butler said:

> *I am against determining the mode of election until the ratio of representation is fixed—if that proceeds on a principle favorable to wealth as well as numbers of free inhabitants, I am content to unite with Delaware (Mr. Read) in abolishing the state legislatures and becoming one nation instead of a confederation of republics.*[10]

In connection with a discussion of the Senate, "he urged that the second branch ought to represent the states according to their property."[11] Later in the sessions of the Convention, he again "warmly urged the justice and necessity of regarding wealth in the apportionment of representation."[12] He was also particularly solicitous about slave property, and he declared that "the security which the

[5] Ibid., Vol. I, p. 100.
[6] Ibid., Vol. I, p. 421.
[7] Ibid., Vol. II, p. 32.
[8] Ibid., Vol. II, p. 33.
[9] Ibid., Vol. II, p. 390.
[10] Ibid., Vol. I, p. 144.
[11] Ibid., p. 529.
[12] Ibid., p. 562.

southern states want is that their Negroes may not be taken from them."[13]

Daniel Carroll favored the popular election of the executive, but he advocated a three-fourths vote in Congress to overcome the executive veto. Speaking on this point, "He remarked that as a majority was now to be the quorum, seventeen in the larger and eight in the smaller house might carry points. The advantage that might be taken of this seemed to call for greater impediments to improper laws."[14] Carroll did not indulge in any philosophic reflections in the Convention so that his "political science," if he had worked out any definite system, is not apparent in the records.

George Clymer entertained the notions of government which were common to the Federalists of his time. He held that "a representative of the people is appointed to think *for* and not *with* his constituents";[15] and invariably, during the course of his career, he "showed a total disregard to the opinions of his constituents when opposed to the matured decisions of his own mind." It was on these principles that he "warmly opposed the proposition introducing a clause in the Constitution which conferred upon the people the unalienable right of instructing their representatives."[16]

W. R. Davie, although he is reputed to have been an accomplished orator and profound student, does not figure extensively in Madison's meager records. At no point does he expound any philosophy of government. His views were always practical. On the proposition to count slaves in apportioning representation, he threw down the gauntlet to the Convention, and declared that if the rate was not at least three-fifths, North Carolina would not federate.[17] As to the basis of government Davie "seemed to think that wealth or property ought to be represented in the second branch; and numbers in the first branch."[18]

Davie fully understood the significance of the obligation of contract clause which was designed as a check on the propensities of popular legislatures to assault private rights in property, particularly personalty. Speaking in the convention of North Carolina on this clause, he said: "That section is the best in the Constitution. It is

[13] Ibid., p. 605.
[14] Ibid., Vol. II, p. 300.
[15] John Sanderson, *Biography,* p. 168.
[16] Ibid., p. 169.
[17] Farrand, *Records,* Vol. I, p. 593.
[18] Ibid., Vol. I, p. 542.

founded on the strongest principles of justice. It is a section, in short, which I thought would have endeared the Constitution to this country."[19] Davie undoubtedly understood and approved the doctrines of balanced classes in the government, as expounded in Adams's *Defence of American Constitutions*.[20]

At no time does Davie appear to have courted popular favor in his native state, for a writer speaking of his candidacy for the legislature in 1798 says:

> *The "true Whigs," as they styled themselves, dined together under the oaks and toasted Mr. Jefferson. The other party, who were called "aristocrats," ate and drank in the house on entirely different principles. General Davie dined in the house with the "aristocrats." The "true Whigs" took offence at this and resolved to oppose his selection, and it was only with much address that they were kept quiet. . . . If any person had had the impudence to dispute the election, General Davie would certainly not have been returned. The rabble, which in all places is the majority, would have voted against him.*[21]

John Dickinson, of Delaware, frankly joined that minority which was outspoken in its belief in a monarchy—an action that comported with his refusal to sign the Declaration of Independence and his reluctance to embark upon the stormy sea of Revolution. At the very opening of the Convention, on June 2, he expressed his preference for a regal government, although he admitted that the existing state of affairs would not permit its establishment in America. Madison records him as saying:

> *A limited Monarchy he considered as one of the best Governments in the world. It was not certain that the same blessings were derivable from any other form. It was certain that equal blessings had never yet been derived from any of the republican form. A limited monarchy, however, was out of the question.*[22]

Dickinson was also among the members of the Convention who wished to establish a property qualification for voters because he thought no other foundation for government would be secure. In the debate on this subject on August 7, according to Madison's notes:

[19] Ibid., Vol. III, p. 350.
[20] McRee, *Life and Correspondence of James Iredell*, Vol. II, pp. 161, 168.
[21] Peele, *Lives of Distinguished North Carolinians*, p. 75. Davie's great collection of papers was destroyed in Sherman's raid. Ibid., p. 78.
[22] Farrand, *Records*, Vol. I, p. 86.

Mr. Dickinson had a very different idea of the tendency of vesting the right of suffrage in the freeholders of the Country. He considered them as the best guardians of liberty; And the restriction of the right to them as a necessary defence agst. the dangerous influence of those multitudes without property & without principle, with which our Country like all others, will in time abound. As to the unpopularity of the innovation it was in his opinion chimerical. The great mass of our Citizens is composed at this time of freeholders, and will be pleased with it.[23]

According to King's notes:

Dickinson—It is said yr. restraining by ye Constitution the rights of Election to Freeholders, is a step towards aristocracy—is this true, No.—we are safe by trusting the owners of the soil—the Owners of the Country—it will not be unpopular—because the Freeholders are the most numerous at this Time—The Danger to Free Governments has not been from Freeholders, but those who are not Freeholders—there is no Danger—because our Laws favor the Division of property—The Freehold will be parcelled among all the worthy men in the State—The Merchants & Mechanicks are safe—They may become Freeholders besides they are represented in ye State Legislatures, which elect the Senate of the U.S.[24]

No member of the Convention distrusted anything savoring of "levelling democracy" more than *Oliver Ellsworth.* Later as Chief Justice he denounced from the bench Jefferson and the French party as "the apostles of anarchy, bloodshed, and atheism."[25] In the Convention, he opposed the popular election of the President[26] and favored associating the judges with the executive in the exercise of a veto power over acts of Congress.[27] He believed in the restriction of the suffrage to those who paid taxes.[28] He was a warm advocate of judicial control, in general, and thoroughly understood the political significance of the system.[29]

Thomas Fitzsimons, the wealthy merchant and stockbroker from Pennsylvania, was, after his kind, not a loquacious man, but rather a man of action—a practical man; and the records of the Convention contain no lengthy speech by him. When Gouverneur Morris, on August 7, proposed to restrain the right to vote to freeholders, Fitz-

[23] Ibid., Vol. II, p. 202.
[24] Ibid., Vol. II, p. 207.
[25] H. J. Ford, *Rise and Growth of American Politics,* p. 113.
[26] Farrand, *Records,* Vol. II, pp. 57, 58, 63, 101, 108, 111.
[27] Ibid., Vol. II, p. 73.
[28] Ibid., Vol. II, p. 207.
[29] Beard, *The Supreme Court and the Constitution,* pp. 71–72.

simons seconded the motion, apparently without saying anything on the point.[30] While he thus sympathized with the movement to set the Constitution frankly on a property basis, Fitzsimons was naturally more interested in such matters as protection to manufactures and harbor improvements.[31]

Benjamin Franklin, who at the time of the Convention was so advanced in years as to be of little real weight in the formation of the Constitution, seems to have entertained a more hopeful view of democracy than any other member of that famous group. He favored a single-chambered legislature,[32] opposed an absolute veto in the executive,[33] and resisted the attempt to place property qualifications on the suffrage.[34] He signed the Constitution when it was finished, but he was accounted by his contemporaries among the doubters, and was put forward by the opponents of ratification in Pennsylvania as a candidate for the state convention, but was defeated.[35]

Elbridge Gerry, of Massachusetts, participated extensively in the debates of the Convention, but his general view of government was doubtless stated in his speech on May 31, when he expressed himself as not liking the election of members of the lower house by popular vote. He said on this point:

> *The evils we experience flow from the excess of democracy. The people do not want virtue; but are the dupes of pretended patriots. In Massts. it has been fully confirmed by experience that they are daily misled into the most baneful measures and opinions by the false reports circulated by designing men, and which no one on the spot can refute. One principal evil arises from the want of due provision for those employed in the administration of Governnt. It would seem to be a maxim of democracy to starve the public servants. He mentioned the popular clamour in Massts. for the reduction of salaries and the attack made on that of the Govr. though secured by the spirit of the Constitution itself. He had, he said, been too republican heretofore: he was still, however, republican, but had been taught by experience the danger of the levelling spirit.*[36]

When the proposition that Senators should be elected by the state legislatures was up for consideration,

[30] Farrand, *Records,* Vol. II, p. 201.
[31] Ibid., pp. 362, 529, 589.
[32] Ibid., Vol. I, p. 48; Vol. III, p. 297.
[33] Ibid., Vol. I, pp. 94, 99.
[34] Ibid., Vol. II, p. 204.
[35] Scharf and Wescott, *History of Philadelphia,* Vol. I, p. 447.
[36] Farrand, *Records,* Vol. I, p. 48.

> *Mr. Gerry insisted that the commercial and monied interest wd. be more secure in hands of the State Legislatures, than of the people at large. The former have more sense of character, and will be restrained by that from injustice. The people are for paper money when the Legislatures are agst. it. Massts. the County Conventions had declared a wish for a depreciating paper that wd. sink itself. Besides, in some States there are two Branches in the Legislature, one of which is somewhat aristocratic. There wd. therefore be so far a better chance of refinement in the choice.*[37]

Nicholas Gilman was by temper and interest a man of affairs, more concerned with the stability of public securities and the development of western land schemes than with political theorizing. From Madison's record he does not appear to have said anything in the Convention.

Nathaniel Gorham was opposed to property qualifications on the suffrage in the federal Constitution and the association of the judiciary with the executive in the exercise of the veto power.[38] Speaking on the latter point, however, he said,

> *All agree that a check on the legislature is necessary. But there are two objections against admitting the judges to share in it which no observations on the other side seem to obviate. The 1st is that the judges ought to carry into the exposition of the laws no prepossessions with regard to them; 2d that as the judges will outnumber the executive, the revisionary check would be thrown entirely out of the executive hands, and instead of enabling him to defend himself would enable the judges to sacrifice him.*

Alexander Hamilton had a profound admiration for the British constitution. "The House of Lords," he said in the Convention, "is a noble institution. Having nothing to hope for by a change and a sufficient interest by means of their property, in being faithful to the national interest, they form a permanent barrier against every pernicious innovation whether attempted on the part of the Crown or of the Commons."[39] Doubtless his maturely considered system of government was summed up in the following words:

> *All communities divide themselves into the few and the many. The first are the rich and well born, the other the mass of the people. The voice of the people has been said to be the voice of God; and however generally*

[37] Ibid., Vol. I, p. 154.
[38] Ibid., Vol. II, p. 122 and pp. 73–79.
[39] Ibid., Vol. I, p. 288.

> *this maxim has been quoted and believed, it is not true in fact. The people are turbulent and changing; they seldom judge or determine right. Give therefore to the first class a distinct, permanent share in the government. They will check the unsteadiness of the second, and as they cannot receive any advantage by a change, they therefore will ever maintain good government. Can a democratic assembly who annually revolve in the mass of the people, be supposed steadily to pursue the public good? Nothing but a permanent body can check the imprudence of democracy. . . . It is admitted that you cannot have a good executive upon a democratic plan.*[40]

In consonance with these principles Hamilton outlined his scheme of government which included an assembly to consist of persons elected for three years by popular vote, a senate chosen for life or during good behavior by electors chosen by the voters, and a president also elected for life or during good behavior by electors chosen by the voters. The Convention failed to adopt his program, and he entertained a rather uncertain view of the Constitution as it was finally drafted, doubting its stability and permanency.

William Houstoun, of Georgia, seems to have spoken only once or twice; but he gave an indication of his political science in a remark which he made to the effect that the Georgia constitution "was a very bad one, and he hoped it would be revised and amended."[41] The constitution to which he alludes was the radical instrument made in 1777, which provided for a legislature with a single chamber and an unusually wide extension of the suffrage.

Jared Ingersoll, in spite of his great abilities as a student and lawyer, seems to have taken no part at all in the debates of the Convention. Such at least is the view to which Madison's records lead. Something is known, however, of the political principles which he entertained. Though he became intimately associated with President Reed on his migration to Philadelphia in 1778, he never accepted the extreme democratic principles embodied in the constitution of that state in 1776.[42] His biographer, after making an exception of Ingersoll's services in the Convention, says:

> *I am not aware that he held or sought a position in any popular or representative body whatever. He was what is called conservative in politics; that is to say, he was not by constitutional temper a rebuilder or*

[40] Ibid., Vol. I, pp. 299 ff.
[41] Ibid., Vol. II, p. 48.
[42] H. Binney, *Leaders of the Old Bar of Philadelphia,* p. 86.

> *reconstructor of anything that had been once reasonably well built; nor was his favorite order of political architecture, the democratic. After the great subversion in 1801 he was found as rarely as anybody in Pennsylvania on the side of the majority. He was known to be inclined to the contrary, so far that with or without his consent he was selected in that state, in the year 1812, as the opposition or anti-Madisonian candidate for the office of Vice-President of the United States.*[43]

Rufus King correctly understood the idea of a balanced government independent of "popular whims" and endowed with plenty of strength. He favored a long term for the President, and speaking on the executive department in the Convention he

> *expressed his apprehensions that an extreme caution in favor of liberty might enervate the government we were forming. He wished the house to recur to the primitive axiom that the three great departments of governments should be separate and independent: that the executive and the judiciary should be so, as well as the legislative: that the executive should be equally so with the judiciary. . . . He* [the executive] *ought not to be impeachable unless he hold his office during good behavior, a tenure which would be most agreeable to him; provided an independent and effectual forum could be devised; But under no circumstances ought he to be impeachable by the legislature. This would be destructive of his independence and of the principles of the constitution. He relied on the vigor of the executive as a great security for the public liberties.*[44]

King also believed in the principle of judicial control—that most effective check on the popular attacks on property through legislatures.[45]

It was largely on King's initiative that the prohibition against interference with contracts was placed in the Constitution.[46]

William Livingston took a middle ground between the "high-toned" system of John Adams and the simple democracy of such writers as "Centinel" of Pennsylvania. *The Defence of the Constitutions* he impatiently characterized as "rubbage"; and a "Humiliating and mortifying acknowledgement that man is incapable of governing himself." But for the opposite party that would set up a simple democratic government through legislative majorities, Livingston had just as little patience.

[43] Ibid., p. 87.
[44] Farrand, *Records,* Vol. II, p. 66.
[45] Beard, *The Supreme Court and the Constitution,* p. 29.
[46] Farrand, *Records,* Vol. II, p. 439.

> *The security of the liberties of a people or state depends wholly on a proper delegation of power. The several component powers of government should be so distributed that no one man, or body of men, should possess a larger share thereof than what is absolutely necessary for the administration of government. . . . The people ever have been and ever will be unfit to retain the exercise of power in their own hands; they must of necessity delegate it somewhere. . . . But it has been found from experience that a government by representation, consisting of a single house of representatives, is in some degree liable to the same inconveniences which attend a pure democracy; a few leading men influence the majority to pass laws calculated not for the public good, but to promote some sinister views of their own. To prevent this, another representative branch is added: these two separate houses form mutual checks upon each other; but this expedient has not been found to be altogether effectual. If the legislative power, even tho' vested in two distinct houses is left without any controul, they will inevitably encroach upon the executive and judicial; . . . But further, as prejudices always prevail, more or less, in all popular governments, it is necessary that a check be placed somewhere in the hands of a power not immediately dependent upon the breath of the people, in order to stem the torrent, and prevent the mischiefs which blind passions and rancorous prejudices might otherwise occasion. The executive and judicial powers should of course then be vested with this check or controul on the legislature; and that they may be enabled fully to effect this beneficial purpose, they should be rendered as independent as possible. . . . Tho' it is so short a time since our governments have been put in motion, yet examples have not been wanting of the prevalence of this dangerous thirst after more power in some of our legislatures; a negative therefore lodged in the hands of the executive and judicial powers, is absolutely necessary in order that they may be able to defend themselves from the encroachments of the legislature.*[47]

Livingston thought that there were some grave defects in the Constitution as drafted at Philadelphia and proposed some emendations. He believed that the President should enjoy the appointing power without any control by the Senate; he thought the Chief Justice should hold office during good behavior and be empowered to appoint his colleagues; and he further held that the President, the Chief Justice, and a superintendent of Finance should be organized into a council of revision to pass upon the acts of Congress.

[47] *Observations on Government, Including Some Animadversions on Mr. Adams's Defence of the Constitutions of Government of the United States of America,* etc., published in 1787, by Livingston, under the pen-name of "A Farmer of New Jersey." The pamphlet is sometimes ascribed to J. Stevens, but there is good authority for believing that Livingston is the author. It is not inconsistent with his notions on judicial control; see American Historical Review, Vol. IV, pp. 460 ff.

James McClurg, of Virginia, left the Convention during the early part of August, and was silent on most of the questions before that body. On July 17th, he proposed that the term of the executive should be changed from seven years to "good behavior";[48] and he was particularly anxious to have the executive independent of the legislature. He said that he

> *was not so much afraid of the shadow of monarchy as to be unwilling to approach it; nor so wedded to republican government as not to be sensible of the tyrannies that had been and may be exercised under that form. It was an essential object with him to make the executive independent of the legislature; and the only mode left for effecting it, after the vote destroying his ineligibility the second time, was to appoint him during good behavior.*[49]

That McClurg had small respect for legislatures in general is shown by a letter which he wrote to Madison from Virginia on August 7, 1787, in which he said:

> *The necessity of some independent power to controul the Assembly by a negative, seems now to be admitted by the most zealous Republicans—they only differ about the mode of constituting such a power. B. Randolph seems to think that a magistrate annually elected by the people might exercise such a controul as independently as the King of G.B. I hope that our representative, Marshall, will be a powerful aid to Mason in the next Assembly. He has observ'd the continual depravation of Men's manners, under the corrupting influence of our Legislature; & is convinc'd that nothing but the adoption of some efficient plan from the Convention can prevent Anarchy first, & civil convulsions afterwards.*[50]

James McHenry belonged to the conservative party of his state and opposed "radical alterations" in the constitution of that commonwealth as it stood in November, 1791.[51]

Writing in February, 1787, on the property qualifications placed on voters and representatives in Maryland, McHenry explained that "These disabilities, exclusions, and qualifications have for their object an upright legislature, endowed with faculties to judge of the things most proper to promote the public good." He was warmly opposed to the doctrine that the people had a right to instruct their representa-

[48] Farrand, *Records,* Vol. II, p. 33.
[49] Ibid., Vol. II, p. 36.
[50] *Documentary History of the Constitution,* Vol. IV, p. 245.
[51] Letter to Hamilton, Library of Congress, *Hamilton Mss.,* Vol. XXIII, p. 93.

tives.[52] Democracy was, in his opinion, synonymous with "confusion and licentiousness."[53]

James Madison was the systematic philosopher of the Convention and set forth his views with such cogency and consistency on so many different topics that no short quotations will suffice to state his doctrines. His general scheme of political science was, however, embodied in the tenth number of *The Federalist*. . . .

Alexander Martin was among the silent members of the Convention, for Madison records only an occasional and incidental participation by him in the proceedings.

Luther Martin was the champion of the extreme states' rights' view, and entertained rather democratic notions for his time, although, in arguing against the clause prohibiting Congress to issue paper money, he held that, "considering the administration of the government would be principally in the hands of the wealthy," there could be little danger from an abuse of this power. Martin was in fact a champion of paper money in his state, and he opposed that part of the Constitution which prohibited the emission of bills of credit. As a representative of the more radical section of his community, he was against the clauses restricting the states to the use of the gold and silver coin of the United States, and was opposed to the clause forbidding the impairment of the obligation of contract. Speaking on the latter point he said:

> *There might be times of such great public calamities and distress, and of such extreme scarcity of specie, as should render it the duty of a government for the preservation of even the most valuable part of its citizens in some measure to interfere in their favor, by passing laws totally or partially stopping the courts of justice, or authorizing the debtor to pay by installments, or by delivering up his property to his creditors at a reasonable and honest valuation. The times have been such as to render regulations of this kind necessary in most or all of the states, to prevent the wealthy creditor and the moneyed man from totally destroying the poor, though even industrious debtor. Such times may again arrive. . . . I apprehend, Sir, the principal cause of complaint among the people at large, is the public and private debt with which they are oppressed, and which in the present scarcity of cash threatens them with destruction, unless they can obtain so much indulgence in point of time that by industry and frugality they may extricate themselves.*[54]

[52] *American Museum*, Vol. IV, p. 333.
[53] Steiner, *Life and Correspondence*, p. 527.
[54] Farrand, *Records*, Vol. III, pp. 214 ff.

As might have been expected, a man entertaining such radical notions about the power and duty of a government to interfere with the rights of personalty in behalf of the debtor could not have accepted the instrument framed at Philadelphia. In fact, Martin refused to sign the Constitution; he wrote a vehement protest against it to the legislature of his state; he worked assiduously against its ratification; and as a member of the state convention, he voted against its approval by his commonwealth—but in vain.

George Mason thoroughly understood the doctrine of a balanced government. Speaking in the Convention on the function of the upper house, he said:

> *One important object in constituting the senate was to secure the rights of property. To give them weight and firmness for this purpose a considerable duration in office was thought necessary. But a longer term than six years would be of no avail in this respect, if needy persons should be appointed. He suggested therefore the propriety of annexing to the office a qualification of property. He thought this would be very practicable; as the rules of taxation would supply a scale for measuring the degree of wealth possessed by every man.*[55]

On another occasion, he presented a motion requiring "certain qualifications of landed property, in members of the legislature."[56] Although Mason refused to sign the Constitution, his reasons were based on personal economic interests, not on any objections to its checks on democratic legislatures.

J. F. Mercer, of Maryland, who opposed the Constitution in its final form and became the belligerent anti-federalist leader in that state, does not appear to have been so warmly devoted to the "people's cause," behind the closed doors of the Convention, for he took exceptions to the proposition that the determination of the qualifications of voters should be left to the several states. But his particular objection was "to the mode of election by the people. The people cannot know and judge of the characters of candidates. The worst possible choice will be made."[57]

Thomas Mifflin took no part worthy of mention in the proceedings of the Convention, and expounded no views of government during the debates.

[55] Ibid., Vol. I, p. 428.
[56] Ibid., Vol. II, p. 121.
[57] Ibid., Vol. II, p. 205.

Gouverneur Morris, of Pennsylvania, was the leader of those who wanted to base the new system upon a freehold suffrage qualification; and, on August 7, he made a motion to this effect. In the course of the discussion which followed, Morris said:

> *He had long learned not to be the dupe of words. The sound of Aristocracy, therefore, had no effect on him. It was the thing, not the name, to which he was opposed, and one of his principal objections to the Constitution as it is now before us, is that it threatens this Country with an Aristocracy. The Aristocracy will grow out of the House of Representatives. Give the votes to people who have no property, and they will sell them to the rich who will be able to buy them. We should not confine our attention to the present moment. The time is not distant when this Country will abound with mechanics & manufacturers who will receive their bread from their employers. Will such men be the secure & faithful Guardians of liberty? Will they be the impregnable barrier agst. aristocracy?—He was as little duped by the association of the words, "taxation & Representation"—The man who does not give his vote freely is not represented. It is the man who dictates the vote. Children do not vote. Why? because they want prudence, because they have no will of their own. The ignorant & the dependent can be as little trusted with the public interest. He did not conceive the difficulty of defining "freeholders" to be insuperable. Still less that the restriction could be unpopular. 9/10 of the people are at present freeholders and these will certainly be pleased with it. As to Merchts. &c. if they have wealth & value the right they can acquire it. If not they don't deserve it.*[58]

In all the proceedings of the Convention, Morris took a deep interest and expressed his views freely, always showing his thorough distrust of democratic institutions. As his biographer, Mr. Roosevelt puts it,

> *He throughout appears as the* advocatus diaboli; *he puts the lowest interpretation upon every act, and frankly avows his disbelief in all generous and unselfish motives. His continual allusions to the overpowering influence of the baser passions, and to their mastery of the human race at all times, drew from Madison, although the two men generally acted together, a protest against his "forever inculcating the utter political depravity of men, and the necessity of opposing one vice and interest as the only possible check to another vice and interest."*[59]

This protest from Madison, however, betrays inconsistency, for on more than one occasion in the Convention he expounded principles

[58] Ibid., Vol. II, pp. 202 ff.
[59] Roosevelt, *Gouverneur Morris*, p. 140.

substantially identical with those which he reprobated in Morris.[60] Indeed, what appeared to be cynical eccentricity on the part of the latter was nothing more than unusual bluntness in setting forth Federalist doctrines.

Robert Morris, the merchant prince and speculator of Pennsylvania, seems to have broken his rule of absolute silence only two or three times in the Convention, and he apparently made no speech at all. He nominated Washington as president of the assembly, and seconded Read's motion that Senators should hold office during good behavior.[61] There is no doubt that Morris appreciated the relative weight of speeches and private negotiations.[62]

In the proceedings of the Convention, *William Paterson* was chiefly concerned with protecting the rights of small states; but he signed the Constitution, and after its adoption became an ardent Federalist, serving as an associate justice of the Supreme Court. On the bench he was one of the most scholarly and eminent supporters of the doctrine of judicial control over legislation.[63]

William Pierce took little part in the proceedings of the Convention. On the question of states' rights he held a broad view, saying,

> *state distinctions must be sacrificed so far as the general government shall render it necessary—without, however, destroying them altogether. Although I am here as a representative from a small state, I consider myself as a citizen of the United States, whose general interest I will always support.*[64]

On no occasion, apparently, did Pierce indulge in any general reflections on the basis of all government. He did not sign the Constitution, but he explained this fact by saying,

> *I was absent in New York on a piece of business so necessary that it became unavoidable. I approve of its principles and would have signed it with all my heart had I been present. To say, however, that I consider it as perfect would be to make an acknowledgement immediately opposed to my judgment.*[65]

[60] See *The Federalist,* No. 51.
[61] Farrand, *Records,* Vol. I, p. 409.
[62] For an example see ibid., p. 11, note. He also entertained Washington during the sessions of the Convention. *American Historical Association Report* (1902), Vol. I, p. 92.
[63] Beard, *The Supreme Court and the Constitution,* p. 37.
[64] Farrand, *Records,* Vol. I, p. 474.
[65] Ibid., Vol. III, p. 100.

Charles Pinckney was among the members of the Convention who thought that it was desirable to fix the property qualifications of members of the national legislature firmly in the Constitution. Speaking on the subject of property and government he said:

> *The Committee as he had conceived were instructed to report the proper qualifications of property for the members of the Natl. Legislature; instead of which they have referred the task to the Natl. Legislature itself. Should it be left on this footing, the first Legislature will meet without any particular qualifications of property; and if it should happen to consist of rich men they might fix such qualifications as may be too favorable to the rich; if of poor men, an opposite extreme might be run into. He was opposed to the establishment of an undue aristocratic influence in the Constitution, but he thought it essential that the members of the Legislature, the Executive, and the Judges—should be possessed of competent property to make them independent & respectable. It was prudent when such great powers were to be trusted to connect the tie of property with that of reputation in securing a faithful administration. The Legislature would have the fate of the Nation put into their hands. The President would also have a very great influence on it. The Judges would have not only important causes between Citizen & Citizen but also where foreigners were concerned. They will even be the Umpires between the U. States and individual States as well as between one State & another. Were he to fix the quantum of property which should be required, he should not think of less than one hundred thousand dollars for the President, half of that sum for each of the Judges, and in like proportion for the members of the Natl. Legislature. He would however leave the sum blank. His motion was that the President of the U.S., the Judges, and members of the Legislature should be required to swear that they were respectively possessed of a clear unincumbered Estate to the amount of ——— in the case of the President, &c &c.—*[66]

Pinckney, in fact, had no confidence in popular government, for on March 28, 1788, he wrote to Madison:

> *Are you not . . . abundantly impressed that the theoretical nonsense of an election of Congress by the people in the first instance is clearly and practically wrong, that it will in the end be the means of bringing our councils into contempt.*[67]

General Charles Cotesworth Pinckney entertained views with regard to the special position that should be enjoyed by property, which were substantially identical with those held by his cousin. He

[66] Ibid., Vol. II, p. 248.
[67] *Madison Mss.*, Library of Congress; date of March 28, 1788.

proposed that no salary should be paid to members of the Senate. As this branch, he said, "was meant to represent the wealth of the country, it ought to be composed of persons of wealth; and if no allowance was to be made the wealthy alone would undertake the service."[68] General Pinckney also wished to extend property qualifications not only to members of the legislature, but also to the executive and judicial departments.[69]

Edmund Randolph was not only fully aware of the distress to which property had been put under the Articles of Confederation, but he also understood the elements of a "balanced" government. Speaking on the subject of the structure of the Senate, he said:

> *If he was to give an opinion as to the number of the second branch, he should say that it ought to be much smaller than that of the first, so small as to be exempt from the passionate proceedings to which numerous assemblies are liable. He observed that the general object was to provide a cure for the evils under which the U.S. Laboured; that in tracing these evils to their origin every man had found it in the turbulence and follies of democracy: that some check therefore was to be sought for agst. this tendency of our governments: and that a good Senate seemed most likely to answer the purpose. . . . Mr. Randolph was for the term of 7 years. The Democratic licentiousness of the State Legislatures proved the necessity of a firm Senate. The object of this 2d. branch is to controul the democratic branch of the Natl. Legislature. If it be not a firm body, the other branch being more numerous, and coming immediately from the people, will overwhelm it. The Senate of Maryland constituted on like principles had been scarcely able to stem the popular torrent. No mischief can be apprehended, as the concurrence of the other branch, and in some measure, of the Executive, will in all cases be necessary. A firmness & independence may be the more necessary also in this branch, as it ought to guard the Constitution agst. encroachments of the Executive who will be apt to form combinations with the demagogues of the popular branch.*[70]

George Read was most outspoken in his desire to see the Articles of Confederation completely discarded. He said that

> *he was against patching up the old federal system: he hoped the idea would be dismissed. It would be like putting new cloth on an old garment. The Confederation was founded on temporary principles. It cannot last; it cannot be amended.*[71]

[68] Farrand, *Records*, Vol. I, p. 426.
[69] Ibid., Vol. II, p. 122.
[70] Ibid., Vol. I, p. 51 and p. 218.
[71] Ibid., Vol. I, p. 136.

He favored vesting an absolute veto power in the executive;[72] and he proposed that Senators should hold office during good behavior.[73]

John Rutledge held that the apportionment of representatives should be on a basis of wealth and population.[74] He favored a property qualification for the legislative, executive, and judicial departments;[75] and he thought that Senators should not be paid.[76] In fact, he was one of the most ardent champions of the rights of property in government in the Convention. He was strictly opposed to the introduction of sentimental considerations in politics, for, speaking on an aspect of slavery and the Constitution, he said:

> *Religion & humanity had nothing to do with this question—Interest alone is the governing principle with Nations—The true question at present is whether the Southn. States shall or shall not be parties to the Union. If the Northern States consult their interests they will not oppose the increase of Slaves which will increase the commodities of which they will become the carriers.*[77]

Roger Sherman believed in reducing the popular influence in the new government to the minimum. When it was proposed that the members of the first branch of the national legislature should be elected, Sherman said that he was "opposed to the election by the people, insisting that it ought to be by the state legislatures. The people, he said, immediately should have as little to do as may be about the government. They want information and are constantly liable to be misled."[78]

Richard Dobbs Spaight does not seem to have made any very lengthy speeches in the Convention, but his occasional motions show that he was not among those who believed in "frequent recurrence to the people." On September 6, he moved that the length of the President's term be increased to seven years, and finding this lost he attempted to substitute six years for four.[79] Spaight was the one member of the Convention, however, who came out clearly and denounced judicial control;[80] but he nevertheless proved a stout

[72] Ibid., Vol. II, p. 200.
[73] Ibid., Vol. I, p. 409.
[74] Ibid., Vol. I, p. 582.
[75] Ibid., Vol. II, p. 249.
[76] Ibid., Vol. I, p. 211.
[77] Ibid., Vol. II, p. 364.
[78] Ibid., Vol. I, p. 48; also p. 154.
[79] Ibid., Vol. II, p. 525.
[80] Beard, *The Supreme Court and the Constitution*, p. 53.

champion of the Constitution in North Carolina—defending it warmly against charges to the effect that it was aristocratic in character.[81]

Caleb Strong carried into the Convention the old Massachusetts tradition in favor of frequent elections. He favored a one-year term for representatives,[82] voted against a seven-year term for President,[83] and also opposed a seven-year term for Senators.[84] He supported the Constitution, however, in his native state, and was a member of the convention that ratified it.

George Washington's part in the proceedings of the Convention was almost negligible, and it does not appear that in public document or private letter he ever set forth any coherent theory of government. When he had occasion to dwell upon the nature of the new system he indulged in the general language of the bench rather than that of the penetrating observer. For example, in his Farewell Address, which was written largely by Hamilton, he spoke of the government's being "the offspring of our own choice, uninfluenced and unawed, adopted upon full investigation, and mature deliberation, completely free in its principles, in the distribution of its powers, uniting security with energy."[85] He feared, however, the type of politics represented by the Democratic Societies which sprang up during his administration, and looked upon criticism of the government as akin to sedition.[86] Like Jefferson, he also viewed with apprehension the growth of an urban population, for in a letter to La Fayette at the time of the French Revlution, he said, "The tumultuous populace of large cities are ever to be dreaded. Their indiscriminate violence prostrates for the time all public authority."[87]

Hugh Williamson was against placing property qualifications on voters for members of Congress;[88] and he was opposed to the association of the judges with the executive in the exercise of the veto power.[89] He preferred to insert a provision requiring a two-thirds vote for every "effective act of the legislature."[90] He was, however, an opponent of the paper money party in North Carolina and in the

[81] Elliot, *Debates,* Vol. IV, p. 207.
[82] Farrand, *Records,* Vol. I, p. 361.
[83] Ibid., p. 72.
[84] Ibid., p. 219.
[85] *Writings* (Sparks ed., 1848), Vol. XII, p. 222; see below, p. 299.
[86] Ibid., Vol. X, p. 429.
[87] Ibid., Vol. X, p. 179.
[88] Farrand, *Records,* Vol. II, pp. 201, 250.
[89] Ibid., Vol. I, p. 140.
[90] Ibid., Vol. I, p. 140.

Convention he supported a proposition forbidding the states to pass ex post facto laws, on the ground that "the judges can take hold of it."[91]

James Wilson was among the philosophers of the period who had seriously pondered on politics in its historical and practical aspects. In the Convention he took a democratic view on several matters. He favored the annual election of representatives by the people,[92] he advocated the popular election of United States Senators,[93] and he believed also in the popular election of the President.[94] He furthermore opposed the proposition to place property qualifications on voters.[95] His check on popular legislation was to be found in judicial control, at first in the association of the judges with the executive in its exercise, and later in its simple, direct form.[96] In fact, Wilson shared the apprehensions of his colleagues as to the dangers of democratic legislatures, though he did not frankly advocate direct property checks.[97] He doubtless believed that judicial control would be sufficient.

George Wythe was a representative of the old school of lawyers in Virginia, and he was a profound student of historical jurisprudence, although he apparently made no attempt to apply his learning to any of the general political questions before the Convention. He was a warm advocate of the doctrine of judicial control and gave practical effect to principles while on the bench in Virginia.[98]

The conclusion seems warranted that the authors of *The Federalist* generalized the political doctrines of the members of the Convention with a high degree of precision, in spite of the great diversity of opinion which prevailed on many matters.

[91] Ibid., Vol. II, p. 376.
[92] Ibid., Vol. I, p. 49 and *passim.*
[93] Ibid., p. 52 and *passim.*
[94] Ibid., p. 68 and *passim.*
[95] Ibid., Vol. I, p. 375; Vol. II, p. 125 and *passim.*
[96] Ibid., Vol. I, p. 98; Beard, *The Supreme Court and the Constitution,* p. 42.
[97] *Lectures on Law* (1804 ed.), Vol. I, pp. 398 ff.
[98] Beard, *The Supreme Court and the Constitution,* p. 48.

Charles Warren

FEARS OF DISUNION

Although Beard's economic interpretation of the origins of the American Constitution became an historical canon for over forty years, there were those who preferred the older interpretation, and some, like Charles Warren, restated it eloquently. His version of the origin of the Constitution is in strong contrast to those of Beard and Parrington and may be said, not unfairly, to represent a "conservative" point of view.

In 1922 Charles Warren won the Pulitzer Prize for the best book in American History with The Supreme Court in United States History, *a work of rich scholarship and still an invaluable treatment of the work of the Court, especially through the chief justiceship of Morrison Remick Waite. It is full of admiration for the majesty of law and generally innocent of the social and economic forces that produced landmark cases. It does not appreciate the service of the Court to men of power and property, and it is disinclined to give true weight and measure to critics of the Federalist orthodoxy that was read into the Constitution by John Marshall. As Warren saw Marshall, his greatest service was the vitalization of the Constitution which he made into a stronger bond of union than it had been, although Warren did admit that by the year of his death in 1835, Marshall was out of touch with the changing times.*

In 1929 Warren published The Making of the Constitution, *from which the following excerpt is taken. Like his earlier work on the Supreme Court,* The Making of the Constitution *tends to see political conflict in terms of legal and constitutional issues and not in terms of the economic and social realities these formulations served. Even his opening story about the interview with Captain Levi Preston of Danvers, Massachusetts—which is intended to show that the Revolutionary soldier cared nothing for high-flown political theory—is interpreted to mean that he was, nevertheless, fighting for "an idea, a principle." It is Warren's theme that it was principles—not economic interests—that led to the Revolution and the formation of the Constitution. The Constitution was the product of feelings of National Union and a "patriotic desire for a united Nation, able to take its place with the other Nations of the world."*

In recent years there has been a tendency to interpret all history in terms of economics and sociology and geography—of soil, of debased currency, of land monopoly, of taxation, of class antagonism, of frontier against seacoast, and the like—and to attribute the actions of

From Charles Warren, *The Making of the Constitution*, Cambridge, Mass.: Harvard University Press, 1947 (reprint edition). First published in 1929 by Little, Brown and Company.

peoples to such general materialistic causes. This may be a wise reaction from the old manner of writing history almost exclusively in terms of wars, politics, dynasties, and religions. But its fundamental defect is, that it ignores the circumstance that the actions of men are frequently based quite as much on sentiment and belief as on facts and conditions. It leaves out the souls of men and their response to the inspiration of great leaders. It forgets that there are such motives as patriotism, pride in country, unselfish devotion to the public welfare, desire for independence, inherited sentiments, and convictions of right and justice. The historian who omits to take these facts into consideration is a poor observer of human nature. No one can write true history who leaves out of account the fact that a man may have an inner zeal for principles, beliefs, and ideals. "It seems to me a great truth," wrote Thomas Carlyle, "that human things cannot stand on selfishness, mechanical utilities, economics, and law courts." Those who contend, for instance, that economic causes brought about the War of the Revolution will always find it difficult to explain away the fact that the men who did the fighting thought, themselves, that they were fighting for a belief—a principle. Sixty-two years after the battle of Concord and Lexington, an able American historian had an interview with one of the men who had been in that battle, and asked him the reasons which impelled him, a plain, simple workingman, to take arms. And this was the colloquy between the historian and the man who fought:[1]

> *"Why did you? . . . My histories tell me that you men of the Revolution took up arms against intolerable oppressions."*
>
> *"What were they? Oppressions? I didn't feel them."*
>
> *"What, were you not oppressed by the Stamp Act?"*
>
> *"I never saw one of those stamps. . . . I am certain I never paid a penny for one of them."*
>
> *"Well, what about the tea tax?"*
>
> *"Tea tax, I never drank a drop of the stuff. The boys threw it all overboard."*
>
> *"Then, I suppose, you had been reading Harrington, or Sidney and Locke, about the eternal principles of liberty?"*
>
> *"Never heard of 'em."*
>
> *"Well, then, what was the matter, what did you mean in going into the fight?"*
>
> *"Young man, what we meant in going for those red-coats, was this:*

[1] *John Adams, the Statesman of the American Revolution* (1898), by Mellen Chamberlain, p. 248, interview with Capt. Levi Preston of Danvers, Mass., in 1837.

we always had governed ourselves and we always meant to. They didn't mean we should."

In other words, it was an idea, a principle—belief in self-government—for which this New England yeoman and his fellow-countrymen were fighting.

In the same manner, the men who urged and framed and advocated the Constitution were striving for an idea, an ideal—belief in a National Union, and a determination to maintain it, and the men who opposed the Constitution were also fighting for the preservation of an idea—self-rule as opposed to control by a central government which they feared would destroy their local governments. Historians who leave these factors out of account and who contend that these men were moved chiefly by economic conditions utterly fail to interpret their character and their acts. To appreciate the patriotic sincerity of the motives which inspired the framing of the Constitution, it is necessary to read the hopes and fears of the leading American statesmen prior to 1787, as expressed in their own words. Thomas Jefferson wrote, one hundred years ago, that "the opening scenes of our present government" would not be "seen in their true aspect until the letters of the day, now held in private hoards, shall be broken up and laid open to public use." Within the last thirty-five years, these letters have been very fully published; and unless their authors, in writing to intimate personal friends, were expressing one reason for desiring a change in the form of government, while in fact moved by other and more selfish reasons, then these letters must portray, with accuracy, the motives which led the writers to advocate a new Constitution. These letters, moreover, embody the principles on which the new Government was to be built—principles which were distinctively American and little connected with economics.

The actual evils which led to the Federal Convention of 1787 are familiar to every reader of history and need no detailed description here. As is well known, they arose, in general, first, from lack of power in the Government of the Confederation to legislate and enforce at home such authority as it possessed, or to maintain abroad its credit or position as a sovereign Nation; second, from State legislation unjust to citizens and productive of dissensions with neighboring States—the State laws particularly complained of being those staying process of the Courts, making property a tender in payment of debts, issuing paper money, interfering with foreclosure of mortgages, setting aside judgments of the Courts, interfering with private concerns, imposing commercial restrictions on goods and citizens of other States. The Articles of Confederation as agreed upon by the Continental Congress on November 15, 1777, had provided for a Government consisting simply of a Congress with a single House, in which each State had equal representation—a Government having no Executive and no adequate Court—a Government in which Congress had no power to tax, to raise troops, to regulate commerce, or to execute or enforce its own laws and treaties—a Government in which each of the various States had power to tax, to make its own money, to impose its own import and export duties, and to conform or not, as it chose, to the acts or treaties of Congress, or to its requisitions for money or troops. Congress could only supplicate; it could not enforce.

> Glendower. *"I can call spirits from the vasty deep."*
> Hotspur. *"Why, so can I, or so can any man.*
> *But will they come when you do call for them?"*

Such a Government could not operate successfully for any length of time and there could be no real Union of the States, except in time of war when need of mutual protection would prevent undue dissensions. From the very outset, and long before economic disturbances had arisen in the States, the voices of American statesmen were heard urging upon the people the necessity of a change. Even before the whole thirteen States had decided to ratify the Articles, Alexander Hamilton formulated the additional authority which Congress ought to possess; and in this comprehensive document, written in 1780 (when he was only twenty-three years old), he anticipated most of the powers which were granted, seven years later, by the Constitution. The ink was scarcely dry on the signatures of the delegates from Maryland—the last of the thirteen States to sign the Articles (on March 1, 1781)—when James Madison, James Duane of New York, and James M. Varnum of Rhode Island were appointed a Committee to report on needful changes. This Committee recommended vesting power in Congress to employ the Continental army and navy "to compel any delinquent State to fulfill its Federal engagement, by restraining its vessels, merchandise, and trade." Another Committee, consisting of Edmund Randolph of Virginia, Oliver Ellsworth of Connecticut and James M. Varnum, five months later, in August, 1781, reported a long list of additional powers for Congress, as necessary in order to make the Government efficient, among which was the important suggestion that Congress be authorized "to distrain the property of a State delinquent in its assigned proportion of men and money." No action was ever taken on this Report. A year later a strong appeal made by Robert Morris, Superintendent of Finance, that Congress be granted power to levy excise, land, and poll taxes, to discharge the Government debts was adversely reported on by a Congressional Committee. In 1783, Congress rejected a motion by Alexander Hamilton and James Wilson that that body should be given power to levy a land tax; but, a month later, Congress voted to ask the States to grant to it the power to levy import duties.

It is also to be noted that the idea of a Convention to revise and amend the Articles of Confederation was no new thing in the year 1787. It had been in the minds of the leading American statesmen, and long before any economic evils appeared in the various States. It arose from their patriotic desire for a united Nation, able to take its place with the other Nations of the world. As Edmund Randolph of Virginia strikingly said: "The American spirit ought to be mixed with American pride, to see the Union magnificently triumphant." What they chiefly feared were dissensions of the States and dissolution of the Union, leaving the States open to attack by foreign power. What they desired was to frame some form of Government which, while safeguarding the liberties of the citizens and the rights of the States, should have power to maintain adequately its own authority and independence. These were the objects which occupied all their correspondence. Conventions of the delegates from various States had gathered several times prior to 1787. In 1777, a Convention from New York and the New England States met at Springfield; in 1778, at New Haven, New Jersey and Pennsylvania were represented in addition to New York and New England. In 1780, New York and New England met at Hartford and suggested a General Convention to revise the Articles. The earliest call for a General Convention came from the Legislature of New York in 1782, under the leadership of Alexander Hamilton and General Philip Schuyler. In 1783, the Continental Congress appointed a Committee to consider these New York resolutions for a Convention, but no further action was ever taken. In 1783 also, Washington wrote to Dr. William Gordon suggesting a Convention of the People, as follows:

> *To suppose that the general concerns of this country can be directed by thirteen heads, or one head without competent powers, is a solecism, the bad effects of which every man who has had the practical knowledge to judge from, that I have, is fully convinced of; tho' none perhaps has felt them in so forcible and distressing a degree. The People at large, and at a distance from the theatre of action, who only know that the machine was kept in motion, and that they are at last arrived at the first object of their wishes, are satisfied with the event, without investigating the causes of the slow progress to it, or of the expenses which have accrued, and which they have been unwilling to pay—great part of which has arisen from that want of energy in the Federal Constitution, which I am complaining of, and which I wish to see given to it by a Convention of the People, instead of hearing it remarked that, as we have worked through an arduous contest with the powers Congress already have (but which, by the by, have been gradually diminishing) why should they be invested with more? . . . For Heaven's sake, who are Congress? Are they not the creatures of the People, amenable to them for their conduct, and dependent from day to day on their breath? Where then can be the danger of giving them such powers as are adequate to the great ends of Government and to all the general purposes of the Confederation (I repeat the word general, because I am no advocate for their having to do with the particular policy of any State, further than it concerns the Union at large).*

In 1784, Richard Henry Lee, then President of the Congress, wrote to Madison: "It is by many here suggested as a very necessary step for Congress to take, the calling on the States to form a Convention for the sole purpose of revising the Confederation so far as to enable Congress to execute with more energy, effect, and vigor the powers assigned to it," and Madison replied to him: "I have not yet found leisure to scan the project of a Continental Convention with so close an eye as to have made up any observations worthy of being mentioned to you. In general, I hold it for a maxim that the Union of the States is essential to their safety against foreign danger and internal contention, and that the perpetuity and efficacy of the present system cannot be confided in." In 1785, the Massachusetts Legislature passed Resolutions, in response to a message from Governor James Bowdoin, recommending to Congress the calling of a General Convention.

Meanwhile, the sentiments and motives which inspired the desire for a change in the form of Government may be seen in the letters of Washington, Hamilton, Jay, Madison, Jefferson and many others, both in the South and the North. Washington, more than any other man, was responsible for calling the attention of the people to the defects of the Confederation. His letters were filled with appeals for a remedy. As early as July, 1780, he wrote: "Our measures are not under the influence and direction of one Council, but thirteen, each of which is actuated by local views and politics. . . . We are attempting the impossible." In December, 1780, he wrote that "there are two things (as I have often declared) which, in my opinion, are indispensably necessary to the well-being and good government of our public affairs; these are greater powers to Congress and more responsibility and permanency in the Executive bodies." In 1782, he wrote that if the powers of Congress were not enlarged, "anarchy and confusion must ensue." In 1783, he wrote that:

> *The experience, which is purchased at the price of difficulties and distress, will alone convince us that the honor, power, and true interest of this country must be measured by a Continental scale, and that every departure therefrom weakens the Union, and may ultimately break the band which holds us together. To avert these evils, to form a Constitution that will give consistency, stability, and dignity to the Union and sufficient powers to the great Council of the Nation for general purposes, is a duty which is incumbent upon every man who wishes well to his Country, and will meet with my aid as far as it can be rendered in the private walks of life.*

On June 8, 1783, he sent to the Governors of the States a message in which he said:

> *There are four things, which, I humbly conceive, are essential to the well-being, I may even venture to say, to the existence of the United States, as an independent power. First: An indissoluble union of the States under one Federal head; secondly: A sacred regard to public justice; thirdly: The adoption of a proper peace establishment; and, fourthly: The prevalence of that pacific and friendly disposition among the people of the United States, which will induce them to forget their local prejudices and policies; to make those mutual concessions, which are requisite to the general prosperity; and in some instances, to sacrifice their individual advantages to the interest of the community. These are the pillars on which the glorious fabric of our independency and National character must be supported.*

And these views, he continued to express in the ensuing years, through a voluminous correspondence with friends in the various States. The letters of other leading Americans showed a realization that a truly National Government which should promote the Union of the States was imperative. John Jay of New York wrote to Gouverneur Morris of Pennsylvania, September 24, 1783:

> *I am perfectly convinced that no time is to be lost in raising and maintaining a National spirit in America. Power to govern the Confederacy, as to all general purposes, should be granted and exercised. The governments of the different States should be wound up, and become vigorous. America is beheld with jealousy, and jealousy is seldom idle. Settle your boundaries without delay. It is better that some improper limits should be fixed, than any left in dispute. In a word, everything conducive to union and constitutional energy of government should be cultivated, cherished and protected, and all counsels and measures of a contrary complexion should at least be suspected of impolitic views and objects.*

Governor John Hancock, in his Message to the Massachusetts Legislature in September, 1783, said: "How to strengthen and improve the Union so as to render it completely adequate, demands the immediate attention of these States. Our very existence as a free nation is suspended upon it." Thomas Jefferson wrote to Madison, in 1784: "I find the conviction growing strongly that nothing can preserve our Confederacy unless the bond of union, their common Council, be strengthened." And to Monroe, Jefferson wrote in 1785: "The interests of the States ought to be made joint in every possible instance, in order to cultivate the idea of our being one Nation." Stephen Higginson, a former Member of Congress from Massachusetts, wrote to John Adams, December 30, 1785, that:

> *Experience and observation most clearly evince that in their habits, manners, and commercial interests, the Southern and Northern States are not only very dissimilar, but in many instances directly opposed. Happy for America would it be if there was a greater coincidence of sentiment and interest among them. Then we might expect those National arrangements soon to take place which appear so essential to our safety and happiness.*

Such were the sentiments which prevailed among the public men of the country, prior to the year 1786, as to the necessity of some alteration in the form of their Government which should promote a more perfect National Union. . . .

Meanwhile, all patriotic Americans who wished to see a united country and a real National Union were now given serious cause for alarm by the increase of sentiment in many parts of the land for a division of the States into two or more Confederacies. The fact that such a dissolution of the existing Confederacy was believed by many men to be the true remedy for the unfortunate conditions prevailing in the Government drove home to many, who had hitherto doubted, the necessity of summoning together the representatives of the States in Convention, in an effort to frame an adequate Government of the whole. During the past three years, this suggestion that the commercial and political interests and conditions of the Southern, Middle, and Eastern States were so divergent that they could be dealt with, fairly and justly, only by a separation, had been made on many occasions in letters and in newspaper articles. In this year, 1786, the sentiment for such a division had been given great impetus by the serious dissension which arose in Congress, between the States of the South and of the East, over a proposal initiated by John Jay, then Secretary of Foreign Affairs, to relinquish (for a term of years) the right which the United States had long and persistently asserted against Spain to the free navigation of the Mississippi River. This right had been a cardinal principle with the Southern States and especially with Virginia; and the suggestion that its maintenance might now be abandoned, through the votes of the Northern States headed by Massachusetts, aroused hot excitement. The dangerous situation was described by James Monroe (then a Member of Congress from Virginia). Writing to Madison, August 14, 1786, he said:

> *It is manifest here that Jay and his party in Congress are determined to pursue this business as far as possible, either as the means of throwing the Western people and territory without the government of the United States and keeping the weight of population and government here, or of dismembering the Government itself, for the purpose of a separate Confederacy. There can be no other object than one of these, and I am, from such evidence as I have, doubtful which hath the influence.*

And to Jefferson, he wrote August 19:

> *I am sorry to inform you that our affairs are daily falling into a worse situation, arising more from the intrigues of designing men than any real defect in our system or distress of our affairs. The same party who advocate this business* [*of the Mississippi River*] *have certainly held in this city Committees for dismembering the Confederacy, and throwing the States eastward the Hudson into one Government. As yet, this business hath not gone far, but that there should be a party in its favor, and a man heretofore so well respected but in my opinion so little known, engaged in it, is to me very alarming.*

And to Patrick Henry he wrote:

> *Certain it is that Committees are held, in this town, of Eastern men and others of this State upon the subject of a dismemberment of the States East of the Hudson from the Union and the erection of them into a separate government. To what lengths they have gone I know not, but have assurances as to the truth of the above position, with this addition to it that the measure is talked of in Mass. familiarly, and is supposed to have originated there. The plan of the Government in all its modifications has even been contemplated by them. I am persuaded these people who are in Congress from that State (at the head of the other business) mean that as a step toward the carriage of this, as it will so displease some of them as to prepare the States for this event. . . . Be assured as to all the subjects upon which I have given you information above, it hath been founded on authentic documents. I trust these intrigues are confined to a few only, but by these men I am assured are not.*

Monroe was probably unjustified in believing that Jay of New York or Nathan Dane or Rufus King (the Massachusetts Congressmen) were in favor of division of the Union; but it was unquestionably true that an increasing number of men in the different States were coming to believe in such a dismemberment as the only solution for their political problems. As early as February 11, 1786, General Benjamin Lincoln of Massachusetts had written to King, describing at length the different interests of the States, and concluding:

> *If the observations I have made are just, the citizens of these States are deceiving themselves, in an expectation that any relief can, or will, be granted them by Congress, under our present system of government. . . . That our interests do and will clash, are troubles which will not be questioned. These are the necessary consequences of our great extent, of our difference of climate, productions, views, etc. I do not see how we shall surmount the evils under which we now labor, and prevent our falling into the utmost confusion, disgrace, and ruin, but by a division, which might be formed upon such principles as would secure our public creditors, and thereby our public faith, and our afterpeace and safety by a firm alliance between the divisions.*

And Theodore Sedgwick of Massachusetts wrote to Caleb Strong, August 6, 1786:

> *No reasonable expectations of advantage can be formed from the Commercial Convention. The first proposers designed none. The measure was originally brought forward with an intention of defeating the enlargement of the powers of Congress. Of this, I have the most decisive evidence. It*

well becomes the Eastern and Middle States, who are in interest one, seriously to consider what advantages result to them from their connection with the Southern States. They can give us nothing, as an equivalent for the protection which they derive from us, but a participation in their commerce. This they deny to us. Should their conduct continue the same, and I think there is not any prospect of an alteration, an attempt to perpetuate our connection with them, which act too will be found ineffectual, will sacrifice everything to a mere chimera. Even the appearance of a Union, cannot, in the way we now are, be long preserved. It becomes us seriously to contemplate a substitute; for if we do not controul events we shall be miserably controulled by them. No other substitute can be devised than that of contracting the limits of the Confederacy to such as are natural and reasonable, and within those limits, instead of a nominal, to institute a real and an efficient Government.

Dr. Benjamin Rush wrote from Philadelphia to Dr. Richard Price, in London, October 27, 1786:

Some of our enlightened men who begin to despair of a more complete union of the States in Congress have secretly proposed an Eastern, Middle and Southern Confederacy, to be united by an alliance offensive and defensive. These Confederacies, they say, will be united by nature, by interest, and by manners, and consequently they will be safe, agreeable, and durable. The first will include the four New England States and New York. The second will include New Jersey, Pennsylvania, Delaware, and Maryland; and the last Virginia, North and South Carolina, and Georgia. The foreign and domestic debt of the United States they say shall be divided justly between each of the new Confederations. This plan of a new Continental Government is at present a mere speculation. Perhaps necessity or rather Divine Providence, may drive us to it.

Madison summed up the situation in his diary, February 21, 1787, as follows:

All [Members of Congress] *agreed and owned that the Federal Government in its existing shape was inefficient and could not last. The members from the Southern and Middle States seemed generally anxious for some republican organization of the system which should preserve the Union and give due energy to the Government of it. Mr. Bingham (of Pennsylvania) alone avowed his wishes that the Confederacy might be divided into several distinct Confederacies, its great extent and various interests being incompatible with a single government. The Eastern Members were suspected by some of leaning towards some anti-republican establishment (the result of their late confusions) or of being less desirous or hopeful of preserving the unity of the empire. For the first time, the idea of separate Confederacies had got into the newspapers. It ap-*

peared today under a Boston head. Whatever the views of the leading men in the Eastern States may be, it would seem that the great body of the people, particularly in Connecticut, are equally indisposed either to dissolve or divide the Confederacy, or to submit to any anti-republican innovations.

This sentiment for dismemberment, however, continued to spread in the spring of 1787. In April, the newspapers in Philadelphia and many other cities published widely the following letter:

Instead of attempting to amend the present Articles of Confederation with a view to retain them as the form of Government, or instead of attempting one General Government for the whole community of the United States, would it not be preferable to distribute the United States into three Republics, who should enter into a perpetual league and alliance for mutual defence? . . . Reflections on the subject in the abstract would have suggested to us, and our experience has fully convinced us, that there can be only one sovereignty in a government; the notion therefore of a government by confederation between several independent States, each State still retaining its sovereignty, must be abandoned, and with it every attempt to amend the present Articles of Confederation. . . . The National concerns of a people so numerous with a territory so extensive will be proportionally difficult and important. This will require proportionate powers in the administration, especially in the Chief Executive; greater, perhaps, than will consist with the democratic form. Our fate, as far as it can depend on human means, is committed to the Convention; as they decide, so will our lot be. It must be the wish of the delegates, and it is certainly both our duty and interest to aid them in the arduous business intrusted to them.

And a Massachusetts newspaper stated that the same suggestion for a division of the Confederacy had appeared in Southern newspapers:

A hint has, in the Southern papers, been suggested to the Deputies to the Federal Convention on the propriety of recommending a dissolution of the Confederation and a division of the States into four Republicks—the first, to contain the States of New Hampshire, Massachusetts, Rhode Island and Connecticut, to which Vermont might be added—the second to contain New York, New Jersey, Delaware, Pennsylvania and Maryland—the third, Virginia, the two Carolinas and Georgia. And the fourth to contain the State of Franklin, Kentucky and the lands lying on the Ohio. This division seems to be pointed out by climates whose effect no positive law ever can surpass. The religion, manners, customs, exports, imports and general interest of each being then the same, no opposition arising from difference in these (as at present) would any longer divide their councils—unanimity would render it secure at home and respected abroad and promote agriculture, manufactures and commerce.

In addition to their fears as to the growth of this policy of division into separate Confederacies, those who were anxious for preservation of the Union were given a new cause for alarm, in the rise of the Shays Rebellion in Massachusetts between September, 1786, and February, 1787. . . . This Shays Rebellion, however, has been somewhat overemphasized by historians as a moving cause of the Federal Convention and of the Constitution; and the desire to protect the propertied interests in the future against such assaults has been alleged by some writers to have been a leading motive inspiring the framers of the Constitution. The desire for the prevention of a recurrence of such a Rebellion was undoubtedly one of the causes for agreement upon the Constitution, but it was by no means the leading motive. It will be noted that the Rebellion did not really become serious before December, 1786; but long before that time, the leading statesmen of the country had determined that a change in the framework of the National Government was absolutely necessary, and they had agreed upon the general lines on which such a change must be made. The Shays Rebellion simply afforded one more proof of the disturbing conditions existing in the States and of the weakness of the Confederacy—which must be remedied if the United States were to continue in existence. As an object lesson, it shocked into action many men who had hitherto been lukewarm towards the subject of a Constitutional Convention. . . .

To Washington, Jay wrote, January 7, that it was not easy to say what should be done; that it was useless to give any further degree of power to the existing Congress, but that he was doubtful about the proposed Convention consisting of delegates elected by the State Legislatures, for, said he, "no alterations in the Government should, I think, be made, nor if attempted will easily take place, unless deducible from the only source of just authority—the People"; moreover, he felt that a Convention having power only to recommend would "produce endless discussion, perhaps jealousies and party heat"; hence, he favored popular Conventions in each State to appoint deputies to a General Convention which should have power to alter and amend the Articles of Confederation.

General Knox wrote from New York to General Benjamin Lincoln in Massachusetts, that the topic of a Convention "engrosses a great portion of the attention of men of reflection"; and to Stephen Higginson, he wrote that "the poor, poor, Federal Government is sick almost to death" and that a Convention had been proposed "to consult on some plan to prevent our utter ruin."

> *Perhaps this Convention originated and has been imbued with ideas far short of a radical reform. Let this have been the case, may it, notwithstanding, be turned to an excellent purpose. Our views are limited in all things; we can only see from point to point. If men, great men, are sent to the Convention, might they not assist the vision of the Southern delegates, in such a manner as to induce the adoption of some energetic plan, in the prosecution of which we might rise to National dignity and happiness?*

Knox suggested that the Convention should submit a plan for a Constitution to State Conventions who should then choose delegates to a new Continental Convention having power to decide upon and put in force a more General Government; and he especially urged Massachusetts to join in the present Convention:

> *. . . The Southern States are jealous enough already. If New England, and particularly Massachusetts, should decline sending delegates to the Convention, it will operate in a duplicate ratio to injure us, by annihilating the rising desire in the Southern States of effecting a better National system, and by adding to their jealousies of the designs of New England. I have dwelt on this subject to you, in order that if your sentiments should correspond with mine, that you should influence a choice of delegates of such characters as would possess the ability of pointing out the road to National glory and felicity.*

Stephen Higginson, in reply to Knox, suggested that the Convention in Philadelphia be empowered to form a Federal Constitution to be submitted to the States in special State Conventions, and to go into operation when ratified by nine:

> *It is an agreed, and, as I conceive, a clear point, that the Confederation is incompetent to the purposes for which it was established, the managing the affairs of the Union. Powers delineated on paper cannot alone be sufficient. The Union must not only have the right to make laws and requisitions, but it must have the power also of compelling obedience thereto, otherwise, our Federal Constitution will be a mere dead letter. To*

delegate rights to Congress, and at the same time to withhold from them the means of exercising those rights, is trifling and absurd. The powers of the Union must be increased, and those of the States individually must be abridged; they cannot both be perfectly sovereign and independent at the same time; the Federal must have power to control the individual Governments of the States, in some points at least; and unless the States shall soon consent to part with some of their rights as Sovereign States, they will very soon be involved in one general scene of disorder and distress. The Government of the Union must be the result of deliberation and choice, or of necessity and chance. By an early adoption of a liberal and extensive system of Government, we may secure to ourselves and posterity every rational felicity; and by wisely conceding a part of our separate independency, and concentrating our views to the Union, we may avert these public calamities, which now threaten the dissolution of the Governments of the several States, and which may eventually involve them in all horrors of a civil War. But in order to this, our present Federal Government must be critically examined, and the causes of the indifference or opposition of some of the States in the Union to Federal measures be well understood, or we never shall be able precisely to determine wherein it is deficient nor discover the true and proper remedies to be applied. . . . There are men in the several States of first rate abilities, who cannot be persuaded to go to Congress, or to engage permanently in public life; but they may be prevailed on to enter upon so important and special a business, as the forming a new Federal Constitution. The collective wisdom of a special Convention may probably therefore be greater than that of Congress.

It is to be noted that both Knox and Higginson particularly stressed the necessity of submitting the new Constitution to the people in State Conventions, rather than to the State Legislatures. It is an extremely significant fact that, throughout, the advocates of the new Constitution believed and trusted in the people and in popular action, to a far greater extent than did their opponents, who preferred action by the State Legislatures. . . .

Meanwhile, many statesmen had been pondering on the nature of the necessary changes in the framework of Government and of the theory on which they must be based. That additional power must be given to Congress, especially power over commerce, was generally acknowledged; and as Jefferson phrased it: "The politics of Europe rendered it indispensably necessary that with respect to everything external we be one nation firmly hooped together; interior government is what each State should keep to itself." That the three functions of Government—the Legislative, Executive, and Judicial—must be vested in separate bodies was the first principle agreed upon by several of the leaders; and Jay wrote to Jefferson, as early as August 18, 1786, that:

> *I have long thought, and become daily more convinced, that the construction of our Federal Government is fundamentally wrong. To vest Legislative, Judicial, and Executive power in one and the same body of men, and that too in a body daily changing its members, can never be wise. In my opinion, those three great departments of sovereignty should be forever separated, and so distributed as to serve as checks on each other. But these are subjects that have long been familiar to you, and on which you are too well informed not to anticipate everything that I might say on them. . . .*

A development of this idea in greater detail was written by Rufus King, a Member of Congress from Massachusetts, to Jonathan Jackson of that State, September 3:

> *It should be remembered that the pressure of a common calamity which induced the present Confederation is now removed, that the individual States are governed by their particular interests. These stand, or are supposed to stand, in opposition to each other, and, so long as the idea obtains, will prevent unanimity in any opinion concerning the corroboration of the Federal Constitution. Others, and by no means the least respectable, answer that nothing can be done in our present form, that the error lies in the original plan. Diminish, say they, the number of States, let those which are to be established be nearly equal, reform their Constitutions, give their Governments more energy, the laws more stability, the magistrates greater authority and responsibility. Let the State Governments be confined to concerns merely internal, and let there be a Federal Government, with a vigorous Executive, wise Legislature, and independent Judicial.*

Jefferson, writing to Madison, December 16, 1786, presented the same ideas as follows:

> *I find by the public papers that your Commercial Convention failed in point of representation. If it should produce a full meeting in May and a broader reformation, it will still be well. To make us one nation as to foreign concerns, and keep us distinct in domestic ones, gives the outline of the proper division of power between the general and particular Governments. But to enable the Federal head to exercise the power given it to best advantage, it should be organized, as the particular ones are, into Legislative, Executive, and Judiciary. The first and last are already separated. The second should also be. . . .*

To Jefferson in Paris, Madison wrote, March 19:

> *What may be the result of this political experiment cannot be foreseen. The difficulties which present themselves are on one side almost sufficient to dismay the most sanguine, whilst on the other side, the most timid are compelled to encounter them by the mortal diseases of the Constitution. . . . They are at present marked by symptoms which are truly alarming, which have tainted the faith of the most orthodox republicans, and which challenge from the votaries of liberty every concession in favor of stable Government, not infringing fundamental principles, as the only security against an opposite extreme of our present situation.*

He stated four principles which he believed essential to embody in a new Government: first, ratification by the people themselves rather than by State Legislatures; second, grant of power to the National Legislatures to negative any Act of a State Legislature in order to preserve the boundary between the Federal and the State powers; third, proportional instead of equal representation of the States; fourth, organization of the Federal powers so as not to blend those which ought to be exercised by distinct departments of Government.

On March 27, Edmund Randolph wrote to Madison, stating his views as to action the coming Convention might take:

> *I have turned my mind somewhat to the business of May next, but am hourly interrupted. At present, I conceive—1. that the alterations should be grafted on the old Confederation. 2. That what is best in itself, not merely what can be obtained from the Assemblies, be adopted. 3. That the points of power to be granted be so detached from each other, as to permit a State to reject one part, without mutilating the whole. With these objects, ought not some general proposition to be prepared for feeling the pulse of the Convention on the subject at large? Ought not an address to accompany the new Constitution?*

In reply to this, Madison wrote to Randolph, on April 8, elaborating his Jefferson letter, and setting forth a comprehensive scheme for a National Government, acting upon individuals and not upon States. The first plan for such a form of Government had been presented by Pelatiah Webster of Philadelphia, who, on February 16, 1783, published a pamphlet entitled, "A Dissertation on the Political Union and Constitution of the Thirteen States of North America, which is Necessary to Their Preservation and Happiness." There is no evidence, however, that Madison ever saw this pamphlet. To Randolph, he now said: "I think with you it will be well to retain as much as possible of the old Confederation, tho' I doubt whether it may not be best to work the valuable articles into a new system, instead of engrafting the latter on the former." Madison thus took the bold step of announcing that the work of the Convention should be to frame a new Constitution and not merely to alter over the old one. And this idea he further developed in a long letter to Washington, a week later, April 16, in which he set forth "some outlines of a new system," and in which he stated succinctly the whole theory on which the Constitution, as finally drafted, was based:

Conceiving that an individual independence of the States is utterly irreconcilable with their aggregate sovereignty, and that a consolidation of the whole into one simple republic would be as inexpedient as it is unattainable, I have sought for some middle ground, which may at once support a due supremacy of the National authority and not exclude the local authorities wherever they can be subordinately useful.

To Edmund Pendleton, Madison wrote, April 22:

The absence of one or two States however will not materially affect the deliberations of the Convention. Disagreement in opinion among those present is much more likely to embarrass us. The nearer the crisis approaches, the more I tremble for the issue. The necessity of gaining the concurrence of the Convention in some system that will answer the purpose, the subsequent approbation of Congress, and the final sanction of the States, presents a series of chances, which would inspire despair in any case where the alternative was less formidable. The difficulty too is not a little increased by the necessity which will be produced by encroachments on the State Constitution, of obtaining not merely the assent of the Legislatures, but the ratification of the people themselves. Indeed, if such encroachments could be avoided, a higher sanction than the Legislative authority would be necessary to render the laws of the Confederacy paramount to the acts of its members. . . .

Jay wrote to Jefferson, April 25, as to the Convention:

I wish their councils may better our situation; but I am not sanguine in my expectations. There is reason to fear that our errors do not proceed from want of knowledge; and, therefore, that reason and public spirit will require the aid of calamity to render their dictates effectual.

And John Adams wrote from London to Jay, May 8:

> *The Convention at Philadelphia is to consist of members of such ability, weight, and experience that the result must be beneficial to the United States. The settlement of so many great controversies such as those between Massachusetts and New York, Pennsylvania and Connecticut, New York and Vermont, &c., show that the Union has great weight in the minds of the people. It is, indeed, an object of such magnitude that great sacrifices ought to be made to its preservation. The consequences of a division of the Continent cannot be foreseen fully, perhaps, by any man; but the most shortsighted must perceive such manifest danger, both from foreign Powers and from one another, as cannot be looked upon without terror.*

Such were the sentiments of the public men of the day. Such were their alarms at the existing situation, and such were their hopes that some method might be found to preserve the Union. That they realized the disastrous economic conditions, that they feared the effect of prevailing unwise and unjust State legislation, and that they expected that a more adequate form of Government would bring an increase of economic prosperity for all classes in the community, cannot be doubted. But it is equally indubitable that their leading motive in desiring a new Constitution was their conviction that, without it, a dissolution of the Union and disappearance of republican government were inevitable.

Robert E. Brown

THE ECONOMIC INTERESTS OF THE MEMBERS OF THE CONVENTION

There were critics of Charles Beard's An Economic Interpretation of the Constitution of the United States *when it appeared in 1913, and there were admirers of the work. The number of admirers eventually came to prevail over the critics and Beard's judgments became an orthodoxy with exceptions, some of which, like the disagreement of Charles Warren, have been noted. The enthusiasm for Beard's interpretation increased with the reprinting of the work in 1935, the time of the Great Depression and the New Deal with its talk of economic royalists and its programs for relief, recovery, and reform, a time of vigorous if sometimes confusing governmental action for social causes. The "progressive" mood that had given inspiration to the Progressive movement and had welcomed* An Economic Interpretation *was reborn in the New Deal era and a new generation of Beard's readers added its endorsement to that of its predecessor of more than two decades earlier.*

But in another twenty years, a third generation of historians challenged the orthodoxy of the previous two. Beginning in 1955, the first of several new statements critical of Beard appeared, and although many of the objections newly raised against Beard had been stated when An Economic Interpretation *was first published, the new criticism was, in general, more detailed, better researched, and more clamorous, for now the matter was not merely a dispute about one book but an attack upon a whole orthodoxy. Many of the specific objections to* An Economic Interpretation *had been stated thirty years before: Beard had failed to show that possession of personalty had defined anyone's position in the Federal Convention or determined his vote; Beard had erroneously relied on Treasury information as of 1790 for propositions about the holdings of the Framers in 1787 and had therefore used unacceptable historical methodology; Beard's work was the product of a particular political inspiration, without substantial value of its own, but understandable (although perhaps unworthy) as an historical artifact of a special period, of interest primarily to historiographers of social conflict and liberal dissent. Such an argument, however, might also conceivably explain the appearance of the new criticism in the 1950s, the Eisenhower years of relative consensus and tranquillity, with the revisionists as much captive to their time as they said Beard was of his.*

But the new critics scored Beard heavily on the specifics of his thesis, and the following is Robert E. Brown's critical analysis of Chapter V of An Economic Interpretation. *Brown here examines the detail of Beard's state-*

From *Charles Beard and the Constitution: A Critical Analysis of "An Economic Interpretation of the Constitution,"* by Robert E. Brown (Princeton, New Jersey: Princeton University Press, copyright © 1956), pp. 73–91, footnotes omitted. Reprinted by permission of Princeton University Press.

ments about the personalty holdings of the Framers and assesses the quality of his investigation and the validity of his conceptions.

Many reviewers of *An Economic Interpretation* as well as writers such as Lerner and Hofstadter have praised Chapter V as the heart of the book and the real foundation of the Beard thesis. Since so much emphasis has been placed on Beard's historical method in his Chapter V, a detailed survey of the chapter is essential. What he was attempting to do was to see whether the men in the Convention possessed the kind of personal property that would be increased in value or made more secure by their efforts in Philadelphia. On page 149 he concluded that "at least five-sixths, were immediately, directly, and personally interested in the outcome of their labors at Philadelphia."

At the risk of becoming tedious, I have followed his delegate-by-delegate approach to see whether his evidence actually justifies his generalization about the men in the Convention. While such an approach may not lend itself to fascinating reading, it is the only way to test Beard's historical method.

Before we start this delegate-by-delegate marathon, however, we should note Beard's denial of purpose on page 73. Here he said his aim was not "to show that the Constitution was made for the personal benefit of the members of the Convention" or "to discover how many hundred thousand dollars accrued to them as a result of the foundation of the new government." Yet he concluded on pages 17, 18, and 149, and in many other places in the book, that the delegates were not disinterested spectators and that they stood to gain by the new government. Furthermore, on pages 35–37 he went to great lengths to prove that the holders of public securities alone, and this included many delegates, stood to gain $40 million by the adoption of the Constitution. The author should have been more consistent. Either the delegates were working for their own interests or they were not.

One other general criticism is essential before we analyze the main thesis of this chapter. In a footnote on page 75, Beard said he was assuming that when a member appeared on the funding books for redemption of public securities under the new government, the member was a public creditor in 1787 at the time of the Convention and had not purchased public securities for speculative purposes. The assumption appears to be unwarranted. Why would members of the Convention not buy public securities for speculation since anyone else could do so and there was no law against it? In fact, one might be surprised if they had abstained, especially if we assume that men act predominantly from economic motives. At the very least, this is one of the problems that Beard should have solved—whether the members of the Convention possessed what public securities they possessed at the time of the Convention, or whether they bought public securities later with the expectation that the value would increase.

Abraham Baldwin of Georgia had $2,500, probably in Continental paper, but there is no record of his holdings before April 1792, so there is no way of telling whether he owned this in 1787 or bought it after the Constitution was adopted. Beard did not say what Baldwin held in real estate, so Baldwin as evidence proves nothing.

Richard Bassett of Delaware owned Bohemia Manor, an estate of 6,000 acres, as well as homes in Wilmington and Dover. There is no evidence that he held any public paper in 1787, and he held only a few hundred dollars' worth in 1796 and 1797. If anything, Bassett represented realty rather than personalty.

Gunning Bedford of Delaware was the son of a substantial landowner. The £16 tax paid by a Bedford of that name might well have represented considerable property if the tax meant £ on the pound of rating as it often did. This would mean a rateable estate of £3,840 and an actual estate of several times this amount. We do not even know whether in 1787 he still had the £400 certificate which he bought in 1779. Bedford proves nothing, but the odds would be in favor of realty.

John Blair of Virginia was apparently a man of some fortune, but Beard did not indicate whether it was realty or personalty. The record shows only £249 in paper before the writing and adoption of the Constitution, which would have been a very minor holding if he were a man of some fortune. What he did after the Constitution went into effect is not evidence, for many a man who opposed the Constitution bought government securities under the new government. We would need to know more about Blair's property to catalogue him, but £249 would not make him a large holder of personalty, so he does not prove much.

William Blount of North Carolina was the son of a man who owned a large estate, but we know nothing of Blount's property interests in 1787. Again, what he did after 1790 proves nothing for 1787. If he had large private means in Tennessee later, and had no securities, his wealth was probably in realty.

David Brearley of New Jersey had a grandfather who owned 1,600 acres near Newton, a 100-acre plantation in Delaware, and several thousand acres near Lawrenceville. How much of this Brearley inherited we do not know, but he had only a small amount of securities. The attempt to include Brearley's relatives proves nothing, for they, too, held few securities. The reader should note that much of Beard's information on Brearley came from secondary works, not sources, and that this is true throughout his account of the other delegates.

Jacob Broom of Delaware was the son of a blacksmith who rose to be one of the gentry—some evidence of economic democracy at work—and who had considerable substance in real estate, silver, and gold. Broom had lands and houses to rent and sell and money to lend on good security. What he did after 1787 is of no consequence, and from what we know of him before 1787, we could not put him definitely on the side of realty or personalty.

Pierce Butler was a gentleman of fortune from South Carolina, but the evidence does not prove that this fortune was personalty. His thirty-one slaves would suggest real estate, and he could easily have purchased securities after 1787 with which to buy United States Bank stock. That Butler was descended from the Duke of Ormond is irrelevant to the question of whether or not he owned personal property.

Daniel Carroll of Maryland had some securities, but Beard did not say what their value was. That Carroll made his chief profit out of the new system by selling land on which the capitol at Washington was located would support the notion of a realty rather than a personalty interest. But even so, Beard would have had to prove that Carroll knew in 1787 that the capitol was going to be located on his land. The $5,000 in paper recorded after 1790 proves nothing for 1787.

George Clymer of Pennsylvania is the first of the ten delegates discussed to this point who seems to have had a large personalty holding. But the fact that he held $3,000 worth of securities in 1791 does not prove what he held in 1787, and of course Beard did not say what realty Clymer owned. If the records do not tell us, we cannot "assume" that Clymer held deferred and funded securities and thus had over $10,000 worth of government paper.

William R. Davie of North Carolina owned a fine plantation at Tivoli and had close connections with the landed proprietors of his region, but Beard did not represent him as the owner of any personalty whatever. Davie's ability to pay $5,000 for a thoroughbred colt probably indicated an interest in improving his livestock. It is not evidence that he favored personalty over realty.

Jonathan Dayton of New Jersey speculated with associates in western lands. If Beard is correct, however, Dayton is a good example of a speculator who should not have wanted the Constitution. The speculators had agreed to pay for part of their land in certificates, the prices of which went up after the adoption of the Constitution, causing the speculators much financial hardship. So Dayton does not prove much for personalty, and his later activities mean nothing for 1787. What a man did in speculation in 1800 is quite a different problem from that of his holdings in 1787.

John Dickinson of Delaware was a member of one of the "established landed families," which ought to have put him on the side of realty. The description of his wife's father's house is strictly irrelevant information and does not in any way show how many securities Dickinson held—in fact, the house is just more realty. Beard admitted that there was no evidence whatever of Dickinson's personalty interests.

Oliver Ellsworth of Connecticut bought lands and houses, loaned money at interest, and in 1791 had some $6,000 in government securities. But we do not know whether he had these securities in 1787 or bought them for speculation between 1787 and 1791. We have no comparison of his realty and personalty, and all the irrelevant material from Brown's *Life of Ellsworth* does not resolve the problem.

William Few of Georgia was a small farmer who practiced law and acquired a plantation, and, as Beard said, his personal interest in the new government was probably rather small. Later he presented $2,170 in securities for funding, but he had purchased this amount from someone else. Beard did not indicate when he made the purchase, whether before or after 1787, for the fact that a certificate was of the 1779 issue does not mean that he bought it in 1779.

Thomas Fitzsimons of Pennsylvania combined mercantile and financial interests, so he could be put down as the second delegate clearly on the side of personalty. But his losses in the Robert Morris speculations do not support the view that the speculators gained by the Constitution, or that they were certain ahead of time that the new government was going to operate in their interests.

Benjamin Franklin was worth about $150,000, and at the beginning of the war he had loaned the government about £3,000 which had depreciated and which he hoped would increase in value under the new government (p. xiv.). Just what the remainder of his property was is not clear, so Franklin as evidence proves nothing. In the Convention he was definitely on the side of the common people, so even if we proved that the bulk of his property was personalty, we could not use him as evidence that the Convention was rigging a government to favor personalty.

Nicholas Gilman of New Hampshire was a third delegate who definitely had personalty interests of consequence before the adoption of the Constitution. Far from working for a particular class, however, Gilman urged every town in New Hampshire to buy up public paper for a possible increase in price if the Constitution were adopted. We do not know what his realty holdings were, making it impossible to compare these with his personalty. Gilman's actions might well be considered economic, but they do not bolster a particular brand of economic determinism which pits personalty against realty.

Elbridge Gerry of Massachusetts was undoubtedly a large holder of public securities, some of them purchased before the Convention. The debates also show that he was interested in protecting the interests of public security holders—not only the wealthy ones, but also the soldiers who had been forced to sell their securities. Gerry believed that the new government *should be obliged* to pay off the debts of the Confederation government, not simply *have the power* to pay them. But as Beard pointed out, here was a man who was obviously a security holder, yet he opposed the Constitution. We also know that Gerry's father was a large holder of real estate, and we would need to know what Gerry himself had in realty to make a fair judgment. But even if we place him among the personalty interests, his presence there is of dubious value, since he opposed the Constitution and gave many reasons for his opposition, most of them noneconomic.

Nathaniel Gorham of Massachusetts was a speculator in western lands in April, 1788, when the Constitution had already been ratified by several states, though there is no evidence that he had much in personalty before the Convention met. But Gorham is another example of a land speculator who did not understand what effect the Constitution was going to have. In April, 1788, Gorham and others contracted for a large tract of land for which they were to pay $1 million in three annual installments in Massachusetts scrip, which was still selling below par at that time. When the price of the scrip went up, the speculators—including Robert Morris, who also was at the Convention—suffered diastrous losses. But this speculation came after the Convention, not before, and the speculators did not prove to be good prognosticators.

Alexander Hamilton of New York, as Beard said, had little to do with the formation of the Constitution. But Beard nevertheless made Hamilton the colossus of the new system, the man who saw the economic interests necessary for the success of the new government and who shaped his policies for their benefit. There are weaknesses in Beard's arguments, however. One is that Hamilton did not get a protective tariff for manufacturers, as his report on manufactures in 1791 proves. The second is that the very land speculators who were supposedly helped by Hamilton's policies went bankrupt, evidence that they did not know how the new system would operate. Beard said that thousands of small farmers and debtors and laboring mechanics were opposed to Hamilton's policies, but that they were partly disfranchised and had no leadership. But again, as Beard said before, workingmen in the cities supported the Constitution, and farmers and debtors were in control of state legislatures. What these groups did after Hamilton's policies were adopted is another story, just as the election of Hoover in 1928 and his defeat in 1932 are two different stories. Furthermore, Beard admitted that Hamilton had only about $800 in securities, and that he did not profit personally from the new government. In fact, said Beard, it must be admitted that Hamilton was swayed "by large policies of government," not by personal interests. Does this mean that even the "colossal genius of the new system" actually acted from "principles" rather than from personal economic interests?

William C. Houston of New Jersey, a professor and lawyer, had no public securities apparently and had invested £20 in a land speculation venture. As evidence of either realty or personalty he is therefore worthless.

William Houstoun of Georgia is similarly worthless as evidence, for nothing is known of his holdings.

Jared Ingersoll of Pennsylvania also had no personalty interests which would benefit by the Constitution, and Beard did not give his realty interests.

Daniel of St. Thomas Jenifer of Maryland was a slaveowner and had at least two plantations. Beard's statement that he "probably" held a small amount of public securities is not evidence, so Jenifer must be counted among the realty interests. That his son Daniel had $6,000 in paper in 1790 does not prove that his father had it in 1787.

William Samuel Johnson of Connecticut cannot be placed in either category, real or personal. That he probably speculated in government securities through his son after the Constitution was adopted proves nothing.

Rufus King of Massachusetts probably had both realty and personalty, and his activities after the Constitution was adopted mean nothing for 1787.

John Langdon of New Hampshire could hardly be accused of operating from economic determinist motives, for win or lose, he was willing to put all of his property behind the Revolution. Beard's evidence on Langdon's security transactions, as with most of the men he dealt with, applies after the adoption of the Constitution, not in 1787. Like Gilman, Langdon wanted his state to benefit by acquiring securities.

John Lansing of New York funded over $7,000 in securities in 1791, but Beard did not say what he had in 1787, or what his realty interests were. In addition, Lansing opposed the Constitution, so even if he had $7,000 in securities in 1787, he could not be used as evidence for the influence of personalty. For future reference, the reader should note Beard's statement that Lansing was at the Convention "long enough however to learn (what was not a very deep secret) the certain effect of an efficient government on continental securities" (p. 123).

William Livingston of New Jersey had no securities as far as we know. What his son did in speculation after the Constitution was adopted does not prove anything, for even the men who opposed the Constitution took advantage of opportunities under the Constitution. If we can try to prove guilt by association, as Beard does by saying that some delegates married merchants' daughters, then Livingston should have favored the landed interests, because his wife's father had been a large proprietor of land. Both propositions are invalid, of course, unless backed by evidence.

James Madison of Virginia obviously belongs under realty, and judging by his disillusionment after the Constitution was adopted, he apparently was not aware of the results which the Constitution would produce. He soon became one of the chief architects of the party which opposed the Federalist interpretation of the Constitution.

Alexander Martin of North Carolina, a well-to-do planter and slave owner, should obviously be placed on the side of realty, for, as Beard said, his tastes did not turn to dealings in public securities, with neither the Treasury Department records nor those of North Carolina listing his name.

Luther Martin of Maryland affords an interesting study in the use of historical method. Because he sympathized with poor debtors and opposed the complete exclusion of paper money, Martin was a bitter opponent of the Constitution. Beard described Martin as owning "only six slaves" and holding public securities which "were apparently meagre—a few thousand dollars at most." Beard appeared to be playing down Martin's holdings in securities, since Martin opposed the Constitution, yet these same holdings were larger than those of the other men discussed by Beard. Martin's securities were also as of June, 1791, not as of 1787.

George Mason of Virginia was a large landowner and land speculator, married the daughter of a well-to-do Maryland merchant (which should have made him pro-personalty), but also opposed the Constitution. Mason's 300 slaves were by far the most enumerated by Beard for any member of the Convention. With $80,000 in personalty and debts due, and large areas of western land, he ought to have been an ardent supporter of the Constitution. Beard explained his opposition on the ground that the Constitution would restore British titles to land, which could certainly have been true; but that was not the only reason for Mason's opposition. As the debates in the Virginia ratifying convention show, his chief objection was that the Constitution would establish a national government which he feared would annihilate the state governments and threaten the rights of the people. Particular items included powers of Congress over taxation, elections, and the military; lack of rotation in office for the president; failure to separate the functions of president and Senate; and absence of checks on the treaty-making powers.

James McClurg of Virginia was another example of the use of evidence after the Constitution was adopted presumably to prove something for 1787. This time, however, Beard admitted that most of the securities which he presented at the loan office had been bought for speculation and were not an original purchase. The same could easily have been true for most of Beard's examples, since most of his evidence comes from the period after 1790.

James McHenry of Maryland had both real and personal property, but there is no evidence, as Beard said, that he was an original holder of securities. If he had a debt of £5,000 due to him, and it was secured by bond, he should not have been interested in a government that would raise prices. What McHenry proves is difficult to say, except that he owned property of various kinds.

John Francis Mercer of Maryland is another example of the curious use Beard made of evidence. As mentioned before in dealing with Luther Martin, Beard said Martin's fortune was never very large for he owned "only six slaves" and had a "meagre" holding of at most a few thousand dollars in securities. But Beard changed his tone in speaking of Mercer. Mercer, he wrote, was "a man of some fortune," for he held "six slaves, and a moderate amount of public securities." Actually Beard should have attempted to show that neither owned any personalty, for they both opposed the Constitution.

Thomas Mifflin of Pennsylvania is still another example of misused evidence. Having said that Mifflin held only a "petty sum" of a few hundred dollars in Continental paper in common with Jonathan Mifflin, Beard then concluded that, on the basis of this evidence, it was apparent Mifflin appreciated the position of the powerful class of security holders who looked to the Convention for relief, and that Mifflin had more than an abstract interest in the establishment of public credit. If Martin with a few *thousand* dollars' worth of securities did not appreciate the position of the security holders, why would a few *hundred* dollars' worth necessarily incline Mifflin in that direction? Perhaps Mifflin's interests were identified with those of artisans who also wanted protection for manufacturing.

Gouverneur Morris of Pennsylvania belonged to the "landed aristocracy" and did not hold any public securities. According to the Beard thesis, he should have opposed the Constitution, but he did not.

There can be little doubt from Beard's account that Robert Morris of Pennsylvania had varied economic interests, or that he was a large holder of personalty. We do not know how much he held, or what the relative weight of his personalty and realty interests were, but even so, if Beard could have proved that all the men in the Convention were Robert Morrises, his thesis would doubtless have been on pretty firm ground. There are no contradictions in the evidence, there is no reason to question the conclusions drawn from this evidence, and the *Records* tell us nothing. There is one problem with regard to Morris, however. Beard gives us the impression that these men in the Convention wanted a government that would help them in their speculative ventures, yet Robert Morris ended his career in poverty and debt after having served a term in a debtors' prison. We could account for this if the Antifederalists had controlled the new government and had adopted policies inimical to the interests of the speculators. Did Morris, like other speculators, promise to pay for western land in securities that rose in value, thus indicating that he did not know how the new government was going to affect economic conditions?

William Paterson of New Jersey was for a time a merchant, but Beard could find out little about his economic interests.

William Pierce of Georgia was likewise evidence for nothing in particular, since we know little about him.

Charles Cotesworth Pinckney of South Carolina, a lawyer and a "considerable" landholder in Charleston, had a country estate and forty-five slaves. His holdings of public securities after the funding system prove nothing, for they could have been original holdings or securities purchased for speculation between 1787 and 1791.

Charles Pinckney of South Carolina was also a large land and slave owner, which would place him on the side of realty. He was the man who pictured American society as particularly democratic, both economically and politically, in his long speech in the Convention, and who believed that all the Convention had to do was to design a reasonably stable government to fit this democratic society.

Edmund Randolph of Virginia furnishes another example of a curious use of evidence. Randolph's grandfather was Sir John Randolph, which seems irrelevant, and we do not know how burdened with debt the three farms, Negroes, and other property were which he inherited. Beard said that Randolph was apparently never very prosperous, yet he enjoyed a magnificent law practice which brought in considerable revenue, held £14,200 Virginia currency in money claims in 1801, and had 7,000 acres of land, several houses, nearly 200 slaves, and ten or fifteen thousand dollars' worth of public securities. Just what a man had to have to be prosperous Beard did not say, but it is interesting to note the contrast with Mercer, who was "a man of some fortune" with six slaves and a moderate amount of public securities, and Pierce Butler, who, with thirty-one slaves, was a gentleman of fortune. Randolph's refusal to sell his excess slaves might well have meant that economic motives were not the only ones. The letter to Hamilton (p. 140) does not necessarily mean that he owed Hamilton a considerable sum. It would appear likelier that Hamilton was negotiating the sale of some of Randolph's securities, for Randolph wanted to sell only a part of his holdings, the remainder to be kept for a rise in price. Beard failed to say that Randolph was one of the delegates who refused to sign the Constitution after it had been accepted by the Convention, but perhaps this refusal accounts for his efforts to disparage Randolph's wealth.

George Read of Delaware was not a wealthy man. He owned a small farm and some slaves, and the records show that he invested $2,000 in securities in 1779, the darkest days of the Revolution and the days when the chances of getting back his money were at the lowest ebb. What he proves is difficult to say, for his farm might easily have been worth more than his securities.

John Rutledge of South Carolina was a plantation owner and had no securities. He should have opposed the Constitution if we follow the Beard interpretation to its logical conclusion.

Roger Sherman of Connecticut cannot be cataloged on the basis of Beard's evidence, for his securities were funded after Hamilton's program and there is no way of knowing from this account when he bought them or what he owned in realty.

Richard Dobbs Spaight of North Carolina was definitely on the side of realty, for he was "among the large planters of his state," held seventy-one slaves, and did not engage in public security transactions. But in spite of this, Beard pictured him as a supporter of personalty on the ground that "an old account of 3 per cents *for the sum of a few dollars,* shows that he was not unaware of the relations of public credit to stable institutions" (p. 143, italics mine). Just what such evidence shows about Spaight is anyone's guess.

Caleb Strong of Massachusetts likewise proves nothing, for he, too, could have purchased securities after the funding program seemed assured. Strong came from middle-class, agricultural Northampton, and the many members of the Strong family were ordinary middle-class farmers, as the tax records show.

Washington was undoubtedly the key figure in the whole movement for the Constitution. Without his prestige, there might not have been a Constitution, so we should be especially interested in

Washington's holdings from the standpoint of the Beard thesis that personalty was the dynamic element. And it does not take more than a glance to see that Washington's wealth was overwhelmingly on the side of realty.

Much of Washington's western holdings had been acquired before the Revolution started. In 1754 Governor Dinwiddie of Virginia issued a proclamation granting lands to officers and soldiers who would enlist for the campaign against the French. Before this land was actually granted, however, the British during the French and Indian War decided to stop all grants of land in the area. This decision was reinforced by the well-known British Proclamation of 1763 dealing with governments, land, and Indians in the West, but the latter also provided for land grants to officers and soldiers who had served during the war. Field officers, of whom Washington was one, were to receive 5,000 acres. In 1770 the grant of 1754 still had not been made, and many officers were selling their shares for a pittance, both because the grant itself seemed so uncertain and because they would have to invest a good deal of money to improve their lands in order to fulfill the terms of the grant. Washington was willing to gamble that the grant would eventually materialize, so he set out to buy twelve or fifteen thousand acres of these officers' grants at from £5 to £7 a thousand acres. In 1771 the Governor and Council finally decided on a division of the 1754 grant, of which Washington received 15,000 acres.

Washington's letters indicate that the grant would probably never have been made at all except for his persistent efforts and expenditure of money, and even then it took nearly twenty years. How much he bought in addition to the 20,000 acres he had coming as an officer would require further study, but in 1773 he was advertising that he had 20,000 acres on the Ohio which he would lease rent-free for a number of years to a tenant who would build on the land and clear a certain amount. From this time until the Revolution, Washington worked feverishly to improve his land so that he could save it according to the terms of his grant. His aim was to get settlers on the land, not just to hold the land for a rise in price. In fact, Washington bought, but very seldom sold, both land and slaves.

This account furnishes the background for an analysis of Beard's figures. These are for 1799, and as Washington never ceased acquiring property, they would necessarily have to be reduced somewhat to get the true amount in 1787. Even so, if we take the figures as they stand, we find that Washington owned 45,404 acres of land in addition to real estate in Washington, Alexandria, Winchester, and Bath, and that this real estate was valued at $266,819. Of personal property he held only $25,212. Using these figures alone, Washington's realty was 91.6 percent and his personalty 9.4 percent, or an advantage of nearly ten to one in favor of realty. In addition, however, we would need to add to the realty the $15,653 in livestock and the tremendous value of his slaves, for his total property amounted to $530,000. As I have said before, and as Beard acknowledged, slaves on plantations must be considered a part of realty. With these figures, the preponderance of realty over personalty is 95.44 to 4.56 percent. If we emphasize government securities, as we shall see that Beard did, the ratio is 1.17 percent for securities to 98.83 percent for realty.

Washington had many financial interests, it is true, but these figures prove beyond doubt that his main economic interest was realty and agriculture, not personalty. No one can read the Washington *Diaries* without coming to this conclusion. So the key figure in the whole move for the Constitution was on the side of realty—the wrong side according to the Beard interpretation.

A few minor points should be noted in Beard's treatment of Washington. If Washington was in arrears two years on back taxes because he could not sell his farm products, he must have been a debtor and he also must have been interested in doing something that would benefit agriculture. Furthermore, even the richest man in the country had been obliged to sell his certificates at the rate of twenty to one. On page 38 Beard made the unsupported statement that the Society of the Cincinnati, representing officers of some means, had not been forced to sacrifice their certificates as had the poor private soldiers. Yet Washington, the richest man, had sacrificed his certificates.

Hugh Williamson of North Carolina might well be placed on the side of personalty because of his mercantile activities, his $2,444.84 worth of securities, and his speculation in western lands. The securities, which of course could have been purchased between 1787 and 1791, were no more than those possessed by some men who opposed the Constitution, and Beard did not say what other realty interests Williamson had. But if Williamson's western lands would be enhanced in value by the new government, so would the lands owned by anyone else in the West.

James Wilson of Pennsylvania proves little, for most of the evidence on his activities came after the Constitution was adopted. Just what his stock in the Insurance Company of North America, 1792, or his speculations in Georgia land in 1795 have to do with 1787 is a problem that Beard did not explain. The only thing that counts is what he had in 1787, and Beard admitted that Wilson had only a "trivial" amount of securities.

George Wythe of Virginia is another example of realty rather than personalty interests. He inherited and married realty, and had only £513 of Virginia certificates which he had purchased from their original owners. His emancipation of his slaves and his provision for their future could mean that men had other than economic motives for their actions, for Wythe could certainly have sold his slaves.

Robert Yates of New York refused to enrich himself by speculating in confiscated estates, took no part in the transactions of public securities, and died poor. He also opposed the Constitution, so he really proves nothing as far as the Beard interpretation is concerned.

Having reviewed all this evidence on the economic holdings of the Convention delegates, the important question is whether Beard's historical method justified his conclusions that personal property was responsible for the Constitution. The answer must be an emphatic no. If we forget Beard's own generalizations and consider only his evidence, we find that actually only six delegates had personal property in excess of their realty (Clymer, Fitzsimons, Gilman, Gerry, Robert Morris, and Williamson), and further research into their holdings might show that even some of these held more realty than personalty. Two of these are of questionable value as evidence, Gilman because he presumably wanted farmers as well as personalty interests to benefit, and Gerry because he opposed the Constitution in spite of his holdings. In contrast with these six, and again strictly on the basis of Beard's evidence, eighteen delegates definitely had realty which greatly outweighed their personalty (Bassett, Bedford, Blount, Carroll, Davie, Dickinson, Few, Jenifer, Madison, Alexander Martin, Mason, Gouverneur Morris, Charles Cotesworth Pinckney, Charles Pinckney, Rutledge, Spaight, Washington, and Wythe). The other thirty (Baldwin, Blair, Brearley, Broom, Butler, Dayton, Ellsworth, Franklin, Gorham, Hamilton, Houston, Houstoun, Ingersoll, Johnson, King, Langdon, Lansing, Livingston, Luther Martin, McClurg, McHenry, Mercer, Mifflin, Paterson, Pierce, Randolph, Read, Sherman, Strong, and Wilson) really prove nothing in particular on the basis of Beard's evidence, for even he could not tell what these men had in the way of economic goods.

In evaluating Beard's historical methods, other criticisms mentioned in connection with the discussion of these various men should be summarized here. There is much material about their lives and background which is either irrelevant or the relevancy of which has not been made clear. A tremendous amount of Beard's material in this chapter comes from secondary writers, not primary sources, including a great deal from uncritical biographers of the delegates. While much of the material on securities was taken from the Treasury records, most of it refers to holdings several years after the Convention met. We have seen that several of these men acquired their securities after the Convention, so we cannot assume, as Beard did, that they held these when the Convention met.

Anyone would concede that the Founding Fathers had education, property, and influence far greater than the average at that time, but the same would be true of colonial legislatures, the Confederation Congress, and legislatures today. Had Beard cited this evidence to prove that the Convention delegates represented property in general and were interested in a government which would protect property, he would have been on firm ground. All of the delegates believed in the sanctity of property; some even believed that the chief function of government was the protection of property. This was undoubtedly important, but it was not their only concern. Beard did not contend, however, that the Convention was rigged to protect property *in general.* What he emphasized was *personalty*, and in fact, a particular kind of personalty which did not include livestock and slaves. We shall see later that he even refined personal property to mean predominantly one kind of personal property—public securities.

In addition to the fact that the evidence in this chapter does not prove the predominance of personalty, the big criticism of this particular economic interpretation is the ease with which Beard dismissed the agricultural interest. Does this mean that farmers had no economic interests? Would a politician in the predominantly agricultural states of North and South Dakota ignore the farm vote in his state? Yet in 1787 all the states were more agricultural than the Dakotas.

As Shays's Rebellion and Washington's inability to pay his taxes demonstrated, the farmers as well as the holders of personalty were not enjoying prosperous times. Why not assume that perhaps they, too, expected conditions to be better under the new government? And why draw such a shrap distinction between realty and various forms of personalty? A man who owns realty is not necessarily less interested in his property than anyone else. The simple fact is that the farmers cannot be ignored in the adoption of the Constitution, for as we shall see, some of the most heavily agricultural states adopted the Constitution the most quickly and by the most nearly unanimous vote. He who leaves the farmers out of the picture of the Constitution is treading on thin ice indeed, especially when such an important man as Washington was so obviously on the side of realty.

Forrest McDonald

A REVALUATION OF THE BEARD THESIS OF THE MAKING OF THE CONSTITUTION

Shortly after the appearance of Brown's book on Beard, Forrest McDonald also published a full-length attack on Beard. His purpose, he said, was not to examine Beard's methodology (which had been of principal interest to Brown), but to report on An Economic Interpretation *as a work of history. McDonald's conclusion was that the "economic interpretation of the Constitution does not work." McDonald's main contribution to the new criticism, however, was not this dictum but rather his pluralization of Beard's concept of property. That is to say, Beard, according to McDonald (and to other critics before McDonald) had employed rather crude classifications of property. His economic groups did not correspond, for example, with those of James Madison, whose classifications were "vertical" rather than "horizontal," that is, based not on class but on distinctions of general substantive economic interest. Now this fact alone would certainly not have disqualified Beard's classifications, but other weaknesses and curiosities of classification diminished their analytical value. For example, his conception of "property" led him to describe three kinds of real property holders in 1787 and four kinds of personalty—money, public securities, manufacturing and shipping, and capital invested in western lands. It is certainly rather odd that Beard should have combined manufacturing and shipping in the same category.*

In McDonald's opinion there were at least twenty basic occupational groups of diverse economic characteristic and need, and six basic forms of capital, besides capital incidental to occupational activity. And he argued that most of the occupational groups and forms of capital could be further subdivided. On the basis of these findings, it was McDonald's opinion that it was not even theoretically possible to present a single set of alignments that would explain ratification as a contest in which "economic self-interest was the principal motivating force." This may indeed be true. McDonald also said, however, that most of the leadership in each state came from three groups—lawyers, planters, and merchants; and he said further that there indeed were struggles for power, and that those striving sought the support of various economic groups having political weight, making appeals to economic self-interest, whether real or imaginary. In his words, "The result of the contest would then seem . . . to have turned largely upon the anticipated effects of the Constitution on economic interest." This conclusion would seem to modify somewhat the statement that an economic interpretation of the Constitution does not work.

Despite this, McDonald was undoubtedly right in his view that there was

Reprinted by permission from *We the People: The Economic Origins of the Constitution*, by Forrest McDonald (Chicago: University of Chicago Press, 1958), pp. 349–57. Copyright © 1958 by The American History Research Center, Inc., Madison Wisconsin.

no clear line of cleavage between personalty and other economic interests either in the Convention or in the contest over ratification, as Beard had argued. He was undoubtedly also right in his denial that public securities were the "dynamic element" among interests of personalty that brought in the new Constitution, which Beard had also argued. But McDonald was thought by some critics to resemble Beard in one respect, at least—McDonald, like Beard, it was said, postulated a relation between economic situation and political behavior without proving the connection. Although he had many more economic categories than Beard, some felt that he had not come any closer than Beard in the establishment of the relations between social class and political opinion. Professor McDonald speaks ably in his own behalf in the last essay in this book.

The following excerpt from McDonald's We the People *is a summary judgment on three "key propositions" of Beard's economic interpretation of the Constitution.*

Professor Beard interpreted the making of the Constitution as a simple, clear-cut series of events. When all the groups that became Federalists are brought together and analyzed, he asserted, and all the anti-Federalists are brought together and analyzed, the events can be seen as mere manifestations of a fundamentally simple economic conflict. His analysis led him to formulate three basic propositions, one regarding the Philadelphia Convention and two regarding the contest over ratification. In the light of the data in the foregoing chapters [of *We the People*], we may now focus our attention upon these three key propositions of Beard's economic interpretation of the Constitution.

The Philadelphia Convention

From his analysis of the Philadelphia Convention, Beard concluded that the Constitution was essentially "an economic document drawn with superb skill" by a "consolidated economic group . . . whose property interests were immediately at stake"; that these interests "knew no state boundaries but were truly national in their scope."

From a thorough reconsideration of the Philadelphia Convention, however, the following facts emerge. Fully a fourth of the delegates in the convention had voted in their state legislatures for paper-money and/or debt-or-relief laws. These were the very kinds of laws which, according to Beard's thesis, the delegates had convened to prevent. Another fourth of the delegates had important economic interests that were adversely affected, directly and immediately, by the Constitution they helped write. The most common and by far the most important property holdings of the delegates were not, as Beard has asserted, mercantile, manufacturing, and public security investments, but agricultural property. Finally, it is abundantly evident that the delegates, once inside the Convention, behaved as anything but a consolidated economic group.

In the light of these and other facts presented in the foregoing chapters, it is impossible to justify Beard's interpretation of the Constitution as "an economic document" drawn by a "consolidated economic group whose property interests were immediately at stake."

The Contest over Ratification, First Proposition

Beard asserted that the ultimate test of the validity of an economic interpretation of the Constitution would rest upon a comparative analysis of the economic interests of all the persons voting for and all the persons voting against ratification. He made an analysis of the economic interests of some of the leaders in the movement for ratification and concluded that "in the ratification, it became manifest that the line of cleavage for and against the Constitution was between substantial personalty interests on the one hand and the small farming and debtor interests on the other."

For the purpose of analyzing this proposition it is necessary to employ Beard's own definitions of interest groups. In the paragraphs that follow, as in the foregoing chapters, the term "men of personalty interests" is used to mean those groups which Beard himself had in mind when he used the term, namely money, public securities, manufacturing and shipping, and western lands held for speculation.

From a thorough reconsideration of the contests over ratification the following facts emerge.

1. In three states (Delaware, New Jersey, and Georgia) the decisions of the ratifying conventions were unanimous, and it is therefore impossible to compare the interests of contending parties. The following analyses of the conventions in these three states may be made, however.

In Delaware almost 77 percent of the delegates were farmers, more than two-thirds of them small farmers with incomes ranging from 75 cents to $5 a week. Slightly more than 23 percent of the delegates were professional men—doctors, judges, and lawyers. None of the delegates was a merchant, manufacturer, banker, or speculator in western lands.

In New Jersey 64.1 percent of the delegates were farmers, 23.1 percent were professional men (physicians, lawyers, and college presidents), and only 12.8 percent were men having personalty interests (one merchant, three iron manufacturers, and one capitalist with diversified investments).

In Georgia 50 percent of the delegates were farmers (38.5 percent slave-owning planters and 11.5 percent small farmers), 11.5 percent were frontiersmen whose economic interests were primarily agrarian, 19.2 percent were professional men (lawyers, physicians, and professional office-holders), and only 11.5 percent had personalty interests (all merchants). The interests of 7.7 percent of the delegates were not ascertained.

Beard assumed that ratification in these states was pushed through by personalty interest groups before agrarian and paper-money groups could organize their forces. The opposite is true. In each of these three states agrarian interests dominated the conventions. In each state there were approximately equal numbers of delegates who had voted earlier for and against paper money.

2. In two states in which the decision was contested (Virginia and North Carolina) the great majority of the delegates on both sides of the question were farmers. In both states the delegates who voted for and the delegates who voted against ratification had substantially the same amounts of the same kinds of property, most commonly land and slaves. A large number of the delegates in the Virginia convention had voted on the question of repudiation of debts due British merchants, and the majority of the delegates who had favored such repudiation voted for ratification of the Constitution. Large numbers of delegates in both North Carolina conventions were speculating in western lands. In the first convention a great majority of these land speculators opposed the Constitution; in the second a substantial majority of them favored ratification.

Beard assumed that ratification in these states represented the victory of wealthy planters, especially those who were rich in personalty other than slaves, over the small slaveless farmers and debtors. The opposite is true. In both states the wealthy planters—those with personalty interests as well as those without personalty interests—

were divided approximately equally on the issue of ratification. In North Carolina small farmers and debtors were likewise equally divided, and in Virginia the great mass of the small farmers and a large majority of the debtors favored ratification.

3. In four states (Connecticut, Maryland, South Carolina, and New Hampshire) agrarian interests were dominant, but large minorities of delegates had personalty interests.

In Connecticut 57.8 percent of the delegates who favored ratification and 67.5 percent of those who opposed ratification were farmers. Ratification was approved by 76.2 percent of all the delegates, by 81.8 percent of the delegates having personalty interests, and by 73.3 percent of the farmers in the convention. Here, then, four delegates out of five having substantial personalty interests favored the Constitution. On the other hand, three of every four farmers also favored the Constitution.

In Maryland 85.8 percent of the delegates who voted for ratification were farmers, almost all of them wealthy slave-owning planters; 27.3 percent of the opponents of ratification were farmers, all of them substantial slave-owning planters. The opponents of ratification included from three to six times as large a proportion of merchants, lawyers, and investors in shipping, confiscated estates, and manufacturing as did the delegates who favored ratification. It is to be observed, however, that because the vote in the Maryland ratifying convention was almost unanimous (63 to 11), statistics on the attitudes of the various interest groups would show that every major interest group except manufacturers favored the Constitution. A majority of the areas and of the delegates that had advocated paper money also favored the Constitution.

In South Carolina 59 percent of the delegates who voted for ratification were large slave-owning planters and 10.7 percent were lesser planters and farmers. Of the delegates who voted against ratification, 41.7 percent were large slave-owning planters and 34.2 percent were lesser planters and farmers. Merchants, factors, and mariners favored ratification, 70 percent to 30 percent, a margin almost identical to the vote of the entire convention—67 percent for, 33 percent against—and manufacturers, artisans, and mechanics were unanimous in support of the Constitution. On the other hand, 35.7 percent of the delegates who favored ratification were debtors who were in a desperate plight or had borrowed paper money from the state. Only 15.1 percent of those who voted against ratification were debtors or had borrowed paper money from the state. No fewer than 82 percent of the debtors and borrowers of paper money in the convention voted for ratification.

As respects New Hampshire, comparisons are difficult because of the lack of adequate information concerning 28.2 percent of the delegates. Of the delegates whose interests are known, 36.9 percent of those favoring the Constitution and 25 percent of those opposing it were farmers; of the known farmers in the convention 68.7 percent favored ratification. If it is assumed, however, that all the delegates whose interests are not ascertainable were farmers (as in all likelihood most of them were), then 49.1 percent of the delegates favoring ratification were farmers, 54.3 percent of those opposing ratification were farmers, and 52.8 percent of the farmers in the convention voted for ratification. Delegates whose interests were primarily in personalty (merchants, tradesmen, manufacturers, and shipbuilders) voted in favor of ratification, 60.9 percent to 39.1 percent. Delegates from the towns which had voted for and against paper money divided almost equally on the question of ratification: 42 percent of the towns that had voted for paper money and 54 percent of those that had voted against paper sent delegates who voted for the Constitution.

Beard assumed that in these states ratification was the outcome of class struggles between commercial and other personalty groups (Federalists) on the one hand and farmers and advocates of paper money (anti-Federalists) on the other. This generalization is groundless. In each of these states a majority of the men having personalty interests favored ratification, but in each of them a similar majority of the farmers also favored ratification. In one of these states there was no great demand for paper money, in another a large majority of the friends of paper money favored ratification, and in the other two the advocates of paper money were divided almost equally on the question of ratification.

4. In four states (Massachusetts, Pennsylvania, New York, and Rhode Island) men having personalty interests were in a majority in the ratifying conventions.

In Massachusetts, in the popular vote (excluding that of Maine) men whose interests were primarily nonagrarian favored the Constitution by about three to two, and men whose interests were primarily agrarian opposed the Constitution by about 55 percent to 45 percent. In the ratifying convention 80 percent of the merchants and shippers engaged in water-borne commerce, 77 percent of the artisans and mechanics, and 64 percent of the farmers favored ratification. About 83 percent of the retail storekeepers, 85 percent of the manufacturers, and 64 percent of the miscellaneous capitalists opposed ratification. One-fourth of those favoring and one-sixth of those opposing the Constitution were farmers. Of the personalty groups combined, 57.5 percent opposed and 42.5 percent favored ratification. The realty groups combined, including artisans and mechanics, favored ratification by 67 percent to 33 percent.

In Pennsylvania only 34.8 percent of the delegates favoring ratification were farmers, and only 26.1 percent of the opponents were farmers. Almost three-fourths—72.7 percent—of the farmers in the convention favored ratification. The great majority of the delegates on both sides, however, 84.7 percent of those favoring and 91.3 percent of those opposing the Constitution, had substantial investments in one or more of Professor Beard's four forms of personalty.

New York delegates are difficult to classify as farmers because almost all farmers in the convention were also landlords with tenants. Delegates to the state's convention may be classified as elected Federalists, converts from anti-Federalism, delegates who abstained from voting, and anti-Federalists. Of the delegates about whom there is sufficient data on which to generalize, fewer than 20 percent of each group consisted of farmers who had no tenants and who owned none of Beard's four forms of personalty.

Rhode Island delegates do not lend themselves to occupational classification because almost everyone in the state normally combined in his own economic activities several kinds of functions. Only 11.8 percent of the delegates favoring ratification and only one of the delegates opposing ratification were found to have no interests except farming. The early opponents of paper money formed the original core of those favoring ratification, yet in the final vote 62 percent of the delegates voting for ratification and 63 percent of those opposing ratification were men who had borrowed paper money from the state.

Beard's thesis—that the line of cleavage as regards the Constitution was between substantial personalty interests on the one hand and small farming and debtor interests on the other—is entirely incompatible with the facts.

The Contest over Ratification, Second Proposition

Beard was less certain of the foregoing point, however, than he was of this next one:

> *Inasmuch as so many leaders in the movement for ratification were large security holders, and inasmuch as securities constituted such a large proportion of personalty, this economic interest must have formed a very considerable dynamic element, if not the preponderating element, in bringing about the adoption of the new system. . . . Some holders of public securities are found among the opponents of the Constitution, but they are not numerous.*

This proposition may be analyzed in the same manner that Beard's more general personalty-agrarian conclusion was analyzed. To repeat, Beard asserted that public securities were the dynamic element within the dynamic element in the ratification. This assertion is incompatible with the facts. The facts are these:

1. In three states (Delaware, New Jersey, and Georgia) there were no votes against the Constitution in the ratifying conventions, and hence no comparisons can be made. If public securities were the dynamic element in the ratification, however, it would be reasonable to expect that the great majority of the delegates in these states which supported the Constitution so unreservedly should have been security holders. But the fact is that in Delaware only one delegate in six owned securities, in New Jersey 34 percent of the delegates, and in Georgia only one delegate.

2. In two states (New Hampshire and North Carolina) the numbers of security holders among the delegates were very small. In New Hampshire only 10.5 percent of those who voted for and only 2.2 percent of those who voted against ratification held securities. In the first North Carolina convention only 2.4 percent of the friends and only 1.1 percent of the opponents of ratification held securities. In the second convention only 2.0 percent of those favoring and only 3.9 percent of those opposing the Constitution were security holders. Superficially these facts tend to substantiate Beard's thesis, for these virtually securityless states were slow to ratify the Constitution. It has been shown, however, that actually the reluctance of these states to adopt the Constitution and their vulnerability to raids on their securities by outsiders were both merely surface manifestations of the same underlying conditions—the isolation, the lack of information, and the lethargy of the majority of the inhabitants of North Carolina and New Hampshire.

3. In three states (Rhode Island, Maryland, and Virginia) where there were contests and considerable numbers of security holders, the advocates and the opponents of ratification included approximately the same percentages of security holders: in Rhode Island, 50 percent of the advocates and 47 percent of the opponents; in Virginia, 40.5 percent of the advocates and 34.2 percent of the opponents; and in Maryland, 17.4 percent and 27.3 percent respectively. The facts relative to these three states clearly contradict Beard's thesis.

4. In two states (Massachusetts and Connecticut) the advocates of ratification included a considerably larger percentage of holders of securities than did the opponents. In Massachusetts 31 percent of the ratificationists and only 10.1 percent of the anti-ratificationists were security owners, and in Connecticut 36.7 percent and 15 percent respectively. The situations in these two states, and in these two states alone, tend strongly to support Beard's thesis.

5. In three states (Pennsylvania, South Carolina, and New York) a considerably larger percentage of the delegates opposing ratification than of the Federalist delegates held public securities. In Pennsylvania 73.9 percent of the opponents and 50 percent of the supporters of ratification were security owners, in South Carolina 71 and 43 percent respectively, and in New York 63 and 50 percent respectively. The facts pertaining to these states not only fail to harmonize with Beard's thesis but indicate that there the precise opposite of his thesis is true.

In the light of the foregoing facts it is abundantly evident that there are no more grounds for considering the holding of public securities the dynamic element in the ratification than for considering this economic interest the dynamic element in the opposition. There were, indeed, some holders of public securities among the opponents of the Constitution and, contrary to Beard's assertion, they were as numerous as the security holders among the supporters of the Constitution.

On all counts, then, Beard's thesis is entirely incompatible with the facts. Beard's essential error was in attempting to formulate a single set of generalizations that would apply to all the states. Any such effort is necessarily futile, for the various interest groups operated under different conditions in the several states, and their attitudes toward the Constitution varied with the internal conditions in their states.

Jackson T. Main
Forrest McDonald

BEARD AND THE CONSTITUTION: A DIFFERENCE OF VIEWS

Forrest McDonald's We the People *was given a very rigorous review by Jackson T. Main when it appeared. He noted that many monographs had been written in the long time since the publication of Beard's* Economic Interpretation *profitably using the theme it expressed. Main said, "Nobody would insist that Beard's thesis be accepted in its entirety, but his fundamental idea—that the Constitution reflected the economic interests of the large property-holders who wrote it—has survived much research, and any book which challenges it ought to be examined with a cautious and skeptical eye. If Forrest McDonald's* We the People . . . *is so scrutinized, it will be found that Beard has survived the attack."*

Main contradicted McDonald's statement that the Convention had been representative of the country at large geographically or in political opinion; criticized McDonald's evidence on grounds of inaccuracy and selectivity; thought that some of it, if properly interpreted, yielded results opposite from those inferred; and said that the true situation in four states closely examined by McDonald was that merchants and other commercial interests favored ratification of the Constitution by an "overwhelming margin," that farmers were opposed, that holders of paper were "predominantly Federal," and that Federalists had far more property than their opponents. The Convention, in short, according to Main, did not represent all geographical areas or shades of opinion, and the ratifying controversies showed that the holders of paper were strongly in favor of the new Constitution. All of this supported Beard.

Forrest McDonald replied to Main's critical review of We the People *in the same issue of the journal in which it appeared. He said that he had not been attempting to "refute" Beard but had been concerned only with "errors, misinterpretations, and overemphases" in* An Economic Interpretation. *He also criticized Main on many points of fact and interpretation and said that Main, like Beard, had attempted to provide a single uniform interpretation of events that were too complex to be so treated. It was McDonald's conclusion that Beard, in order to convey the simple truth that history does not take place in a vacuum, and to overcome the antiseptic and heroic interpretation of the work of the Framers that had been fashionable, had made things more simple than they were, overstated the case in order to make the point clear, and came close—in doing both—to proclaiming an*

Reprinted by permission of the authors and publisher from: "Charles A. Beard and the Constitution: A Critical Review of Forrest McDonald's *We the People*," by Jackson T. Main; and "A Rebuttal," by Forrest McDonald, *William and Mary Quarterly*, Ser. 3, Vol. XVII (1960): 86–110 (footnotes omitted).

American version of universal law, like one in physics, quantifiable and exact. The error, as McDonald saw it, was that Beard's followers did not have his imagination and applied, as rule, what Beard had offered as creative explanation.

Both Main's review of McDonald and McDonald's reply to the review are set out in the following pages.

It is a little strange that, when dozens of monographs during twoscore years have profitably used Beard's interpretation of the Constitution, an attempt utterly to refute him has aroused scarcely a whimper of protest. Nobody would insist that Beard's thesis be accepted in its entirety, but his fundamental idea—that the Constitution reflected the economic interests of the large property-holders who wrote it—has survived much research, and any book which challenges it ought to be examined with a cautious and a skeptical eye. If Forrest McDonald's *We the People: The Economic Origins of the Constitution* (Chicago, 1958), is so scrutinized, it will be found that Beard has survived the attack. Since a complete criticism would require a volume of equal length, this discussion will review only a few of the most important aspects.

Beard's work was an early attempt to test the hypothesis "that economic elements are the chief factors in the development of political institutions." He therefore assembled data concerning the real and personal property owned by those who wrote the Constitution and those who favored its ratification. Since, as he wrote, a complete survey "would entail an enormous labor," Beard relied chiefly on secondary accounts and published documents, except that he did undertake to identify the holders of the Federal debt. In addition, he discussed the political ideas of the members of the Federal Convention insofar as these related to his general purpose. This chapter is not discussed by McDonald. Beard found that most of the members of the Convention were lawyers, that they came from towns or regions near the coast where public securities were concentrated, that they were not farmers, and that they would be economically benefited by ratification because they possessed public securities, land held for speculation, money at interest, slaves, or property in commerce, manufacturing, and shipping. The same observations applied to the Federal members of the various state ratifying conventions. In general, the division on this issue "was between substantial personalty interests on the one hand and the small farming and debtor interests on the other."

McDonald set himself the task of testing Beard's conclusions. In doing so he made far greater use of primary materials and has substantially increased our knowledge, especially concerning the economic interests of the men involved. It is this contribution which immediately impresses the reader and has led to the general praise which the book has hitherto received. Nevertheless the research is far from complete. The facts cited are those which tend to refute Beard, while those which would support his views are often omitted; and the interpretation of the facts is likewise open to dispute.

The first part of the book attempts to prove that the Federal Convention, far from reflecting exclusively the ideas of certain well-to-do economic groups, was a truly representative body. McDonald seeks first to show that the delegates came from most of the major geographical areas; second, that they reflected all "shades of political opinion"; and third, that they themselves were of diverse economic interests, often in debt, less rich than Beard had suggested, and less influenced by ownership of public securities.

The first contention is "proved" by defining geographical areas in a way which achieves the desired result and by counting as present at the Convention anyone who was chosen as a delegate even when he did not attend. This faulty methodology may be illustrated by the case of Massachusetts. On the basis of physical location one might expect that the major areas would be described as (1) the maritime coast and its immediate hinterland; (2) Maine; and (3) the agricultural, upland interior; with perhaps (4) the Connecticut Valley towns distinguished as a fourth section. Such a division would reflect political and economic realities, for the seacoast towns were in fact usually opposed to those of the interior, while the lower Connecticut Valley usually supported the east and Maine went its own way. If this were done, then of the four delegates who attended, three came from the east and one from the Valley, leaving most of the state, including Maine and all of the interior, unrepresented. However, McDonald divides the coastal towns into four separate areas in such a way that all but one of them were represented; counts Rufus King as doubling for Maine as well as Newburyport, although King no longer lived in either place (being in fact a resident of New York) and had left Maine when he was twelve; considers that a group of interior towns connected with Boston were present through Francis Dana, although Dana did not attend the Convention; and concludes that six out of the nine areas into which he divides the state were represented at

Philadelphia. In this manner the fundamental fact, which Beard recognized, is concealed, namely, that the commercial East Coast was represented and the agrarian West was not. In like fashion he says that three out of four New Hampshire regions were represented, although the only two delegates who attended were from Portsmouth and Exeter, both within ten miles of the coast!

In Virginia as in Massachusetts, McDonald divides the Tidewater eastern part of the state into four separate areas, all represented; in addition the "Upper James" is counted present through Edmund Randolph who lived in Richmond, a fall-line town; and the rest of the interior is also considered to be present through Patrick Henry, who did not attend. McDonald can then cheerfully concede that the three sections west of the Blue Ridge were not represented, for he has discovered a majority of six out of nine. It can be argued with equal if not superior evidence that in truth all of Virginia's delegates to the Convention represented only one section: the Tidewater, or perhaps more accurately the eastern river valley area, leaving four sections to be counted as not present.

McDonald's proof that "all shades of political opinion" were present rests upon his division of the country into "factions," which are supposed to include all political groupings. He then finds that most of the major factions were represented. The argument depends, of course, upon whether the idea of "factions" adequately describes post-Revolutionary politics, and whether his particular identification of factions is valid. His conclusions therefore follow only if his definitions be accepted and if in addition it is granted that all those chosen as delegates should be counted even though they rejected the election. Massachusetts may again serve as an illustration. McDonald finds two major factions, led by John Hancock and James Bowdoin, and several minor ones headed by Samuel Adams, Theodore Sedgwick, Benjamin Lincoln, Benjamin Austin, and the Cushing family. Since both of the major factions were represented, he declares his point proved. But Massachusetts politics cannot be explained in terms of the personal leadership of individuals, of whom all but one lived near the coast, and that one (Sedgwick) a supporter of the conservative, commercial Bowdoin group. What about the vast majority of small interior towns? Surely a delegation which contained not a single man to express the views of small farmers—not a Shaysite or Shaysite sympathizer—did not reflect all of the various political opinions, but fundamentally only one. Similarly in Virginia, McDonald declares that "all four major and three independent factions were represented." But R. H. Lee and Henry did not attend, so that even accepting his definition of factions the true figure is two out of four major groups. Moreover, once again there was not a single delegate who spoke for the small farmers. In state after state the only "factions" represented were those of the mercantile, large landholding, well-to-do easterners, and it certainly is not true that the Convention represented all shades of political opinion. Once again Beard's analysis is the more nearly correct one.

The attempt to refute Beard's views concerning the property interests of the delegates is equally open to question, even though McDonald has gathered much additional data. The refutation is attempted by placing the emphasis upon those facts which depreciate the property held and by continually minimizing the delegates' wealth. Now every historian is required to select such facts as he believes significant and to arrange them in such a way as to convey a meaning: to interpret. Yet it is not always easy for the reader to remember that he is being presented an interpretation rather than an exact re-creation of reality. It will be instructive to compare, in a few cases, the accounts given by Beard and McDonald. The latter emphasizes that Robert Morris was heavily in debt and died bankrupt; Beard barely mentions this and concentrates upon describing his great wealth in 1787. Beard stresses James Wilson's large estate, McDonald his debts and ultimate poverty. To McDonald, Hamilton was "perpetually in debt"; to Beard, he is the principal spokesman for the rich, who "lived well, and had a large income." Madison is depicted by McDonald as the owner of "560 ill-kept acres," by Beard as the son of a wealthy planter, relieved thereby from the necessity of earning a living (actually the Madison estate included 5,748 acres and 99 slaves). Richard Bassett appears in *We the People* as a man of moderate means who lived "in comfort"; in Beard he is one of the wealthy men of the state who "entertained lavishly." In a number of other instances the two accounts differ, sometimes radically.

Throughout *We the People*, men of means are made to appear quite the opposite. Hamilton, Robert Morris and Wilson were not the only ones to die in debt; so also did Nathaniel Gorham, who in 1787—the date that matters—was one of the country's wealthiest men. We read that Pierce Butler, who owned 143 slaves, was "in rather desperate circumstances." William Houstoun, "the richest member of the Georgia delegation," could scarcely support himself, the implication being that the rest of the delegates from that state must have been truly impoverished; yet in truth Houstoun was one of the wealthy planter aristocracy with extensive lands. Gouverneur Morris's family estate is called "magnificent" when he fails to inherit it, but in the next paragraph, having passed into Morris's hands, it becomes "debt-laden." Jared Ingersoll, we read, had in 1787 "besides a wealthy father-in-law, a moderately successful practice, a fourth interest in a 30-ton sloop in the coasting trade, *and little else*" (italics mine). Edmund Randolph was in "great need," "beset with economic difficulties," impoverished it seems by thousands of acres and over a hundred slaves. Indeed to McDonald the rich man had less wealth than the poor, for we learn that John Rutledge's 243 slaves "were apparently more of a burden than an asset " When a man's basic wealth enabled him to borrow money in a time of great currency shortage, this is interpreted as a sign of poverty Washington becomes "land- and slave-poor," a debtor, who borrowed £10,000 to cover expenses when he went to New York as President. McDonald lists thirteen members who were "debtors for significant amounts" and whose condition "ranged from acute embarrassment to desperation and outright bankruptcy," including such impecunious figures as Rutledge, Robert Morris, James Wilson, Washington, Madison, Randolph, Butler, Houstoun, and both Pickneys.

This is absurd. If the reader will take the trouble to examine the facts which McDonald himself provides, the true situation will become apparent. The fact is that over two dozen of the sixty-five elected delegates, and more than half of those who signed the Constitution, were rich, and others were well-to-do. Not more than nine—less than one-seventh of the elected delegates—were of only modest means. Almost all of the delegates, moreover, were merchants, large landholders, or lawyers representing these groups, comprising precisely what Beard said they were: a "consolidated economic group."

McDonald also attempts to disprove the influence of public securities upon the Founders. The real question, it might be urged, is not whether a member of the Convention held securities, but the distribution of these in the country at large and the extent to which delegates reflected the desires of security-holders. However, since Beard did not do this, McDonald is justified in restricting his inquiries to the holdings of the delegates. In doing so he emphasizes that few of them held large amounts, and he tries, by gratuitous remarks, to disparge the importance of the profit received. Nicholas Gilman made $500 which is "roughly $10 per month from 1787 to 1791." Rufus King made "only" about $1,300 in four years. Thomas Fitzsimons retained "only" $2,668.10 worth. Oliver Ellsworth's profit of $3,240 "would hardly seem large enough to write a Constitution to protect," and McDonald's concession that in Ellsworth's case the motive probably did exist merely emphasizes the impression he conveys that in all other cases no such amount would suffice. It was Beard's point, however, that even a small holding might well create sympathy with the needs of public creditors. The question was not, he wrote, "how many hundred thousand dollars accrued to them," but whether they represented "distinct groups whose economic interest they understood and felt in concrete, definite form through their own personal experience with identical property rights." Furthermore the stake of the delegates was by no means as small as McDonald implies. No argument can conceal the fact that nearly half of the delegates made over $500 each from the appreciation of these certificates, and no fewer than thirteen held $5,000 worth apiece (face value) in 1787. It would certainly seem that once again Beard is closer to the mark than McDonald.

In addition to this effort to reinterpret the nature of the Convention, McDonald tries to disprove Beard's contention concerning the alignment for and against ratification—"to test," as he puts it, "the validity of Beard's class struggle interpretation," by demonstrating through a description of the members of the ratifying conventions that men on both sides had the same economic interests and the same amount of property. In his anxiety to prove his point, McDonald sometimes (1) minimizes the property held by Federalists and exaggerates that owned by Antifederalists; (2) defines, in ways open to question, the professions of men on both sides so as to make it appear that they were of similar status; (3) omits, doubtless inadvertently, some relevant biographical data; (4) prints summary tables which appear to support his views, but neglects to publish tables which might have proved the contrary; and lastly (5) includes those facts which support his opinions but overlooks some which do not. The reader is drawn into an uncritical acceptance of all this because McDonald has done some excellent research and goes into great detail upon subjects which uphold his interpretation.

The first chapter of the three (chapters five, six, and seven) devoted to this subject is the least liable to objection. Most of the states discussed did not contain a large Antifederal party, and so, few challenging comparisons are made. There are, however, some doubtful generalizations, and the discussion of the Connecticut ratifying convention introduces the line of argument which McDonald follows throughout. It is emphasized that the wealthy Federalist merchant Jeremiah Wadsworth had to give up some of his tax-delinquent land, and this is evidently supposed to cast doubt upon his financial position. Nearly everyone, rich or poor, was affected by the financial difficulties of the period. The question therefore is not who was in financial straits at the time—everybody was—but whether Federalists or Antifederalists had more property. In this case the fact of greatest significance is that Wadsworth was the richest man in the state. In the ratifying convention, we are told, both sides came from "similar economic backgrounds" in spite of the fact that twenty-nine out of thirty-three lawyers and ten out of twelve merchants were Federalists. The admission that among Antifederalists "less than half as many were public security-holders" turns out to be McDonald's way of expressing the fact that forty-five Federalists and only six Antifederalists held part of the national debt.

Chapter six will furnish most of the examples of the way in which the true situation is disguised. The treatment of the alignment in Pennsylvania is typical. Property held by the Federalists is minimized. Robert Coleman is listed merely as the "proprietor of an ironworks"; one would not guess that this was the Elizabeth Furnace, which covered part of a 4,000-acre property, and that Coleman was one of the wealthy men of the state. Less than justice is done to the holdings of such men as Yeates and Rush, while Neville and Scott certainly cannot be characterized merely as frontier farmers, for both were men of means, economic leaders of their community. Colonel Thomas Bull, whom McDonald calls a farmer, managed an iron furnace so successfully that he was able to erect a fine mansion, a gristmill, a sawmill, and a blacksmith shop, and to retire. On the other hand, among the Antifederalists, Nicholas Lotz, who was a weaver, becomes "the proprietor of a clothing business." Adam Orth is called an iron manufacturer although he did not own a forge until 1793. James Martin is stated to have been engaged in "miscellaneous promotional and speculative deals" elevating him above the farmer rank, but these high-sounding phrases mean, upon examination, only that he owned a couple of small farms and some public securities.

Federalists such as Barclay, Neville, and Scott, who outdealt Martin by a wide margin, remain merely "farmers." Summarizing his information in a table, McDonald introduces an occupation called "manufacturing capitalist," which turns out to mean someone who had a mill, the idea evidently being that these small property-holders should be considered among the economic elite. Six Federalists and seven Antifederalists are placed in this category, which makes it appear that, if anything, the Antifederalists were more likely to be "capitalists." But the fact is that six additional Federalists, identified only as farmers, also had mills (Allison, Bull, Hannum, J. Morris, Wynkoop, and Yardley). In addition, if the Antifederalist Whitehill is elevated out of the farmer ranks because he owned an inn, the same ought to apply to the Federalist Barclay. The total result is that McDonald's summary table is misleading, for whereas it states that 35 percent of the Federal ratifiers were farmers, the true figure, accepting his definition of what constituted a farmer, is 15 percent.

McDonald also tries to demonstrate that the Antifederalists held more public securities than their opponents by comparing the certificates held by the delegates. The fact that a few of the important Antifederalists owned certificates really proves little. Popular parties typically derive their leadership from men of large property, and in nearly every state, including Pennsylvania, the Antifederalists were led by men of means. A few of them were indeed large holders, but the evidence is strong that most of the securities were owned by Federalists. Philadelphians owned as much as 90 percent of the debt, and Philadelphians of all professions and classes were Federal; pro-Constitution candidates to the ratifying convention received an average of 1,200 votes each compared with 160 each for the Antifederalists. Among the largest ($10,000 plus) holders whose political affiliations could be determined, three out of five were Federalists.

Finally (and this is the most important point of all), whereas only two or three Antifederal delegates were men of large property, more than a dozen of their opponents were wealthy. In short the delegates on both sides did not hold "about the same amounts of the same kinds of property." Again Beard is more nearly correct than McDonald.

A similar procedure is followed in the case of Massachusetts. Federalists are downgraded and their property minimized. Elijah Dwight was more than a retail shopkeeper; he was a prominent and wealthy judge. Ebenezer Janes, who is called a maker of gravestones, was also a miller and a deacon who had an imposing house. T. J. Skinner, "carpenter," was a prominent Williamstown merchant. John Ashley, identified by McDonald merely as a farmer, was a merchant, a lawyer, and a large landowner (and Harvard, 1754). Noah Porter, also called a farmer, had the first chair in town, later added a chaise, had £100 loaned at interest, was Harvard 1761, and was sheriff of Hampshire County. Tristam Dalton was not just a lawyer but a wealthy merchant who married the daughter of another wealthy merchant. Morison writes that when Dalton went to New York as one of Massachusetts' first senators, he drove "in Newburyport style, in his own four-horse coach, emblazoned with the Dalton arms, and attended by servants in the Dalton livery." Other examples could be given. Among the Federalists whom McDonald could not identify, George Payson of Walpole and Moses Richardson of Medway were both innkeepers, while John Winthrop and Caleb Davis were both prominent merchants of Boston. On the Antifederal side there are also some errors in the assigning of occupations.

An important question of interpretation concerns the category of "gentleman-capitalists," who were "men of means, large landowners, renters, money-lenders, and investors in various local business ventures." Among the thirteen Federalists identified as such, many undoubtedly belong to this group, among them Francis Dana, Benjamin Greenleaf (who was from Newburyport, incidentally, not Salem), Nathaniel Barrell, Benjamin Lincoln, William Pynchon, William Heath, and Richard Cranch. Whether all or even any of the fifteen Antifederalists are properly assigned to this category is of course a matter of judgment, but it is clear from the records that they did not as a group compare in wealth with their Federal equivalents.

McDonald's summary table and his conclusions, being based in part upon doubtful facts, can be seriously challenged. If the changes in occupation noted above are made, it appears that thirty merchants and tradesmen favored ratification and only eight opposed it. At the other end of the social scale most of the men whose occupations are unknown may safely be presumed to have been farmers, and if they are added to those known to have been such, then 38 percent of the Federalists and 58 percent of the Antifederalists were farmers. Therefore, despite McDonald, the Federalists were not more successful in winning the support of these men. McDonald omits any mention of the relative property holdings of the opposing sides, but it is certainly important to observe that almost all of the wealthy men in the convention were Federal. He does concede that the vast majority of public security-holders favored ratification. His figures (in assembling which he has done a real service) show, indeed, that only three Antifederalists held $500 worth whereas forty-one Federalists did so. Outside of the convention, virtually all of the securities were concentrated in Boston and a few other seacoast centers; most of the large owners were merchants and, insofar as their politics are known, they were Federalists.

South Carolina is discussed without providing the usual table summarizing the alignment. Had such a table been constructed it might have caused McDonald to modify his conclusions. Two key generalizations are offered. First, "The majorities by which merchants, factors, lawyers, planters, and farmers favored ratification was for each group about the same as the overall majority in the convention—about two to one." Let us accept the data given, but among the Federalists changing John Chesnut and Henry Laurens from planters to merchants and John Kean from unknown to merchant. The proportions are as follows: merchants, 3:1 for ratification; among artisans and mechanics, 7:1, lawyers 5:1, doctors 5:1, and large planters 3:1, but in significant contrast small planters and farmers 2:1 *against* ratification. The truth therefore is diametrically opposed to his statement. Secondly, he continues, "They had, proportionately, about the same amounts of the same kinds of property." Let us construct our own table of slave-ownership, since none is furnished:

No. of Slaves	*Federalists*	*Antifederalists*
Unknown	18	8
None	2	2
1–9	16	21
10–19	25	14
20–49	23	13
50–99	30	12
100 plus	35	3

It will be seen that 43.6 percent of the Federalists and only 20.5 percent of the Antifederalists owned fifty slaves. So also the very great majority of large landholders and of large public security-holders were Federalists. Once again McDonald's conclusions are contrary to the evidence.

Chapter six closes with a discussion of the ratification in New Hampshire. The shortage of biographical information prevents any confident generalizations. McDonald concedes that public securities were held mainly by the Federalists. All of the merchants in the convention were Federalists; 60 percent of the Antifederalists and 53 percent of the Federalists were farmers or of unknown occupation. No summation is made of the proportion of large property-holders on either side, although such information as is provided makes it obvious that the Federalists had far more wealth, a conclusion which contemporaries shared.

To summarize the critique of this key chapter, the true situation is as follows: in all four of these states, among members of the conventions, (1) merchants and those connected with the commercial interest favored ratification by an overwhelming margin; (2) farmers took the opposite side; (3) public security-holders were predominantly Federal; (4) the Federalists had far more property. This is precisely what Beard argued, yet McDonald, through the omission of pertinent data and the distortion, doubtless unconscious, of the facts he does give, arrives at an opposite conclusion.

The analysis which has been presented here could be extended through the third chapter on ratification, but enough has perhaps been said to prove the points at issue. A few additional remarks may be made. In Virginia, the delegates held properties in counties other than those which they represented, and these are not always noted—twenty-five Federalists and seventeen Antifederalists had more property than is shown. Some errors are made in regard to the professions of the delegates: among the Federalists, Simms, Z. Johnston, and Tomlin were merchants; T. Lewis, McClerry, and Bushrod Washington were lawyers; while Antifederalists R. Williams and R. Lawson were also lawyers. Federal delegates did have more slaves than the Antifederalists, and more of them were large public security-holders, but it is true that the division of property among the delegates in the Virginia convention was more equal than was ordinarily the case. McDonald's concluding generalizations, as elsewhere, do not always follow from the evidence. The discussion of New York's ratification also contains some errors. His description of the convention delegates omits altogether the wealthy Federalist lawyer Richard Morris, while Philip Livingston was a merchant in addition to his other occupations. The impression is given that Federalist John Hobart was merely a debtor, but in fact he inherited a considerable estate. As usual the conclusion is drawn that the members were about equal in wealth and economic interest. No table is provided, so it is necessary to construct one:

	Federal	*Elected Anti, voted Fed.*	*Elected Anti, did not vote*	*Antifederal*
Merchants	5	1	0	0
Lawyers and large landowners	3	3	0	1
Lawyers	5	0	4	7
Large landowners	2	1	1	2
Millers	0	1	0	1
Obscure men	4	3	2	9
Farmers	0	3	0	6

Obviously there was no such equality. It should also be noted that on the final alignment eleven Federalists and six Antifederalists held public securities worth over $500.

The last three chapters consider the economic origins of the Constitution from a more general point of view, and some more general criticisms are in order. In the first place, it can be seen from the foregoing that the attack upon Beard has been unsuccessful. The Federal Convention did not represent all or even most of the economic interests and political opinions. Analysis of the delegates to the ratifying conventions shows conclusively that the influence of the merchants, lawyers, and large landowners was pro-Constitution while most farmers were on the other side; that the Federalists held far more wealth than their opponents; and that the influence of public security-holders was strongly on the side of ratification. The evidence upon which the final interpretative chapters is based therefore lacks validity and the conclusions themselves are of course invalid.

A second general criticism concerns the introductory paragraphs which precede the descriptions of the delegates in each state. These are designed to analyze some of the local factors which were involved in the ratification process. In some cases McDonald has uncovered new material, and parts of his introductions are very good, but they usually deal with only a few of the causative factors. Those which do not support his general thesis are omitted, although the reader is sometimes left with a different impression. Particular attention is given to the state paper-money controversy, in discussing which McDonald tries to show that the Federalists were more deeply in debt than the Antifederalists and that they supported debtor bills. Several observations must be made here. The first is that by selecting particular votes and ignoring others, the evidence is "stacked." In the case of South Carolina, for example, all of the attention is concentrated on the debates in 1785. Yet it is conceded that two years later the planters had changed their minds (indeed the situation in 1785 was abnormal, not typical). It would seem pertinent therefore to examine a series of votes recorded on economic matters during 1787–88, in which the sectional division, correlating with the vote on the Constitution, is revealed. Secondly, the fact that men borrowed money, as did the South Carolina planters, does not make them debtors in the Beardian sense. The difference between the man of means, who borrows of his free will, or to avoid disposing of some of his less fluid wealth (as Washington borrowed £10,000), and the small property-holder, who unwillingly falls into debt, or is forced to borrow from one creditor in order to pay another, is fundamental; and to treat them alike is as absurd as it would be to condemn United States Steel because its indebtedness is greater than that of a corner filling station. Thirdly, McDonald's anxiety to prove that Federalists were debtors leads him into some misstatements. We are informed for example that "virtually all of the fourteen delegates" from the Shenandoah Valley were debtors, but according to his source only five were in debt. Fourthly, in spite of what McDonald says, paper-money advocates did tend to oppose the Constitution: (1) most of the Antifederal strength in Connecticut came from paper-money districts; (2) the correlation in Massachusetts exceeds 80 percent; (3) the correlation in New Hampshire is not high, but it exists; (4) the paper-money forces in Rhode Island were Antifederal; (5) the alignment in New York is well known; (6) the correlation in North Carolina is very high (the situation there is not described by McDonald); and (7) paper-money supporters in both Maryland and Virginia usually opposed ratification. There are certainly many cases in which the generalization does *not* hold, but it cannot be denied altogether. To do so, finally, is also to ignore a great deal of contemporary testimony. If the debtors did not, on the whole, oppose, and the creditors did not, by and large, support the Constitution, it would come as a great surprise to informed observers on both sides.

Another general critical observation stems from what is in many ways an excellent suggestion: namely, that the economic aspects of the Constitution be studied by classifying Americans in terms of their occupations, of which McDonald distinguishes four major categories and over two dozen subgroups. Beyond doubt this kind of an investigation is needed and will be most rewarding. However, American society in 1787–88 can be structured in other ways than by occupation, of which one of the most important is by class, or (if the existence of classes be denied) at least by relative income or property held. It is not sufficient to distinguish, for example, between the occupations of subsistence farmers and merchants unless it is recognized also that the former were poor by comparison with the latter. Despite McDonald, it can be maintained that the Constitution was written by large propertyowners and that the division over its acceptance followed, to some extent, class lines. There is much evidence that this was the case, and the thesis is stated explicitly in many contemporary letters and newspaper articles. At the very least the subject warrants investigation, and no program for research can be successful which ignores it.

A final point; the procedure adopted by McDonald and others of conducting their research with the intent of disproving someone's thesis is not likely to reveal the truth, because one's conclusions are prejudiced in advance. The facts of history do not, as a rule, all point inescapably in a single direction; interpretations are made by balancing the evidence. When one sets out deliberately to gather evidence on only one side the desired result can generally be achieved, for along the way first the "facts" and then the judgment are unconsciously distorted. McDonald has done much valuable research, and his errors are doubtless honest errors; yet no better example can be found of the pitfalls inherent to this methodology. (Beard, of course, can be criticized on the same basis, but this does not justify the method.) The full story of the Constitution and its ratification remains to be written. Until this is done, the historian seeking an interim interpretation will be better advised to follow Beard than McDonald.

FORREST McDONALD'S REBUTTAL

It is with some reluctance that I undertake a reply to Jackson T. Main's critique of *We the People*, for with much of what Mr. Main says I entirely agree. Like him, I have been distressed by the absence of critical reviews of the book (I have seen only two, and he wrote both). Like him, I have been surprised that an attempt to correct some of the errors, misinterpretations, and overemphases in Charles A. Beard's pioneering work (by no means an attempt "utterly to refute" it) has, in Mr. Main's words, "aroused scarcely a whimper of protest." Furthermore, Mr. Main has, in some instances, correctly pointed out some of my factual errors, though he has missed others that I have discovered since publication. The book, it should be said, is based upon several thousand scraps of miscellaneous information, most of it obscure and much of it drawn from sources that were not written with the most scrupulous accuracy, and though I triple-checked each statement of fact some errors were inevitable. Thus where Mr. Main himself has been accurate (which is not always), I gratefully accept the correction.

With other parts of his review, however, I am less happy. Though I feel that chapter two—on factions and areas represented in the Philadelphia Convention to which Mr. Main devotes approximately one-fifth of his paper—is the weakest part of the book, as well as not being entirely germane, Mr. Main's undocumented comments about it seem to me as naive as they are inaccurate. Most of his observations here concern Massachusetts. My analysis of that state was based upon the tabulation and mapping of every vote, popular and legislative, cast on statewide issues from 1781 to 1790, and upon an intensive study of the patterns of internal trade and transportation. And, until he or someone else goes through this material, I shall prefer to believe what I have derived from my research rather than his bare assertion that I am wrong.

Similarly, I am unhappy with Mr. Main's practice of building logical conclusions upon self-contradictory assumptions, and changing his assumptions to suit his convenience. For example, consider the matter of how property-holding is supposed to have influenced attitudes toward the Constitution. At the outset he approves Beard's assertion that the line of division for and against the Constitution was between substantial personalty interests on the one hand and real property interests (particularly small farmers) and debtors on the other. However, Mr. Main omits Beard's explicit qualification that what was meant was personalty *other than slaves.* Later, he goes on to construct a new definition of division that entirely abandons Beard's fundamental distinction between personalty and realty. To Mr. Main the fight becomes one between rich guys and poor guys. And even as he shifts the main argument, Mr. Main finds it convenient to change assumptions frequently. At one point he is with Beard on the proposition that it is not so much the *amount* of public security or other personalty holdings that counts; rather, what "really" matters is merely having had experience with various kinds of property, as a result of which "even a small holding might well create sympathy" with the needs of suffering public creditors or other personalty groups. Two paragraphs later he changes his mind and decides that what is really important is neither who was suffering nor who had experience with different kinds of property, "but whether Federalists or Antifederalists had more property." As this bewildering display of illogic proceeds, it is difficult for me to understand just what thesis Mr. Main is defending. It is certainly not Charles A. Beard's thesis.

But let us get down to specifics. Mr. Main's first volley, after his critique of my second chapter, is directed against my account of the economic interests of the members of the Philadelphia Convention. He begins with a reluctant admission that my sketches contain "much additional data." But he then forgets this and compares my analysis of the delegates with Beard's, as if we were merely placing different emphasis (mine a distorted emphasis) upon precisely the same data. To substantiate his charge, he mentions by name thirteen of the delegates, and asserts that I attempted to depreciate their property holdings. He made an unfortunate choice. If the reader will compare my statements with Beard's on these thirteen delegates, he will find that I have shown at least eight of them to have had considerably *more* property than Beard had indicated. I found and reported that all four delegates from South Carolina had far more property than Beard had stated: Butler had 112 more slaves than Beard had said (about this, more later); Beard credited Rutledge with only 26 slaves, whereas I show the number to have been 243; Beard records Charles Pinckney as holding 52 slaves, which I corrected to 111, and C. C. Pinckney as holding only 45 slaves, which I revised upward to 70. In addition, I found and reported considerable personal property holdings, overlooked by Beard, in the cases of Houstoun, Wilson,

Ingersoll, and Randolph. Yet it is in precisely these cases that Main charges me with twisting Beard's data so as to depreciate the property-holdings of the delegates. To quote a phrase used by Mr. Main, "This is absurd." But if he had chosen a different set of delegates, or considered them all, the result would have been the same, since for a vast majority of the delegates I found and reported more property than did Beard.

As to the use of adjectives to disparage property holdings, Mr. Main makes great sport over my characterizing Edmund Randolph as in "great need," "beset with economic difficulties," and, in Mr. Main's words, "impoverished it seems by thousands of acres and over a hundred slaves." Main neglects to tell us that Beard himself described Randolph as a man "burdened with debt," "apparently never very prosperous," and one whose slaves "had long been an incumbrance."

My aim was not to depreciate but to clarify and fill in the details, details which were, in the main, unavailable when Beard wrote his book. To illustrate, let us consider the case of Pierce Butler, one of Mr. Main's thirteen. Beard described Butler as a plantation aristocrat; so do I (pp. 81–82). But because of the paucity of available manuscripts when he wrote, Beard was able to add only two items of factual information, both of which happened to be wrong. He lists Butler as owning only thirty-one slaves. I corrected this, revising Beard upward, not downward, and showed that Butler owned 143 slaves. But then I went on to add more precise data about Butler's economic affairs during the years 1783–87. Butler was financially embarrassed. Just after the war he had negotiated a large loan in Holland on the security of his very large plantation, but then misfortune overtook him. He suffered a succession of crop failures and it was not until the crop of 1787, harvested and marketed some months after the Convention, that he began to pay off his postponed obligations. From 1785 to 1787 he was rich but a debtor—a debtor, unable to pay his debts—and during 1785 and 1786 his perilous circumstances led him to vote for an issue of paper money, for the Pine Barren Act, and for various other emergency measures for the relief of debtors. Beard's polarization of his data in this instance was, in my opinion, justifiable and probably unavoidable. Mr. Main's effort to re-polarize is neither.

As to the problems that confront a debtor, Mr. Main is extremely confused. The seriousness or safety of a debtor's situation do not depend upon the amount of his debt or of his other property, but upon whether he is in a position to pay when debts fall due. Mr. Main's distinction between "the man of means, who borrows of his own free will, or to avoid disposing of some of his less fluid wealth, and the small property-holder, who unwillingly falls into debt, or is forced to borrow from one creditor in order to pay another," is not, as he asserts, "fundamental." It is merely inaccurate. Some of the largest debtors of all are precisely described by his statement about the "small property-holder," and many of the small property-holders borrowed of their own free will to avoid selling their farms or other holdings. Bray Hammond settled this myth of the poor debtor in his work published two years ago, and if Mr. Main has not read Hammond's work, he should.

Before passing on to the next section of Mr. Main's effort, one might observe that regarding the Philadelphia Convention, Main neglects to mention that in my summary I drew the extremely reserved conclusion that Beard's analysis merely requires "a large number of qualifications." He also neglects to mention that I state (p. 95) that, though the value of the agricultural holdings of the delegates far outweighed their personalty, delegates having personalty interests outnumbered delegates having primarily realty interests thirty-one to twenty-four. He also neglects to consider my fourth chapter, in which it is rather conclusively demonstrated, I believe, that there was virtually no correlation between economic interests and voting behavior in the Convention. One would suspect that Mr. Main is attacking one book and defending another without having read either.

The rest of Mr. Main's efforts are devoted to my chapters on ratification. He begins with another demonstration that he has apparently not read my book. My description of Jeremiah Wadsworth's condition, Main speculates, "is evidently supposed to cast doubt upon his financial position." To anyone who can comprehend the English language, the passage in question, if read in context (pp. 138–40), is a description of Connecticut's economic problems during the Confederation period, pointing out why Connecticut had abundant economic reasons for supporting the Constitution. It forms the primary basis for my conclusion that, with only minor modifications (particularly that the majority of Connecticut's farmers apparently favored ratification), Beard's thesis is applicable in the case of Connecticut.

Otherwise Mr. Main focuses upon my chapter six, concerning

ratification in Pennsylvania, Massachusetts, South Carolina, and New Hampshire. As to Massachusetts, I see no point in quibbling, for Mr. Main's efforts are again beside the point. If he will read the "Significance of the Data" chapters which he dismisses without a hearing, he will learn that in chapters eight and ten I conclude that for Massachusetts, as for Connecticut—but only for these two states—Beard's thesis is fundamentally sound, though it can be clarified in numerous details.

As to Pennsylvania, rather than argue with Mr. Main's corrections, and point out where he is often, though sometimes subtly, mistaken, let us suppose that he is correct in every detail. If one applies Mr. Main's suggested corrections to my summary table regarding the Pennsylvania delegates (p. 181), one learns that the Federalists and anti-Federalists were economically even more nearly equal than I had indicated! That is, in every respect except public security holdings, which Beard regarded as the superdynamic element in the ratification. Nothing Main has said is designed to, or could, alter the facts (a) that 73.9 percent of anti-Federalists in the Pennsylvania ratifying convention held securities, as against 50 percent of the Federalists; (b) that the average and mean holdings of the anti-Federalists were far greater than those of the Federalists; and (c) that the twenty-three anti-Federalists in the convention held, between them, securities of a face value greater than those of the forty-six Federalists combined.

In his comments regarding South Carolina, Mr. Main demonstrates that he is no better at arithmetic than he is at reading. First he corrects my lists of merchants, adding Chesnut, Laurens, and Kean as Federalist merchants. Since I do not have available the source he cites for Chesnut, I accept that correction for present purposes. Regarding Laurens, however, Mr. Main is some years out of date, for Laurens had definitely retired from mercantile activity before 1788. As to Kean (whom Main mistakenly says he is transferring from the "unknown" classification, whereas actually I have classified him as a planter), it depends upon the Kean we are talking about. John Kean, merchant (obviously the one to whom Main refers, since he cites the *Biographical Directory of the American Congress* as his source), was born and lived in Charleston; he died in 1795. The other John Kean, a planter (and obviously a different person, since the tax records of St. Helena's Parish indicate that he was alive in 1798), was the one to whom I referred, and he lived in St. Helena's Parish. I assumed that the latter was the delegate to the ratifying convention, since the delegate represented St. Helena's, not Charleston. I may be wrong, but I have seen no evidence demonstrating it. This means that we add 1 merchant, not 3, to the Federalist ranks, and that at best Main may be 33⅓ percent accurate, roughly the extent to which he is accurate throughout. But even if he were right in asserting that 3 should be added, that would bring the total number of Federalist merchants to 9, as opposed to 4 anti-Federalist merchants. Nine to four, according to Mr. Main's system of reckoning, is equivalent to 3 to 1. Similarly, from his own table, constructed from my data, he concludes that small planters and farmers in South Carolina opposed the Constitution, 2 to 1. He does not define small planters and farmers. If this means those owning less than 10 slaves, the number (according to Mr. Main's table) is 23 anti-Federalists to 18 Federalists. Twenty-three to eighteen is, according to Mr. Main's system of reckoning, equivalent to 2 to 1. If he means those owning 19 slaves or less, the number (according to Mr. Main's table) is 37 anti-Federalists to 43 Federalists. Thirty-seven, according to Mr. Main's system of reckoning, is twice as many as 43. Similarly, regarding the artisans and mechanics in the convention, all 7 of whom were Federalists, 7 to 0 is, according to Mr. Main's system of reckoning, equivalent to 7 to 1. Finally, having arrived at these various ratios by a method unknown to ordinary mortals, Mr. Main is ready for comparisons. To disprove my statement regarding (1) merchants; (2) factors; (3) lawyers; (4) planters; and (5) farmers; Main compares his own ratios for (1) merchants; (2) artisans and mechanics; (3) lawyers; (4) doctors; (5) large planters; and (6) small planters. He thus places his logic on a footing with his arithmetic.

In summarizing South Carolina Mr. Main overlooks two small details: that 68.5 percent of the anti-Federalists held securities, as against 41.6 percent of the Federalists; and that 26.8 percent of the Federalists had borrowed state paper money, whereas only 10.9 percent of the anti-Federalists had borrowed paper money. Please let us remember that Beard maintained that it was personalty other than slaves, and particularly public securities, that was the dynamic element in the ratification, and that it was friends of paper money who furnished the principal leadership against ratification.

Next Mr. Main takes up New Hampshire. Except for the snide aside that I "concede" that public securities were held mainly by Federalists (as a matter of fact I "conceded" nothing throughout; I merely reported the facts as I found them), Main has nothing to argue about here. He does neglect to mention, however, that only 7 of the 104 voting delegates in the convention, 6 of them Federalists, held any securities at all. The interesting thing about Main's paragraph on New Hampshire is that he states that more than half (53 percent) of the Federalists were farmers, then tells us in the very next paragraph that he has just demonstrated that an overwhelming majority of the farmers in this and three other states opposed the Constitution. (This after having previously suggested changes in the Pennsylvania sketches that would still leave a majority of the farmers in that convention opposed to ratification, and after suggesting no changes whatever as to the numbers of farmers in the South Carolina convention.)

It is by similar reasoning Mr. Main draws the other three conclusions in this last paragraph about the chapter in question. For example, regarding securities: I reported that in Massachusetts, which had a large number of security-holders, and in New Hampshire, which had a small number, security-holders favored ratification. I also reported that in Pennsylvania and South Carolina, where there were large numbers of security-holders, a far greater percentage of anti-Federalists than of Federalists held securities. Mr. Main says nothing even aimed at contradicting this information. But he summarizes what he has said by telling us that he has just shown that "public security-holders were predominantly Federal." This paragraph is too ludicrous for description.

After this bit of nonsense, Mr. Main has little in the way of substantive comment, and certainly not enough to warrant further discussion here. Instead, let us consider the paper as a whole. Suppose we assume that even his most fanciful and maladroit claims were well founded; what would be the result? Main concedes that I was right, or close to it, in four of the five states considered in chapter five; he admits that in Virginia (per his own researches), despite my being guilty of making some miscellaneous factual errors, property was pretty evenly distributed between the contending sides; and finally, he allows North Carolina and Rhode Island to go entirely unchallenged. Even if we give Mr. Main New Hampshire, which he does not really claim, this means that Main concedes that Beard was wrong in at least seven of the thirteen states. It seems to me that even if I were as bad as Mr. Main makes out, it remains a certainty that Beard's thesis cannot hold up. After all, a general interpretation that is at best, and by admission of its staunchest defender, more than 50 percent invalid is not the most universal truth imaginable. The essential point of my book was just that: Beard's fundamental error (not an uncommon one in our profession) lay in attempting to postulate a single, uniform system of interpretation for an event that was just too complex to admit of such.

Charles A. Beard made one great and lasting contribution to American historiography: he pointed out something that should have been obvious, that American political history has not taken place in a vacuum. To convey this simple truth to the diehards in his profession, Beard found it expedient to employ radical means. He polarized his data almost to the point of suggesting that politics unfold according to mechanistic economic laws, calculable with a slide rule. The great irony is that many of his fellows and followers, lacking his imagination, failed to profit from his contribution because they took for Gospel the means by which he made it. My humble effort was directed at getting us back on the path. Apparently Mr. Main prefers the wilderness.

Suggestions for Additional Reading

Historians have been so inclined to write into their accounts of the Revolution and the Federal Convention the historical perspectives of their own times—slavery, the frontier, economic classes, consensus and so on—that the reader who would learn more about the issues of the late eighteenth century in America should read as widely as possible in contemporary materials. Excellent collections of documents in this period are B. P. Poore, ed., *The Federal and State Constitutions, Colonial Charters, and Other Organic Laws of the United States* (Washington, 1877, 2 vols.); Benjamin F. Wright, Jr., ed., *A Source Book of American Political Theory* (New York, 1929); and *Documents Illustrative of the Formation of the Union of the American States* (House Document No. 398, 69th Congress, 1st session, 1927).

Although they may tend to contradict each other, good older accounts of the political and legal theory of the American Revolution are provided in Charles H. McIlwain, *The American Revolution* (New York, 1923); Carl L. Becker, *The Declaration of Independence* (New York, 1922); and Arthur M. Schlesinger, *New Viewpoints in American History* (New York, 1922). Also valuable are C. Edward Merriam, *A History of American Political Theories* (New York, 1903), and the excellent discussion of the natural-law background of revolutionary thought in Benjamin F. Wright, Jr., *American Interpretations of Natural Law* (Cambridge, Massachusetts, 1931).

On the ideological origins of the Revolution, the works referred to in the body of this book should be read in their entirety, that is, Bernard Bailyn, *The Ideological Origins of the American Revolution* (Cambridge, Massachusetts, 1967); Bernard Bailyn, *The Origins of American Politics* (New York, 1968); Bernard Bailyn, *Pamphlets of the American Revolution* (Cambridge, Massachusetts, 1965); and Gordon S. Wood, *The Creation of the American Republic, 1776–1787* (Chapel Hill, 1969). The accounts of Bailyn and Wood may be said to have superseded that of Becker on the ideological origins of American revolutionary thought. On political ideas preceding the Revolution see also Clinton L. Rossiter, *Seedtime of the Republic* (New York, 1953).

On the question of whether economic and social class divisions were significant elements in the political and legal changes that took place from the Revolution to the Constitution, there are various views. Robert E. Brown, *Middle-Class Democracy and the Revolution in Massachusetts* (Ithaca, 1955) says that sharp class divisions did not exist. Richard B. Morris, *The American Revolution Reconsidered* (New York, 1967) does find classes in the period but no class war. Jackson T. Main, *The Antifederalists, Critics of the Constitution, 1781–1788* (Chapel Hill, 1961) says that the existence of classes was clearly recognized in the eighteenth century, and that it was the well-to-do among the Federalists and Antifederalists to whom the new Constitution appealed most. Staughton Lynd, writing in the radical tradition, says in *Class Conflict, Slavery, and the United States Constitution* (Indianapolis, 1967) that class divisions were sharp and decisive, and that the United States Constitution was a compromise between "men of wealth in the cities and men of wealth on the land."

The standard work on the Federal Convention of 1787 is Max Farrand, ed., *The Records of the Federal Convention of 1787* (New Haven, 1937, 4 vols.). Also useful are Farrand's earlier works, *The Framing of the Constitution of the United States* (New Haven, 1913) and *The Fathers of the Constitution* (New Haven, 1921). Indispensable contemporary documents and proceedings are available in Jonathan Elliot, *The Debates in the Several State Conventions on the Adoption of the Federal Constitution* (revised edition, 5 vols., 1836–1845 and later reprints), and in Paul Leicester Ford, ed., *Pamphlets on the Constitution of the United States* (Brooklyn, 1888) and *Essays on the Constitution of the United States* (Brooklyn, 1892). *The Federalist* is available in several editions. For a collection of Antifederalist writings and speeches, see Cecilia M. Kenyon, ed., *The Antifederalist* (Indianapolis, 1966); and for an early voting study, O. G. Libby, *Geographical Distribution of the Vote of the Thirteen States on the Federal Constitution, 1787–88* (Volume 1 of the University of Wisconsin Economics, Political Science and History Series, Madison, 1897).

Other economic interpretations of the work of the Federal Convention than those cited in the preceding pages of this book are Fred Rodell, *Fifty-five Men* (2d ed., New York, 1936); and Louis B. Boudin, *Government by Judiciary* (New York, 1932). It was not a view peculiar only to liberal and radical writers, however, that there were economic stakes to be won and lost under the Constitution. This fact was also well known to such defenders of the Federalist view as Albert Beveridge, *Life of John Marshall* (Boston, 1919, 4 vols.).

1 2 3 4 5 6 7 8 9 10